GLOW
vs THE STAR PRIMAS

GLOW

IDW

Chris Ryall, President and Publisher/CCO
John Barber, Editor-In-Chief
Cara Morrison, Chief Financial Officer
Matt Ruzicka, Chief Accounting Officer
David Hedgecock, Associate Publisher
Jerry Bennington, VP of New Product Development
Lorelei Bunjes, VP of Digital Services
Justin Eisinger, Editorial Director, Graphic Novels & Collections
Eric Moss, Senior Director, Licensing and Business Development

Ted Adams and Robbie Robbins, Founders of IDW

ISBN: 978-1-68405-473-2   22 21 20 19   1 2 3 4

Originally published as GLOW issues #1–4.

Special thanks to Charlotte Infinger and Shannon Schram for their invaluable assistance.

For international rights, contact licensing@idwpublishing.com

COVER ARTIST
HANNAH
TEMPLER

COLLECTION EDITS BY
JUSTIN EISINGER
AND
ALONZO SIMON

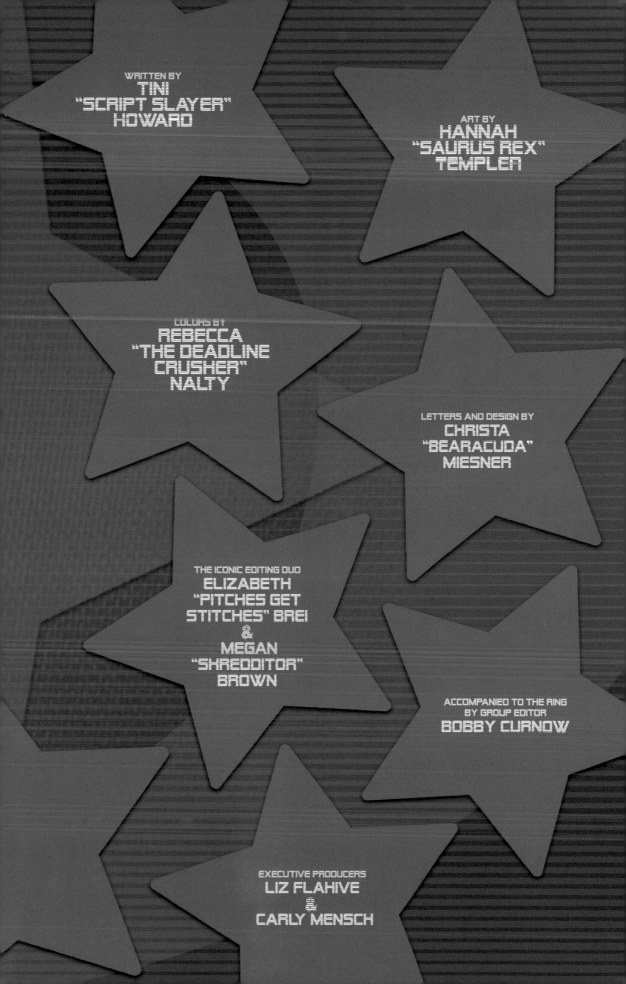

WRITTEN BY
TINI
"SCRIPT SLAYER"
HOWARD

ART BY
HANNAH
"SAURUS REX"
TEMPLER

COLORS BY
REBECCA
"THE DEADLINE
CRUSHER"
NALTY

LETTERS AND DESIGN BY
CHRISTA
"BEARACUDA"
MIESNER

THE ICONIC EDITING DUO
ELIZABETH
"PITCHES GET
STITCHES" BREI
&
MEGAN
"SHREDDITOR"
BROWN

ACCOMPANIED TO THE RING
BY GROUP EDITOR
BOBBY CURNOW

EXECUTIVE PRODUCERS
LIZ FLAHIVE
&
CARLY MENSCH

CASTING CALL

MELANIE ROSEN
A.K.A. MELROSE

SAM SYLVIA
A.K.A. THE DIRECTOR OF GLOW

RUTH WILDER
A.K.A. ZOYA THE DESTROYA

RHONDA RICHARDSON
A.K.A. BRITANNICA

CHERRY BANG
A.K.A. BLACK MAGIC

SHEILA THE SHE-WOLF
AS HERSELF

YOLANDA RIVAS
A.K.A. JUNKCHAIN

CARMEN WADE
A.K.A. MACHU PICCHU

TAMMÉ DAWSON
A.K.A. THE WELFARE QUEEN

DAWN & STACEY
A.K.A. THE TOXIC TWINS

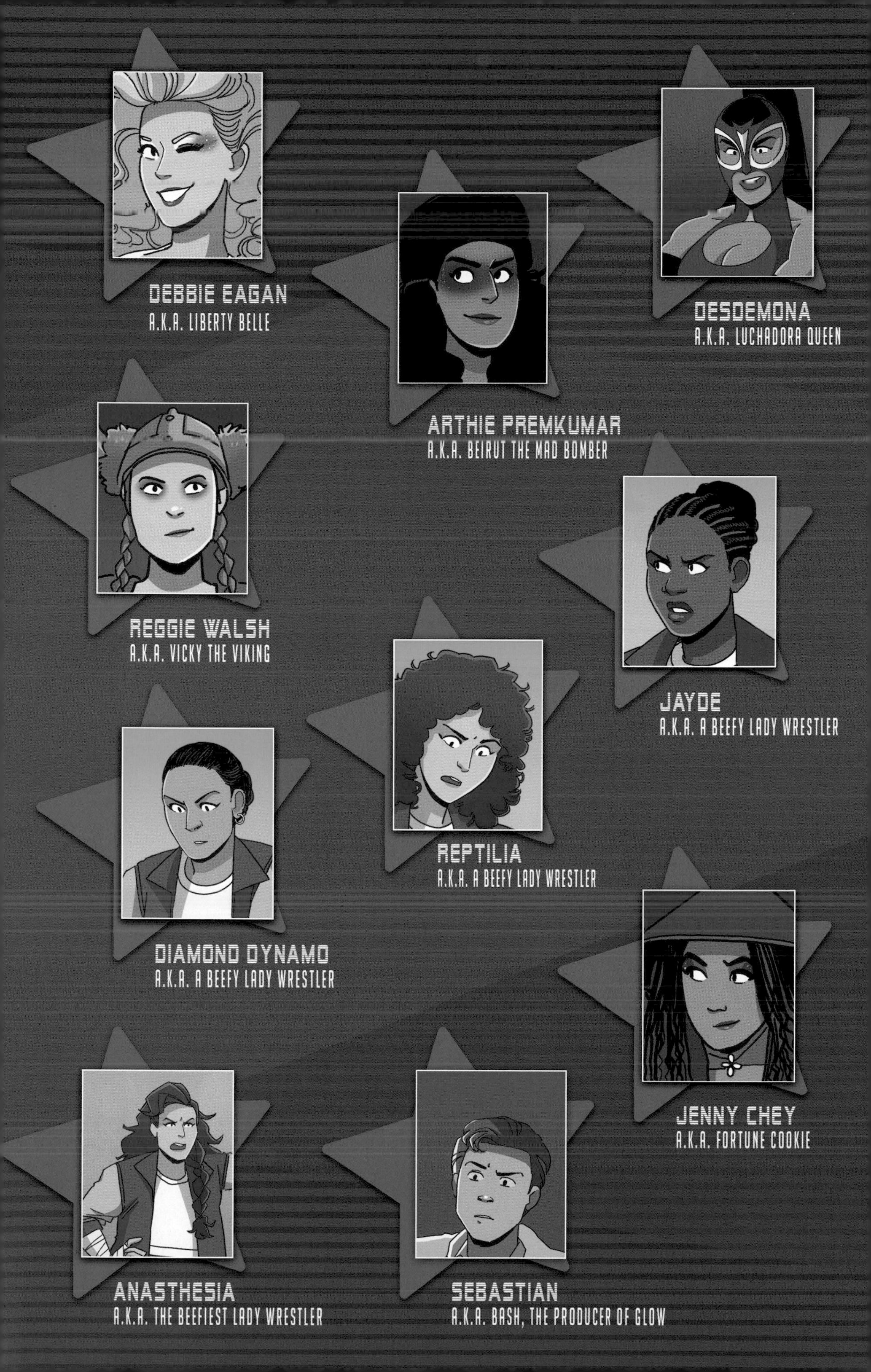
DEBBIE EAGAN
A.K.A. LIBERTY BELLE
DESDEMONA
A.K.A. LUCHADORA QUEEN
ARTHIE PREMKUMAR
A.K.A. BEIRUT THE MAD BOMBER
REGGIE WALSH
A.K.A. VICKY THE VIKING
JAYDE
A.K.A. A BEEFY LADY WRESTLER
REPTILIA
A.K.A. A BEEFY LADY WRESTLER
DIAMOND DYNAMO
A.K.A. A BEEFY LADY WRESTLER
JENNY CHEY
A.K.A. FORTUNE COOKIE
ANASTHESIA
A.K.A. THE BEEFIEST LADY WRESTLER
SEBASTIAN
A.K.A. BASH, THE PRODUCER OF GLOW

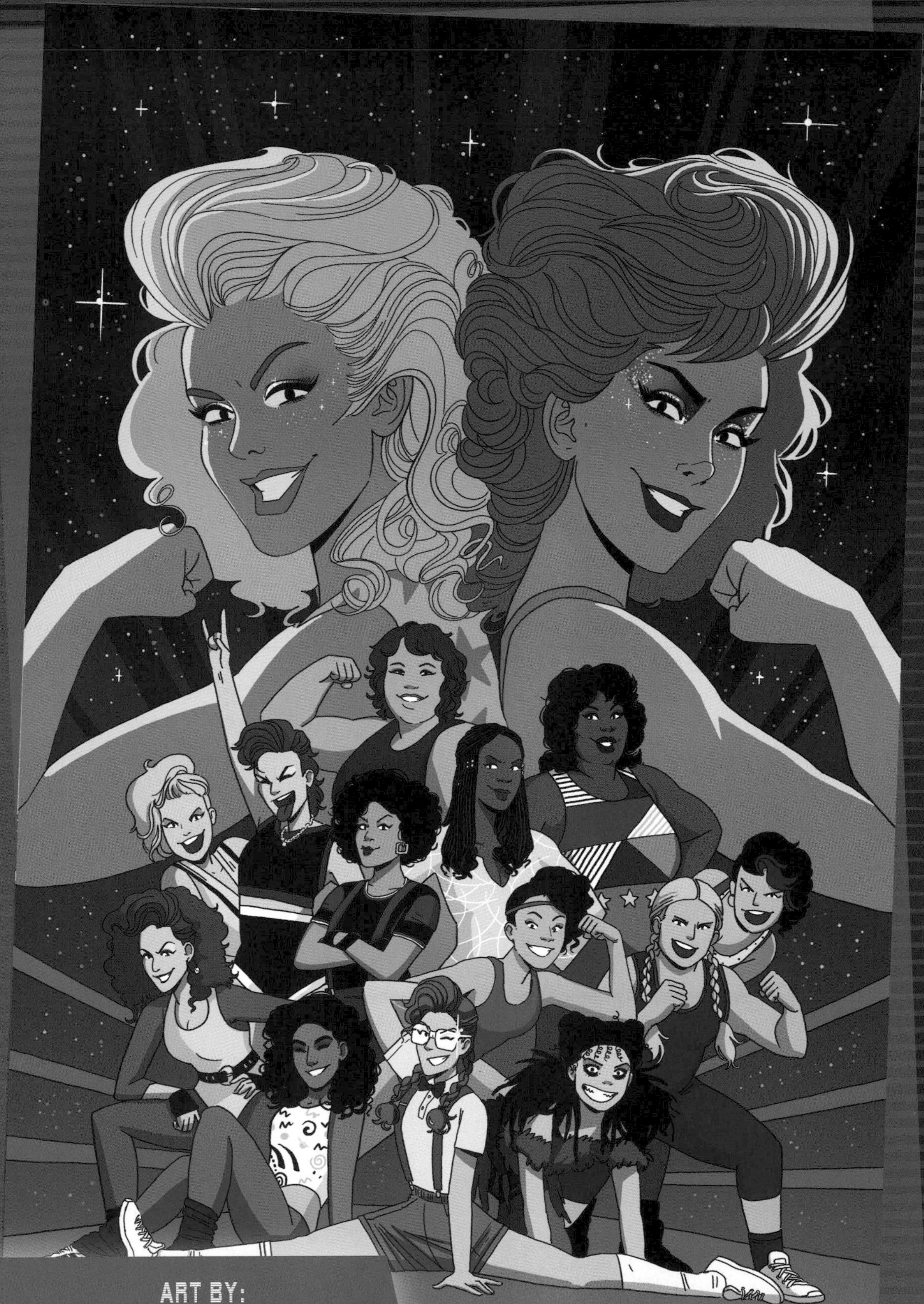

ART BY:
HANNAH TEMPLER

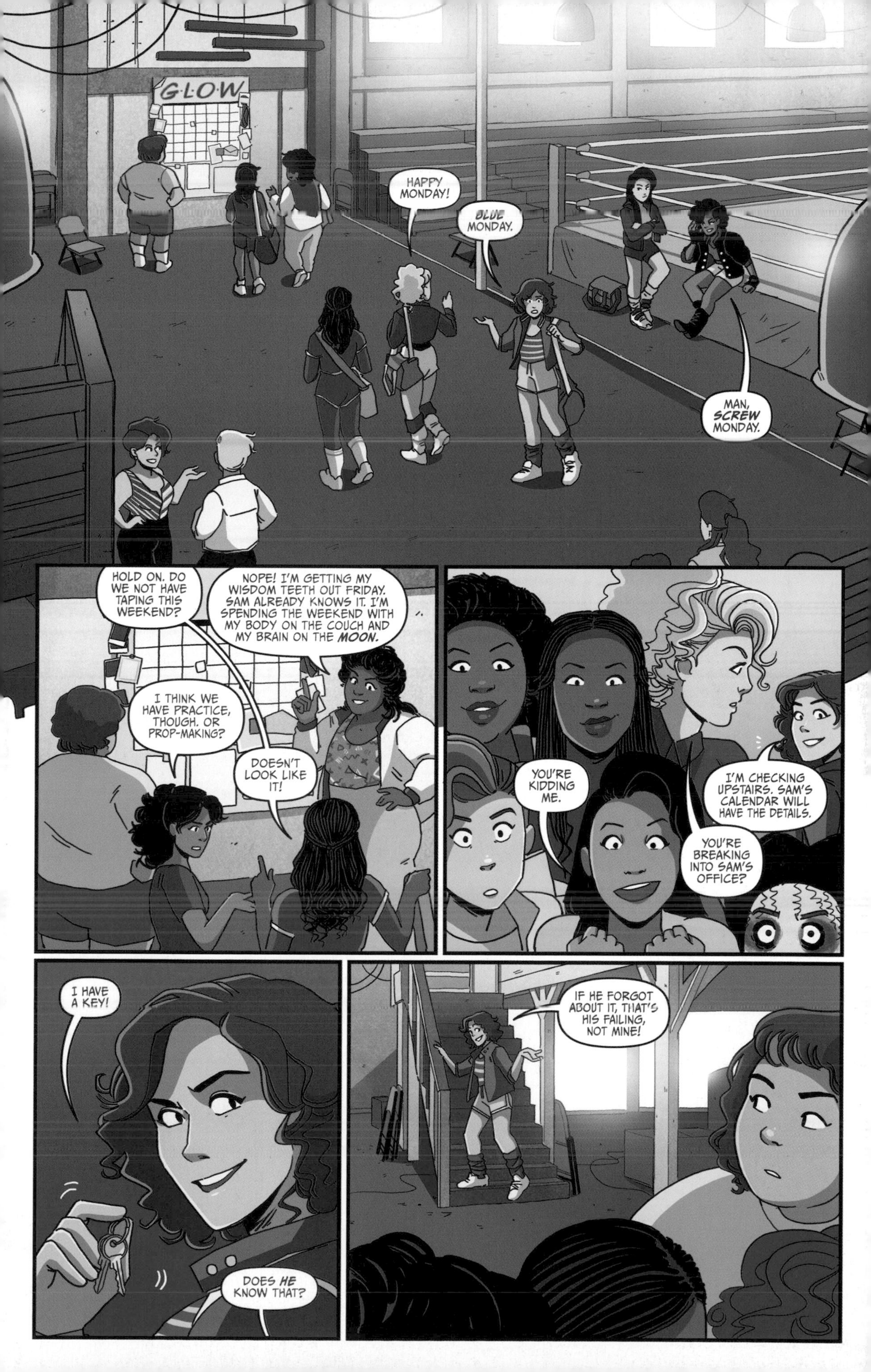
G·L·O·W
HAPPY MONDAY!
BLUE MONDAY.
MAN, SCREW MONDAY.
HOLD ON. DO WE NOT HAVE TAPING THIS WEEKEND?
NOPE! I'M GETTING MY WISDOM TEETH OUT FRIDAY. SAM ALREADY KNOWS IT. I'M SPENDING THE WEEKEND WITH MY BODY ON THE COUCH AND MY BRAIN ON THE MOON.
I THINK WE HAVE PRACTICE, THOUGH. OR PROP-MAKING?
DOESN'T LOOK LIKE IT!
YOU'RE KIDDING ME.
I'M CHECKING UPSTAIRS. SAM'S CALENDAR WILL HAVE THE DETAILS.
YOU'RE BREAKING INTO SAM'S OFFICE?
I HAVE A KEY!
DOES HE KNOW THAT?
IF HE FORGOT ABOUT IT, THAT'S HIS FAILING, NOT MINE!

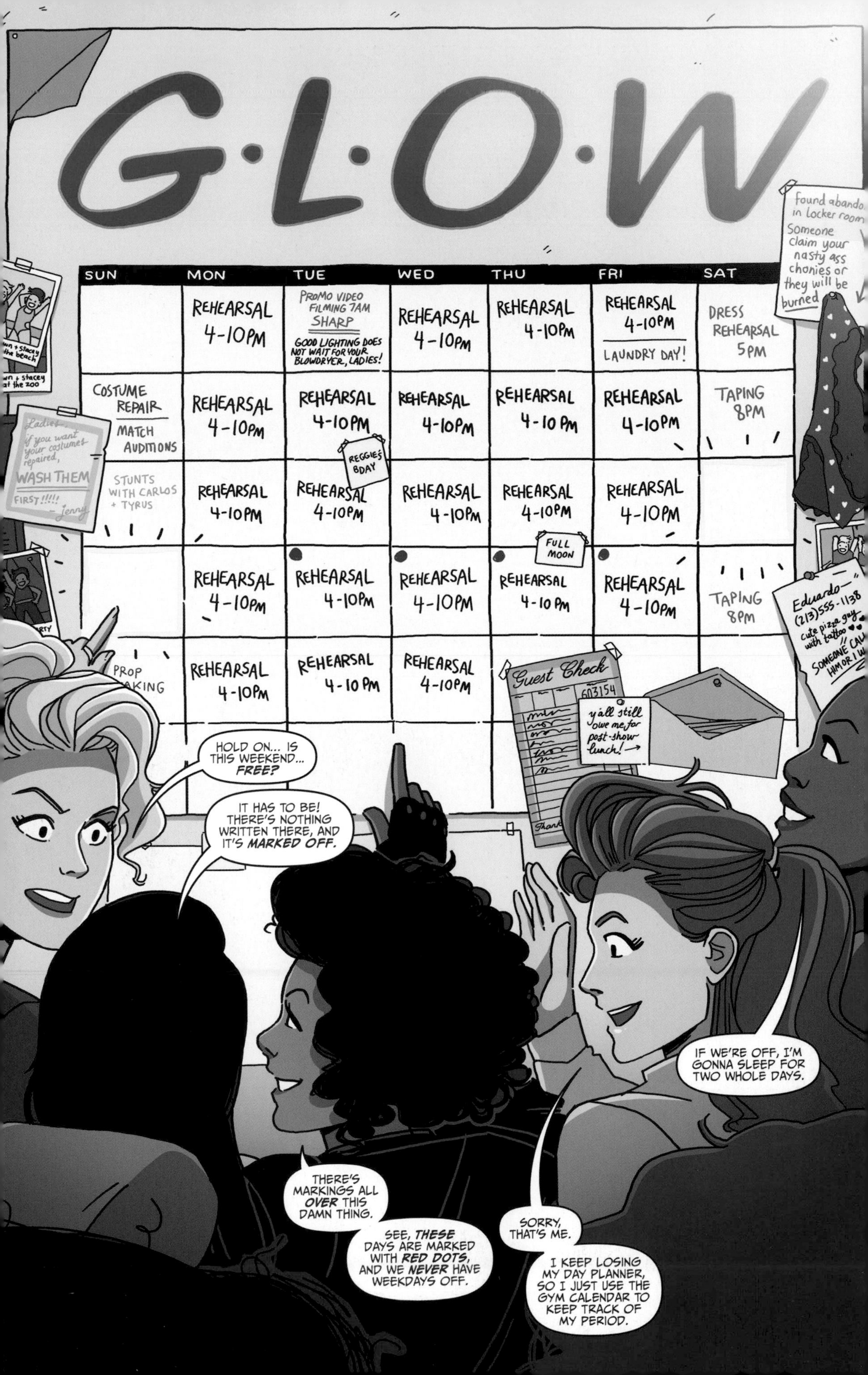
G·L·O·W
SUN
MON
TUE
WED
THU
FRI
SAT
REHEARSAL 4-10PM
PROMO VIDEO FILMING 7AM SHARP
GOOD LIGHTING DOES NOT WAIT FOR YOUR BLOWDRYER, LADIES!
REHEARSAL 4-10PM
REHEARSAL 4-10PM
REHEARSAL 4-10PM
LAUNDRY DAY!
DRESS REHEARSAL 5PM
COSTUME REPAIR
MATCH AUDITIONS
REHEARSAL 4-10PM
REHEARSAL 4-10PM
REHEARSAL 4-10PM
REHEARSAL 4-10 PM
REHEARSAL 4-10PM
TAPING 8PM
REGGIE'S BDAY
STUNTS WITH CARLOS + TYRUS
REHEARSAL 4-10PM
REHEARSAL 4-10PM
REHEARSAL 4-10PM
REHEARSAL 4-10PM
REHEARSAL 4-10PM
FULL MOON
REHEARSAL 4-10PM
REHEARSAL 4-10PM
REHEARSAL 4-10PM
REHEARSAL 4-10 PM
REHEARSAL 4-10PM
TAPING 8PM
PROP MAKING
REHEARSAL 4-10PM
REHEARSAL 4-10 PM
REHEARSAL 4-10PM
Ladies, if you want your costumes repaired, WASH THEM FIRST!!!!! - Jenny
Found abando... in locker room. Someone claim your nasty ass chonies or they will be burned
Eduardo— (213)555-1138 cute pizza guy with tattoo
Guest Check 603154
y'all still owe me for post-show lunch!
HOLD ON... IS THIS WEEKEND... FREE?
IT HAS TO BE! THERE'S NOTHING WRITTEN THERE, AND IT'S MARKED OFF.
IF WE'RE OFF, I'M GONNA SLEEP FOR TWO WHOLE DAYS.
THERE'S MARKINGS ALL OVER THIS DAMN THING.
SEE, THESE DAYS ARE MARKED WITH RED DOTS, AND WE NEVER HAVE WEEKDAYS OFF.
SORRY, THAT'S ME.
I KEEP LOSING MY DAY PLANNER, SO I JUST USE THE GYM CALENDAR TO KEEP TRACK OF MY PERIOD.

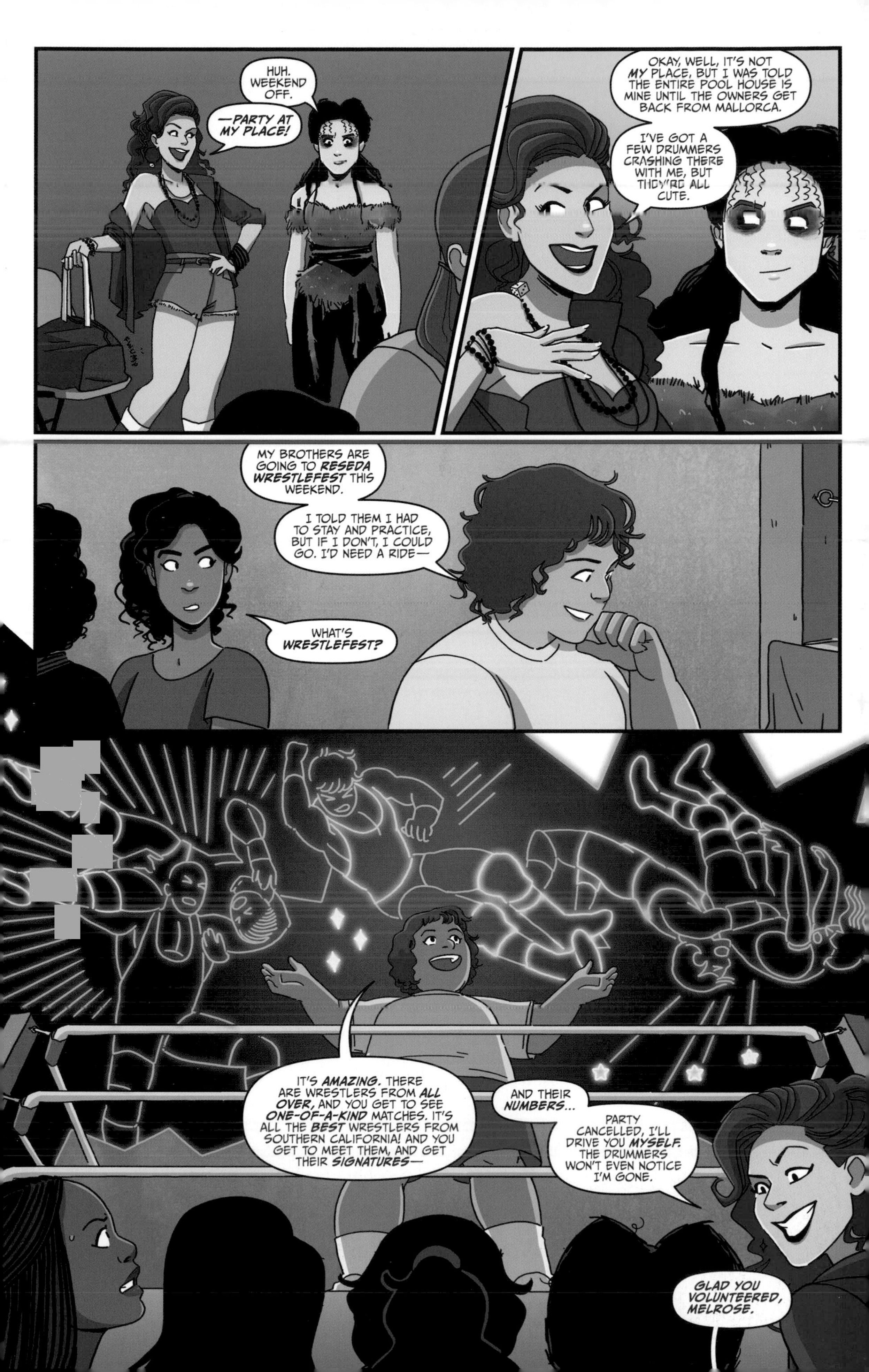
—PARTY AT MY PLACE!
HUH. WEEKEND OFF.
OKAY, WELL, IT'S NOT MY PLACE, BUT I WAS TOLD THE ENTIRE POOL HOUSE IS MINE UNTIL THE OWNERS GET BACK FROM MALLORCA.
I'VE GOT A FEW DRUMMERS CRASHING THERE WITH ME, BUT THEY'RE ALL CUTE.
MY BROTHERS ARE GOING TO RESEDA WRESTLEFEST THIS WEEKEND.
I TOLD THEM I HAD TO STAY AND PRACTICE, BUT IF I DON'T, I COULD GO. I'D NEED A RIDE—
WHAT'S WRESTLEFEST?
IT'S AMAZING. THERE ARE WRESTLERS FROM ALL OVER, AND YOU GET TO SEE ONE-OF-A-KIND MATCHES. IT'S ALL THE BEST WRESTLERS FROM SOUTHERN CALIFORNIA! AND YOU GET TO MEET THEM, AND GET THEIR SIGNATURES—
AND THEIR NUMBERS...
PARTY CANCELLED, I'LL DRIVE YOU MYSELF. THE DRUMMERS WON'T EVEN NOTICE I'M GONE.
GLAD YOU VOLUNTEERED, MELROSE.

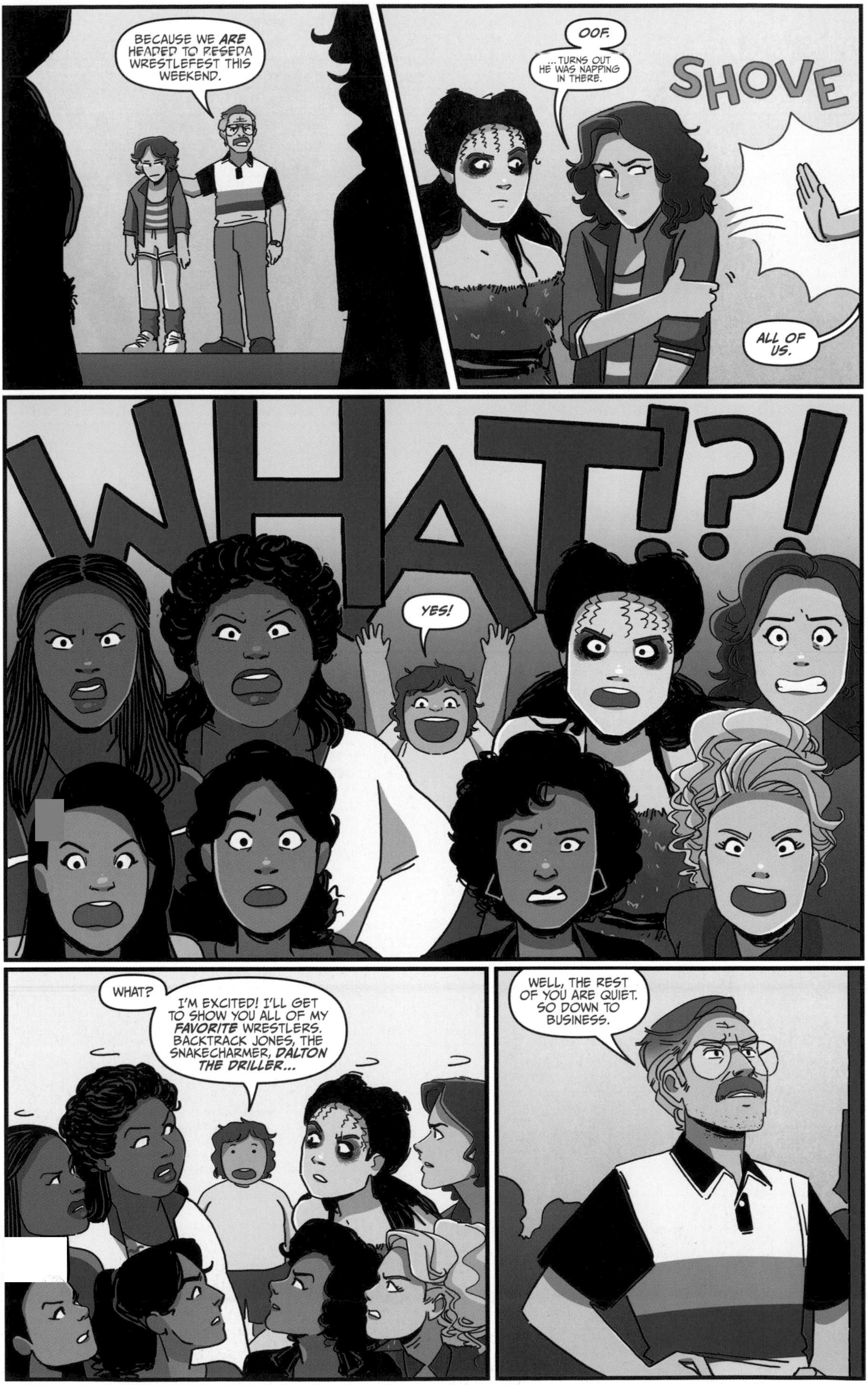
BECAUSE WE ARE HEADED TO RESEDA WRESTLEFEST THIS WEEKEND.
OOF.
...TURNS OUT HE WAS NAPPING IN THERE.
SHOVE
ALL OF US.
WHAT!?!
YES!
WHAT?
I'M EXCITED! I'LL GET TO SHOW YOU ALL OF MY FAVORITE WRESTLERS. BACKTRACK JONES, THE SNAKECHARMER, DALTON THE DRILLER...
WELL, THE REST OF YOU ARE QUIET. SO DOWN TO BUSINESS.

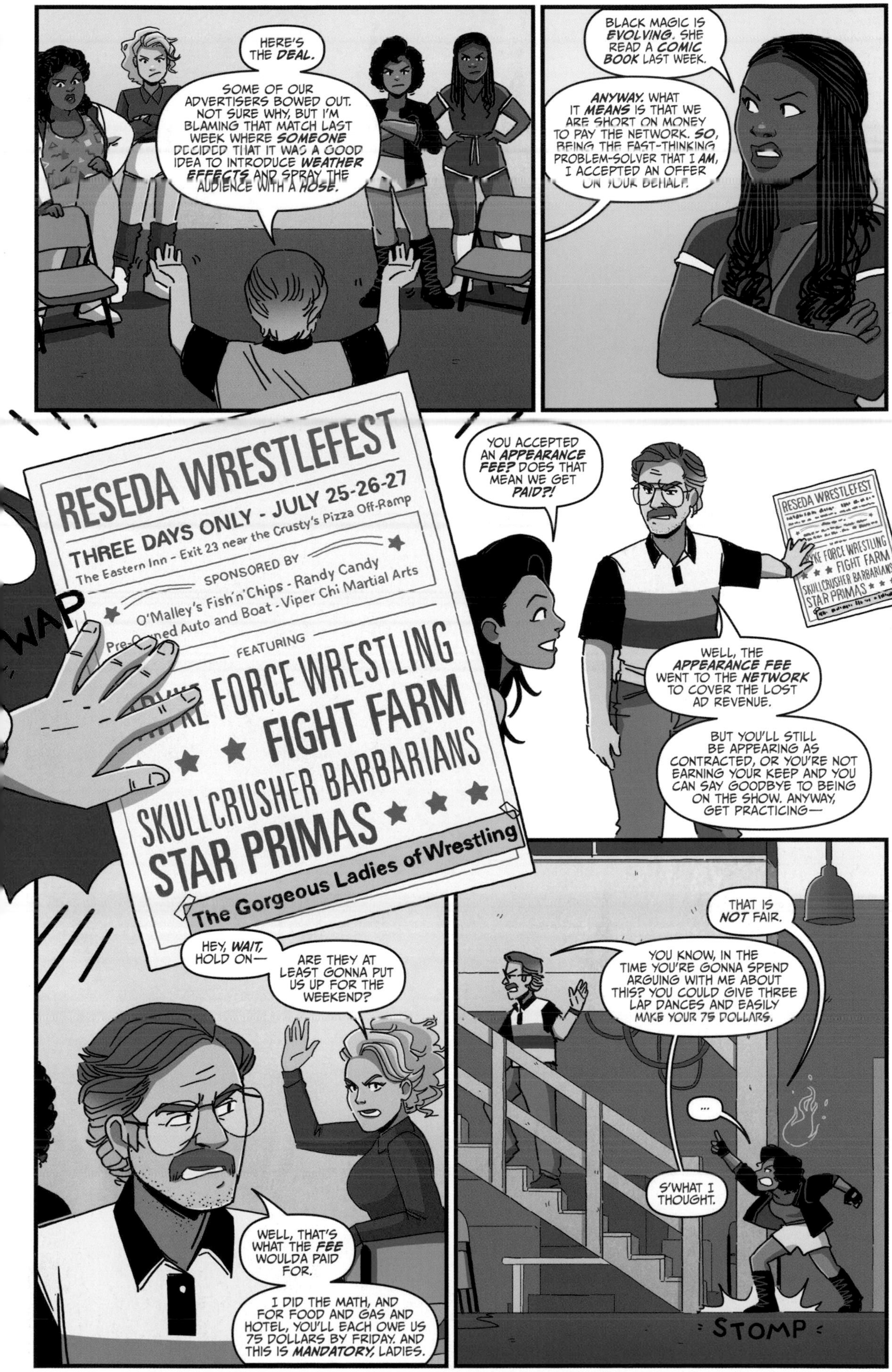
HERE'S THE *DEAL.*
SOME OF OUR ADVERTISERS BOWED OUT. NOT SURE WHY, BUT I'M BLAMING THAT MATCH LAST WEEK WHERE *SOMEONE* DECIDED THAT IT WAS A GOOD IDEA TO INTRODUCE *WEATHER EFFECTS* AND SPRAY THE AUDIENCE WITH A *HOSE.*
BLACK MAGIC IS *EVOLVING.* SHE READ A *COMIC BOOK* LAST WEEK.
ANYWAY. WHAT IT *MEANS* IS THAT WE ARE SHORT ON MONEY TO PAY THE NETWORK. *SO,* BEING THE FAST-THINKING PROBLEM-SOLVER THAT I *AM,* I ACCEPTED AN OFFER ON YOUR BEHALF.
WAP
RESEDA WRESTLEFEST
THREE DAYS ONLY - JULY 25-26-27
The Eastern Inn - Exit 23 near the Crusty's Pizza Off-Ramp
SPONSORED BY
O'Malley's Fish'n'Chips - Randy Candy
Pre-Owned Auto and Boat - Viper Chi Martial Arts
FEATURING
FORCE WRESTLING
FIGHT FARM
SKULLCRUSHER BARBARIANS
STAR PRIMAS
The Gorgeous Ladies of Wrestling
YOU ACCEPTED AN *APPEARANCE FEE?* DOES THAT MEAN WE GET *PAID?!*
RESEDA WRESTLEFEST
WELL, THE *APPEARANCE FEE* WENT TO THE *NETWORK* TO COVER THE LOST AD REVENUE.
BUT YOU'LL STILL BE APPEARING AS CONTRACTED, OR YOU'RE NOT EARNING YOUR KEEP AND YOU CAN SAY GOODBYE TO BEING ON THE SHOW. ANYWAY, GET PRACTICING—
HEY, *WAIT,* HOLD ON—
ARE THEY AT LEAST GONNA PUT US UP FOR THE WEEKEND?
WELL, THAT'S WHAT THE *FEE* WOULDA PAID FOR.
I DID THE MATH, AND FOR FOOD AND GAS AND HOTEL, YOU'LL EACH OWE US 75 DOLLARS BY FRIDAY. AND THIS IS *MANDATORY,* LADIES.
THAT IS *NOT* FAIR.
YOU KNOW, IN THE TIME YOU'RE GONNA SPEND ARGUING WITH ME ABOUT THIS? YOU COULD GIVE THREE LAP DANCES AND EASILY MAKE YOUR 75 DOLLARS.
...
S'WHAT I THOUGHT.
STOMP

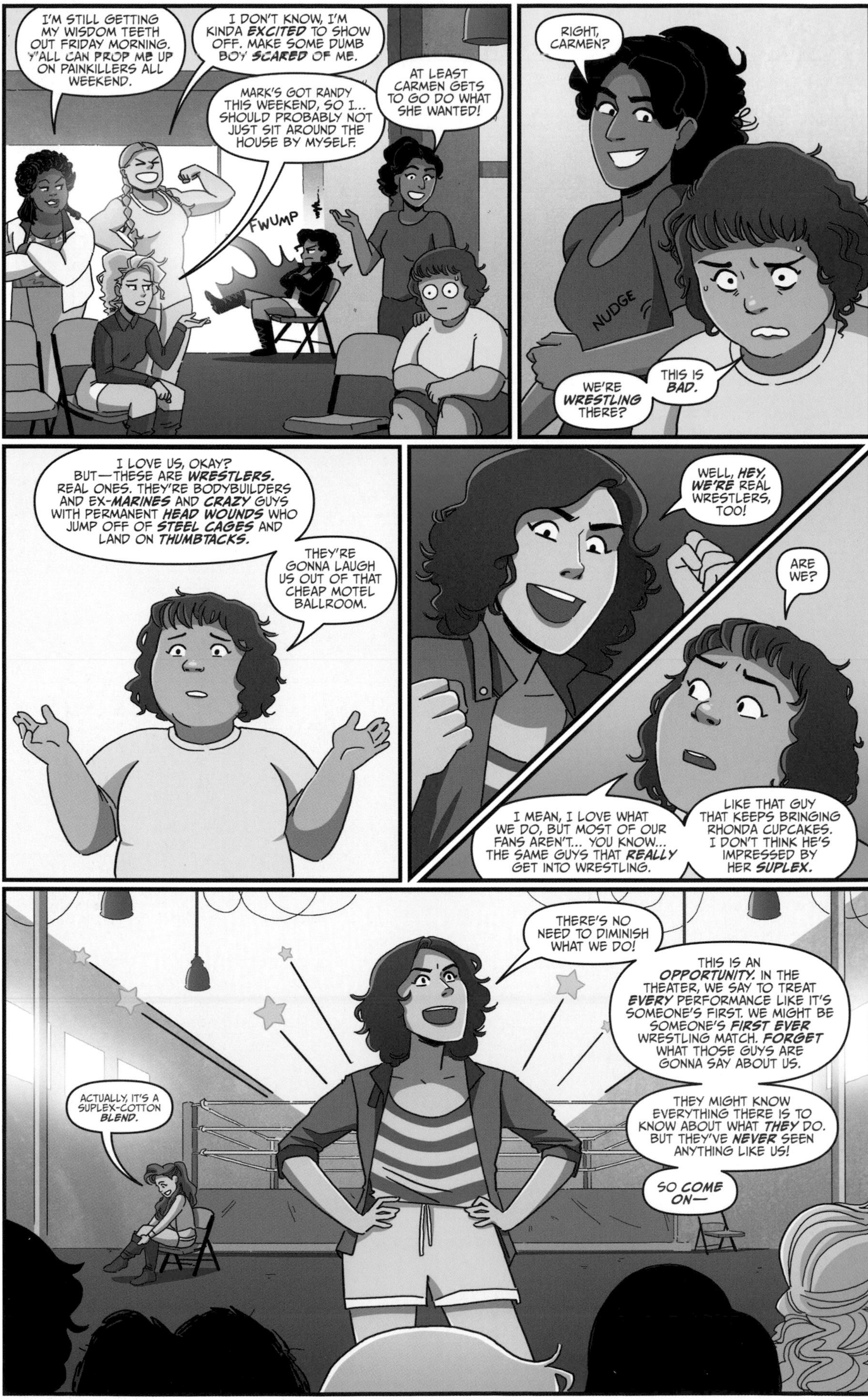
I'M STILL GETTING MY WISDOM TEETH OUT FRIDAY MORNING. Y'ALL CAN PROP ME UP ON PAINKILLERS ALL WEEKEND.
I DON'T KNOW, I'M KINDA EXCITED TO SHOW OFF. MAKE SOME DUMB BOY SCARED OF ME.
MARK'S GOT RANDY THIS WEEKEND, SO I... SHOULD PROBABLY NOT JUST SIT AROUND THE HOUSE BY MYSELF.
AT LEAST CARMEN GETS TO GO DO WHAT SHE WANTED!
FWUMP
RIGHT, CARMEN?
NUDGE
THIS IS BAD.
WE'RE WRESTLING THERE?
I LOVE US, OKAY? BUT—THESE ARE WRESTLERS. REAL ONES. THEY'RE BODYBUILDERS AND EX-MARINES AND CRAZY GUYS WITH PERMANENT HEAD WOUNDS WHO JUMP OFF OF STEEL CAGES AND LAND ON THUMBTACKS.
THEY'RE GONNA LAUGH US OUT OF THAT CHEAP MOTEL BALLROOM.
WELL, HEY, WE'RE REAL WRESTLERS, TOO!
ARE WE?
I MEAN, I LOVE WHAT WE DO, BUT MOST OF OUR FANS AREN'T... YOU KNOW... THE SAME GUYS THAT REALLY GET INTO WRESTLING.
LIKE THAT GUY THAT KEEPS BRINGING RHONDA CUPCAKES. I DON'T THINK HE'S IMPRESSED BY HER SUPLEX.
THERE'S NO NEED TO DIMINISH WHAT WE DO!
THIS IS AN OPPORTUNITY. IN THE THEATER, WE SAY TO TREAT EVERY PERFORMANCE LIKE IT'S SOMEONE'S FIRST. WE MIGHT BE SOMEONE'S FIRST EVER WRESTLING MATCH. FORGET WHAT THOSE GUYS ARE GONNA SAY ABOUT US.
ACTUALLY, IT'S A SUPLEX-COTTON BLEND.
THEY MIGHT KNOW EVERYTHING THERE IS TO KNOW ABOUT WHAT THEY DO. BUT THEY'VE NEVER SEEN ANYTHING LIKE US!
SO COME ON—

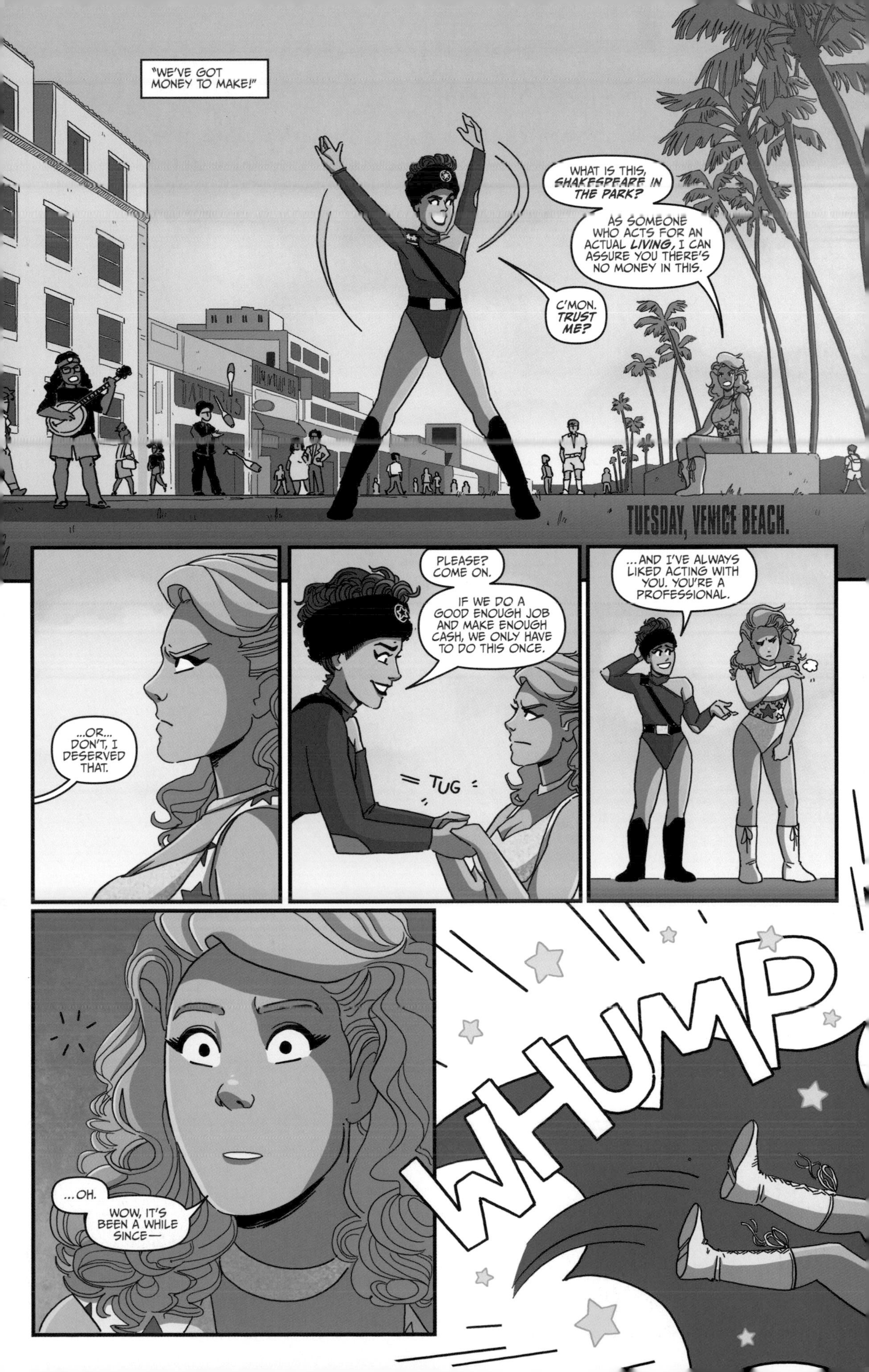
"WE'VE GOT MONEY TO MAKE!"
WHAT IS THIS, SHAKESPEARE IN THE PARK?
AS SOMEONE WHO ACTS FOR AN ACTUAL LIVING, I CAN ASSURE YOU THERE'S NO MONEY IN THIS.
C'MON. TRUST ME?
TUESDAY, VENICE BEACH.
...OR... DON'T, I DESERVED THAT.
PLEASE? COME ON.
IF WE DO A GOOD ENOUGH JOB AND MAKE ENOUGH CASH, WE ONLY HAVE TO DO THIS ONCE.
TUG
...AND I'VE ALWAYS LIKED ACTING WITH YOU. YOU'RE A PROFESSIONAL.
...OH.
WOW, IT'S BEEN A WHILE SINCE—
WHUMP

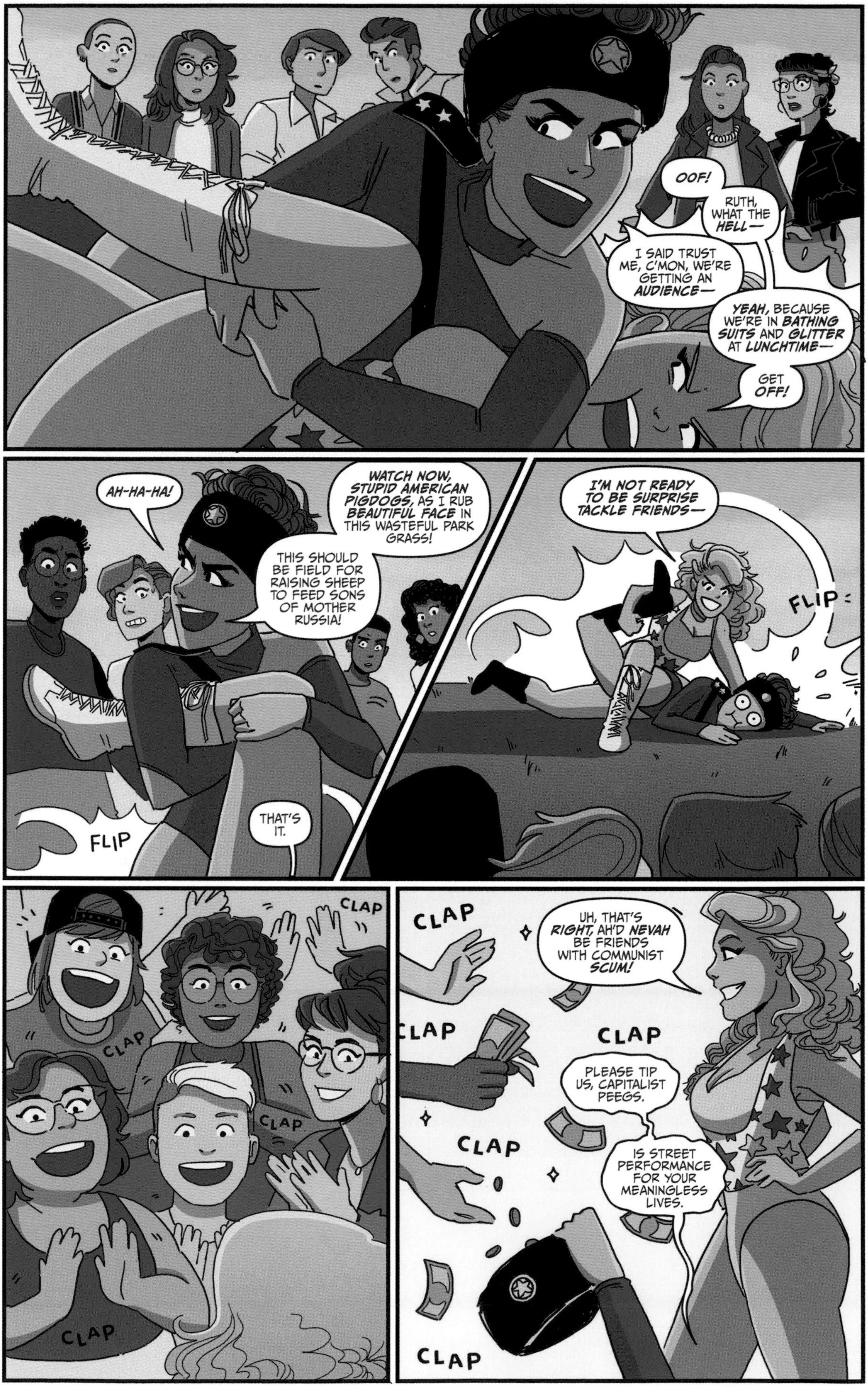
OOF!
RUTH, WHAT THE HELL—
I SAID TRUST ME, C'MON, WE'RE GETTING AN AUDIENCE—
YEAH, BECAUSE WE'RE IN BATHING SUITS AND GLITTER AT LUNCHTIME—
GET OFF!
AH-HA-HA!
WATCH NOW, STUPID AMERICAN PIGDOGS, AS I RUB BEAUTIFUL FACE IN THIS WASTEFUL PARK GRASS!
THIS SHOULD BE FIELD FOR RAISING SHEEP TO FEED SONS OF MOTHER RUSSIA!
FLIP
THAT'S IT.
I'M NOT READY TO BE SURPRISE TACKLE FRIENDS—
FLIP
CLAP
CLAP
CLAP
CLAP
CLAP
UH, THAT'S RIGHT, AH'D NEVAH BE FRIENDS WITH COMMUNIST SCUM!
CLAP
CLAP
PLEASE TIP US, CAPITALIST PEEGS.
CLAP
IS STREET PERFORMANCE FOR YOUR MEANINGLESS LIVES.
CLAP

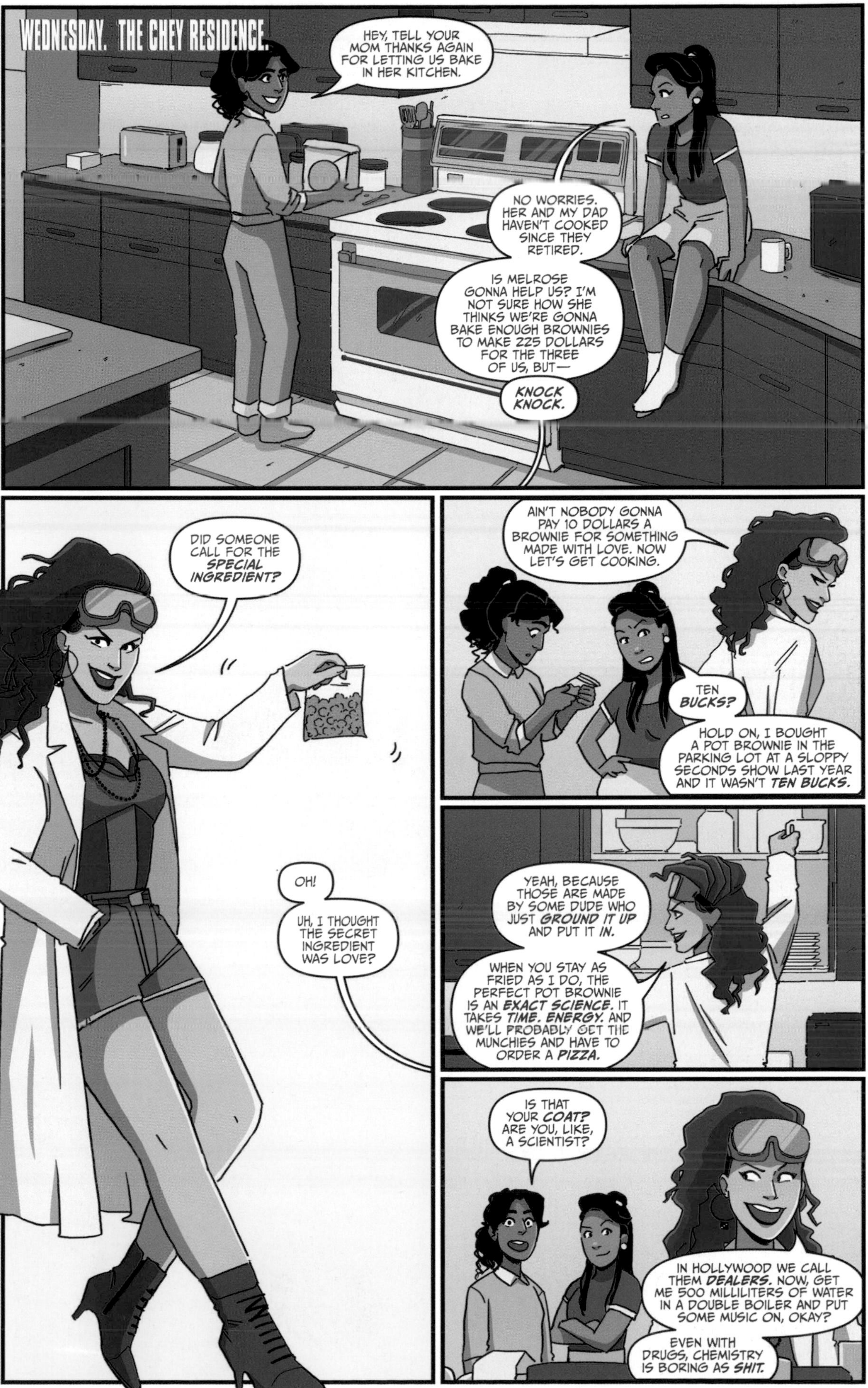
WEDNESDAY. THE CHEY RESIDENCE.
HEY, TELL YOUR MOM THANKS AGAIN FOR LETTING US BAKE IN HER KITCHEN.
NO WORRIES. HER AND MY DAD HAVEN'T COOKED SINCE THEY RETIRED.
IS MELROSE GONNA HELP US? I'M NOT SURE HOW SHE THINKS WE'RE GONNA BAKE ENOUGH BROWNIES TO MAKE 225 DOLLARS FOR THE THREE OF US, BUT—
KNOCK KNOCK.
DID SOMEONE CALL FOR THE SPECIAL INGREDIENT?
OH!
UH, I THOUGHT THE SECRET INGREDIENT WAS LOVE?
AIN'T NOBODY GONNA PAY 10 DOLLARS A BROWNIE FOR SOMETHING MADE WITH LOVE. NOW LET'S GET COOKING.
TEN BUCKS?
HOLD ON, I BOUGHT A POT BROWNIE IN THE PARKING LOT AT A SLOPPY SECONDS SHOW LAST YEAR AND IT WASN'T TEN BUCKS.
YEAH, BECAUSE THOSE ARE MADE BY SOME DUDE WHO JUST GROUND IT UP AND PUT IT IN.
WHEN YOU STAY AS FRIED AS I DO, THE PERFECT POT BROWNIE IS AN EXACT SCIENCE. IT TAKES TIME. ENERGY. AND WE'LL PROBABLY GET THE MUNCHIES AND HAVE TO ORDER A PIZZA.
IS THAT YOUR COAT? ARE YOU, LIKE, A SCIENTIST?
IN HOLLYWOOD WE CALL THEM DEALERS. NOW, GET ME 500 MILLILITERS OF WATER IN A DOUBLE BOILER AND PUT SOME MUSIC ON, OKAY?
EVEN WITH DRUGS, CHEMISTRY IS BORING AS SHIT.

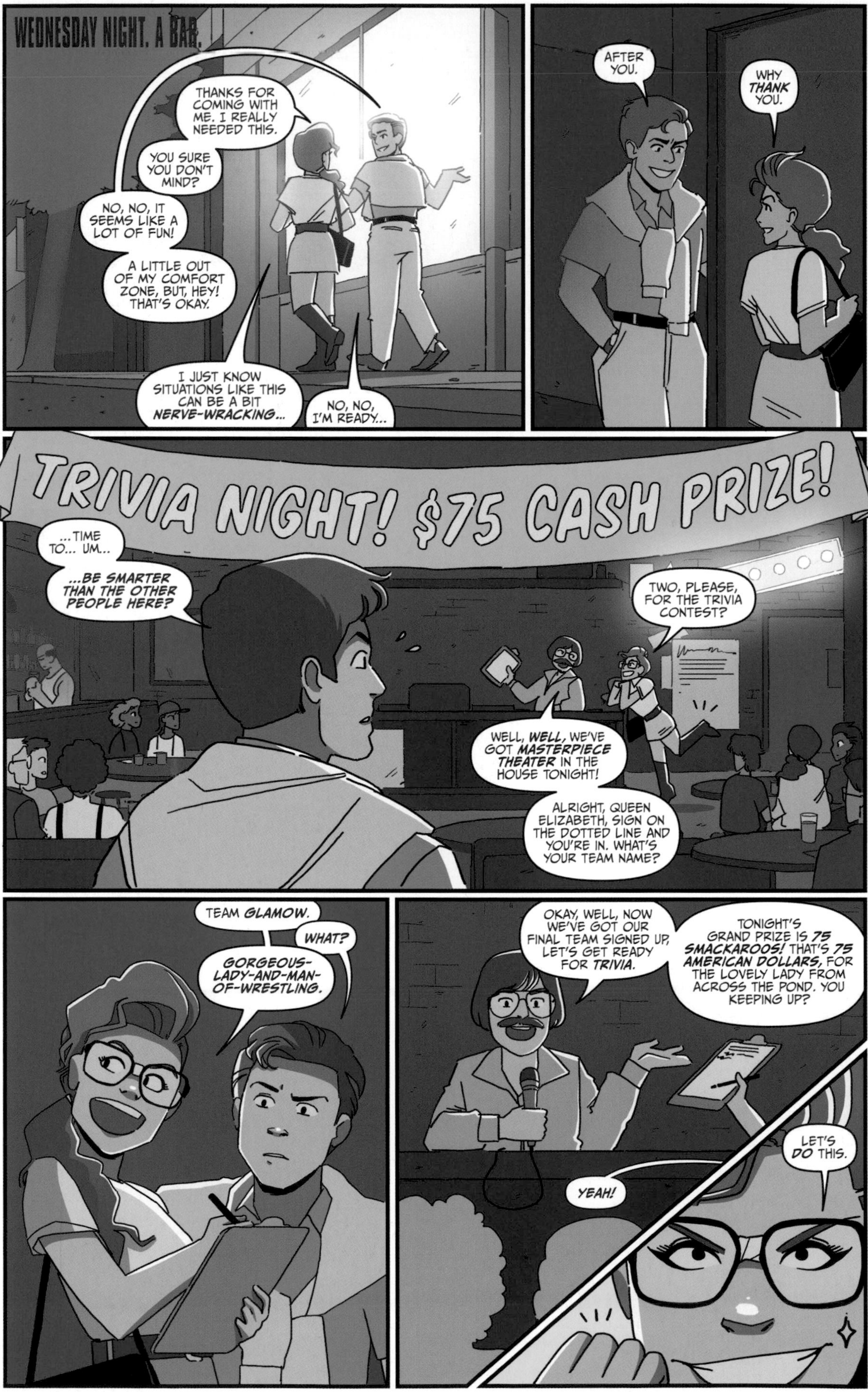

WEDNESDAY NIGHT. A BAR.
THANKS FOR COMING WITH ME. I REALLY NEEDED THIS.
YOU SURE YOU DON'T MIND?
NO, NO, IT SEEMS LIKE A LOT OF FUN!
A LITTLE OUT OF MY COMFORT ZONE, BUT, HEY! THAT'S OKAY.
I JUST KNOW SITUATIONS LIKE THIS CAN BE A BIT NERVE-WRACKING...
NO, NO, I'M READY...
AFTER YOU.
WHY THANK YOU.
TRIVIA NIGHT! $75 CASH PRIZE!
...TIME TO... UM...
...BE SMARTER THAN THE OTHER PEOPLE HERE?
TWO, PLEASE, FOR THE TRIVIA CONTEST?
WELL, WELL, WE'VE GOT MASTERPIECE THEATER IN THE HOUSE TONIGHT!
ALRIGHT, QUEEN ELIZABETH, SIGN ON THE DOTTED LINE AND YOU'RE IN. WHAT'S YOUR TEAM NAME?
TEAM GLAMOW.
WHAT?
GORGEOUS-LADY-AND-MAN-OF-WRESTLING.
OKAY, WELL, NOW WE'VE GOT OUR FINAL TEAM SIGNED UP, LET'S GET READY FOR TRIVIA.
TONIGHT'S GRAND PRIZE IS 75 SMACKAROOS! THAT'S 75 AMERICAN DOLLARS, FOR THE LOVELY LADY FROM ACROSS THE POND. YOU KEEPING UP?
YEAH!
LET'S DO THIS.

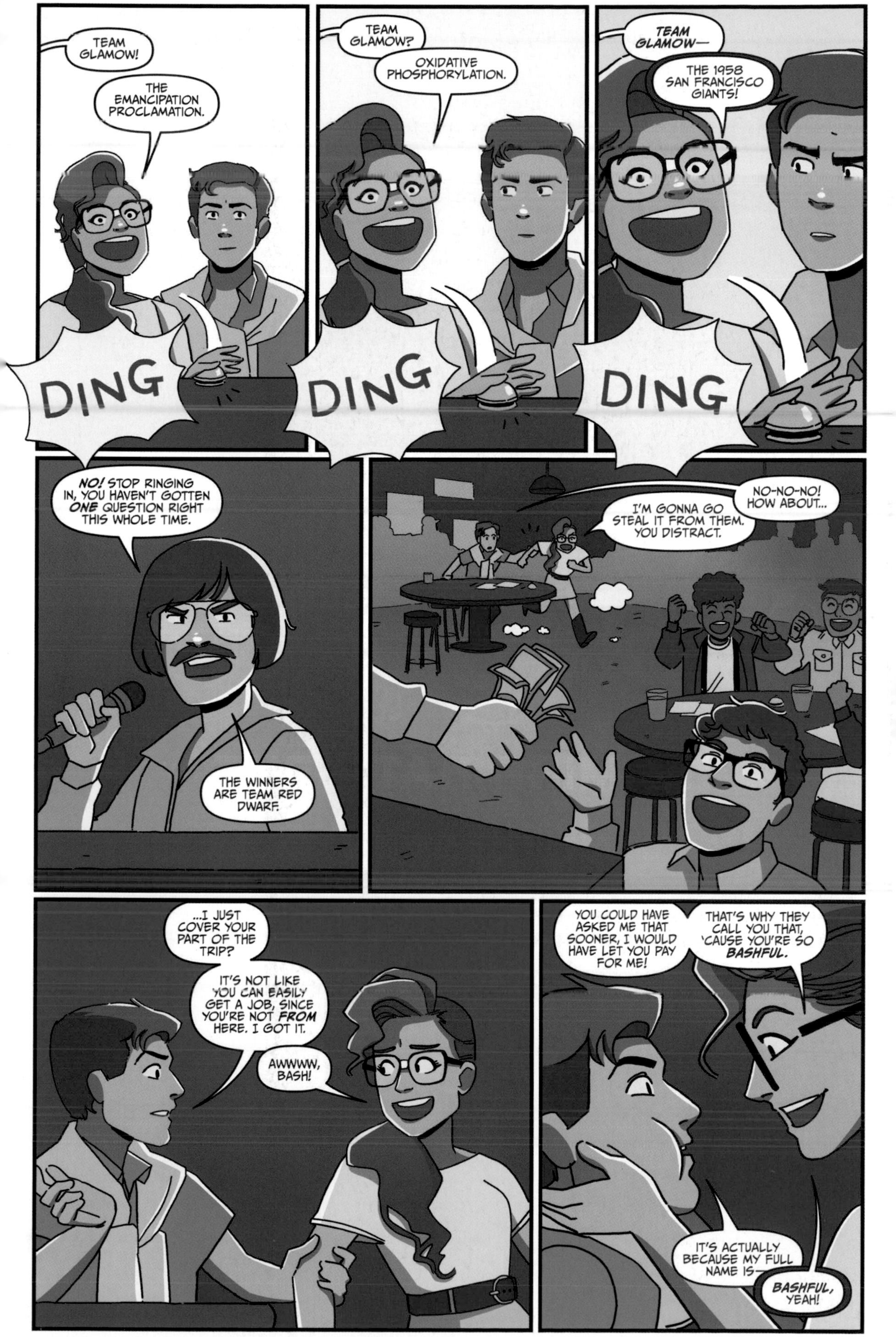
TEAM GLAMOW!
THE EMANCIPATION PROCLAMATION.
DING
TEAM GLAMOW?
OXIDATIVE PHOSPHORYLATION.
DING
TEAM GLAMOW—
THE 1958 SAN FRANCISCO GIANTS!
DING
NO! STOP RINGING IN, YOU HAVEN'T GOTTEN ONE QUESTION RIGHT THIS WHOLE TIME.
THE WINNERS ARE TEAM RED DWARF.
NO-NO-NO! HOW ABOUT...
I'M GONNA GO STEAL IT FROM THEM. YOU DISTRACT.
...I JUST COVER YOUR PART OF THE TRIP?
IT'S NOT LIKE YOU CAN EASILY GET A JOB, SINCE YOU'RE NOT FROM HERE. I GOT IT.
AWWWW, BASH!
YOU COULD HAVE ASKED ME THAT SOONER, I WOULD HAVE LET YOU PAY FOR ME!
THAT'S WHY THEY CALL YOU THAT, 'CAUSE YOU'RE SO BASHFUL.
IT'S ACTUALLY BECAUSE MY FULL NAME IS—
BASHFUL, YEAH!

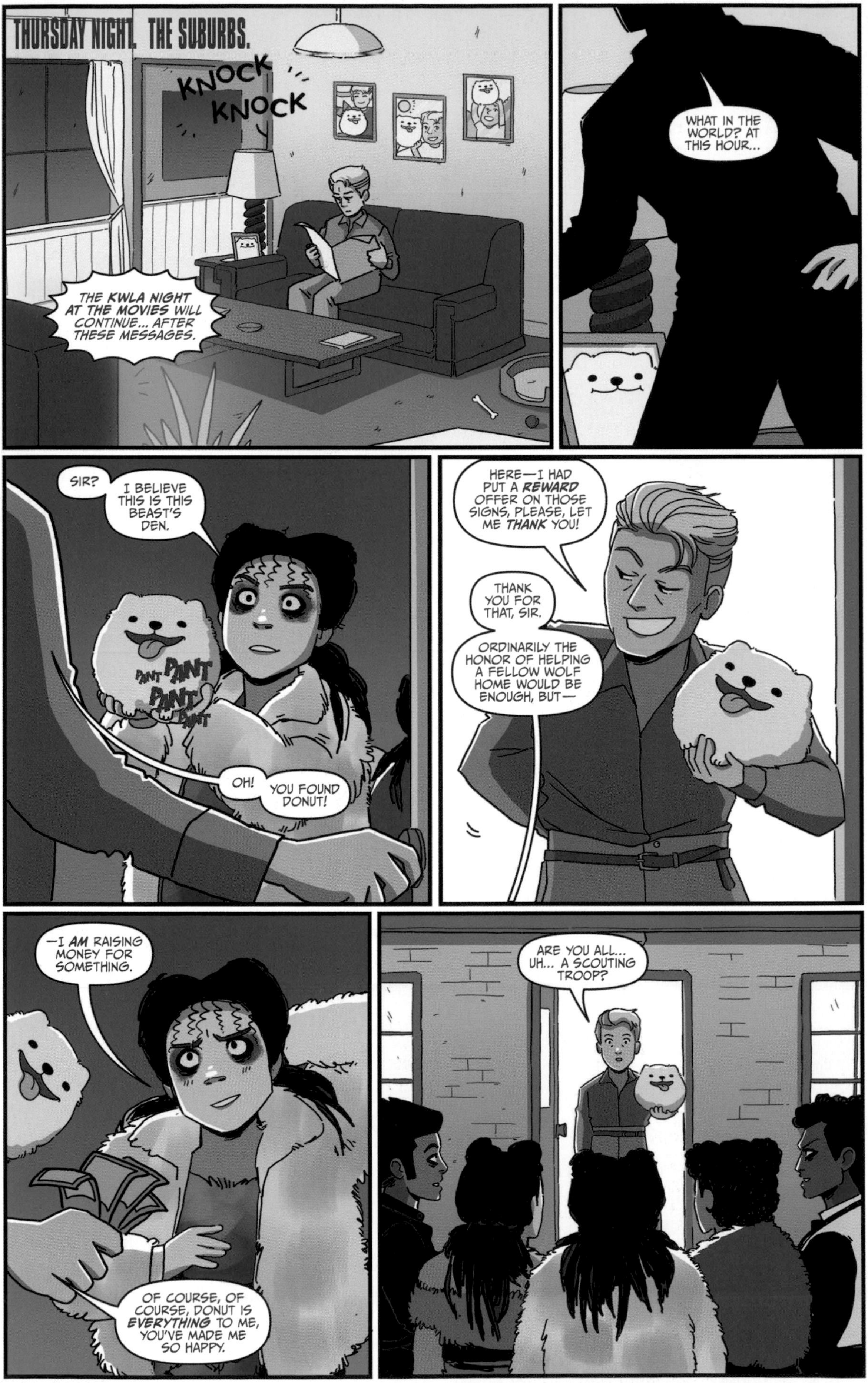
THURSDAY NIGHT. THE SUBURBS.
KNOCK KNOCK
THE KWLA NIGHT AT THE MOVIES WILL CONTINUE... AFTER THESE MESSAGES.
WHAT IN THE WORLD? AT THIS HOUR...
SIR?
I BELIEVE THIS IS THIS BEAST'S DEN.
PANT PANT PANT PANT
OH!
YOU FOUND DONUT!
HERE—I HAD PUT A REWARD OFFER ON THOSE SIGNS, PLEASE, LET ME THANK YOU!
THANK YOU FOR THAT, SIR.
ORDINARILY THE HONOR OF HELPING A FELLOW WOLF HOME WOULD BE ENOUGH, BUT—
—I AM RAISING MONEY FOR SOMETHING.
OF COURSE, OF COURSE, DONUT IS EVERYTHING TO ME, YOU'VE MADE ME SO HAPPY.
ARE YOU ALL... UH... A SCOUTING TROOP?

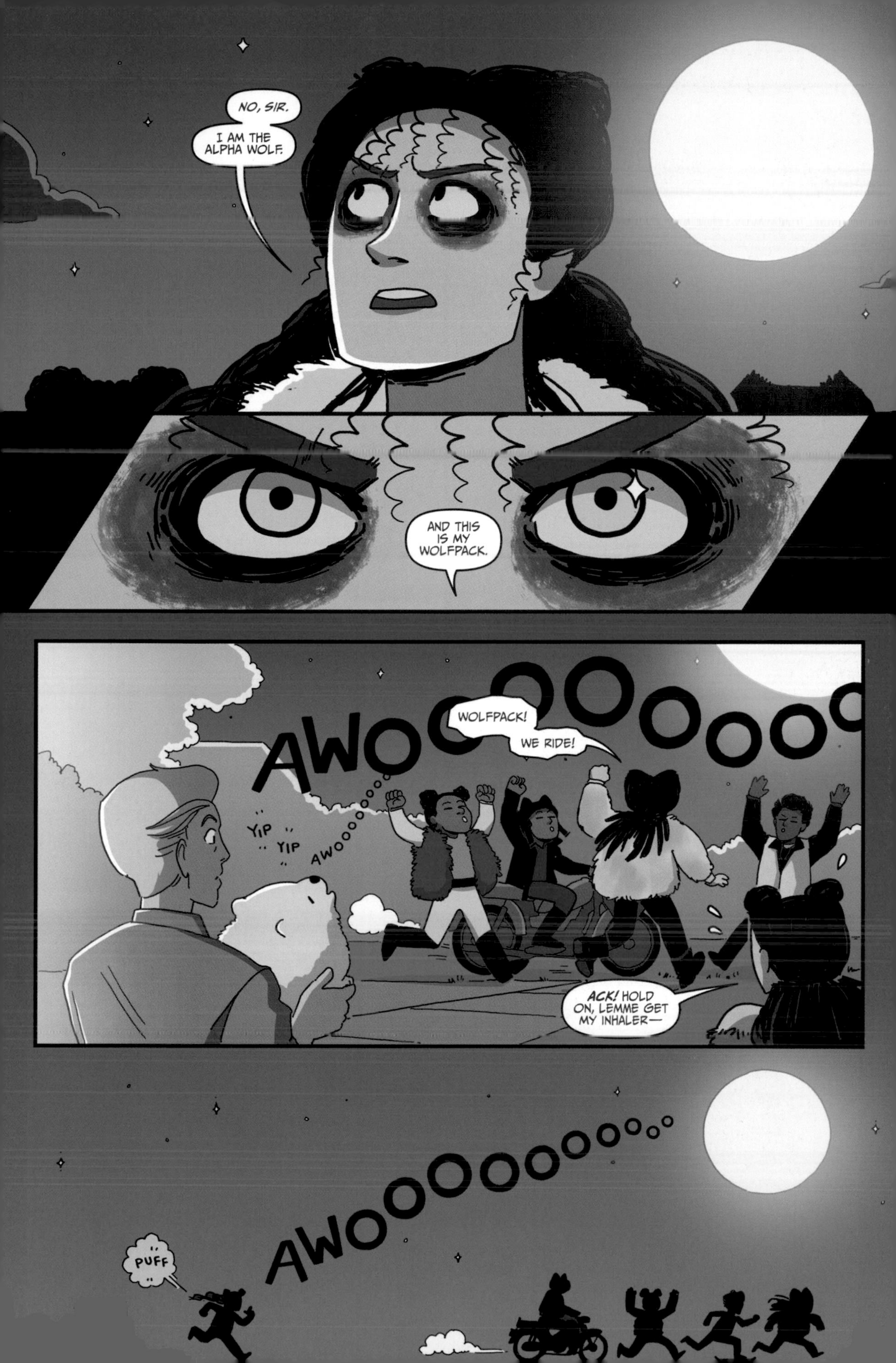
NO, SIR.
I AM THE ALPHA WOLF.
AND THIS IS MY WOLFPACK.
AWOOOOOOOOO
WOLFPACK!
WE RIDE!
YIP YIP
AWOOOOOO
ACK! HOLD ON, LEMME GET MY INHALER—
AWOOOOOOOOOOOO
PUFF

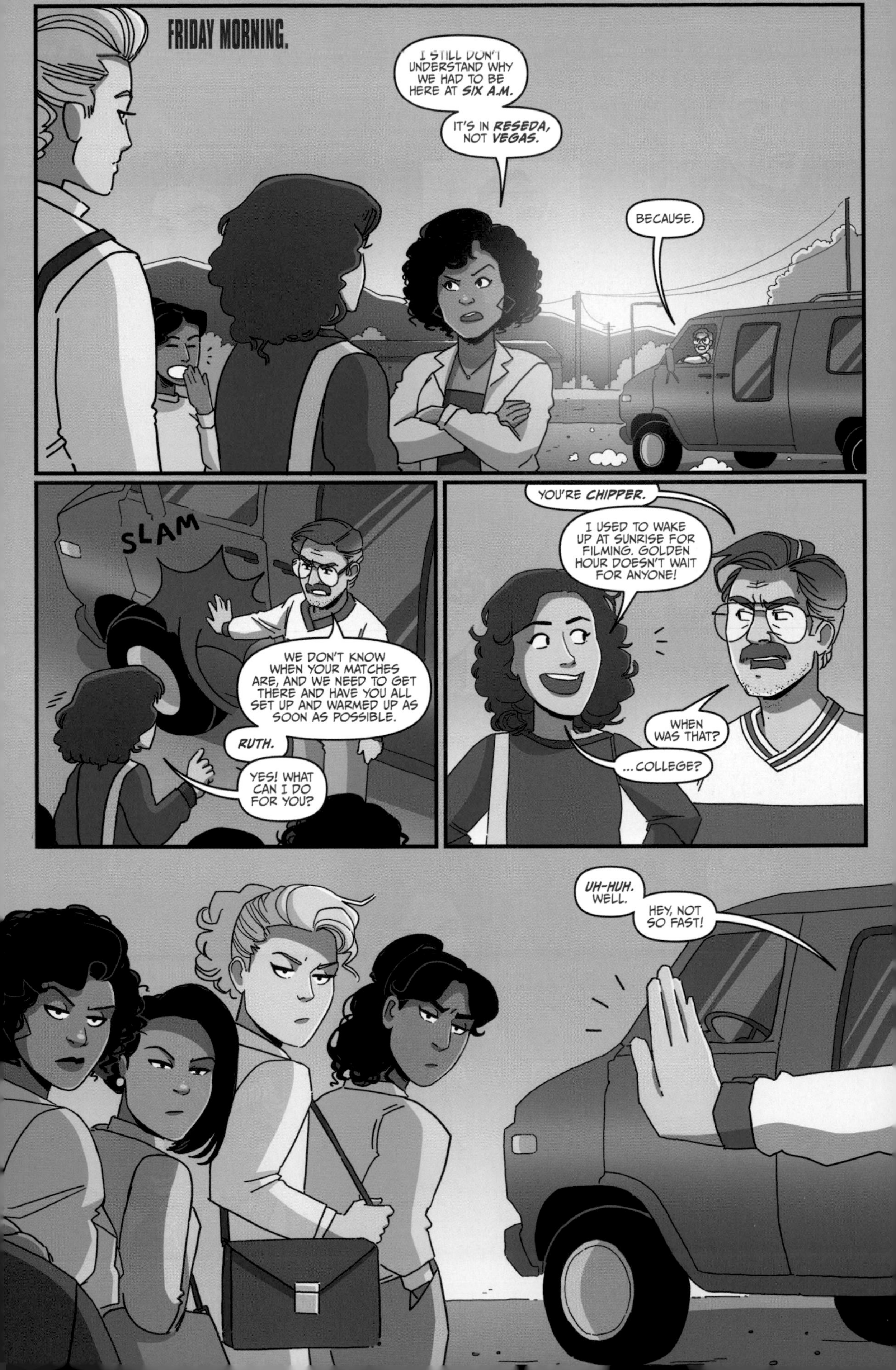
FRIDAY MORNING.
I STILL DON'T UNDERSTAND WHY WE HAD TO BE HERE AT SIX A.M.
IT'S IN RESEDA, NOT VEGAS.
BECAUSE.
SLAM
WE DON'T KNOW WHEN YOUR MATCHES ARE, AND WE NEED TO GET THERE AND HAVE YOU ALL SET UP AND WARMED UP AS SOON AS POSSIBLE.
RUTH.
YES! WHAT CAN I DO FOR YOU?
YOU'RE CHIPPER.
I USED TO WAKE UP AT SUNRISE FOR FILMING. GOLDEN HOUR DOESN'T WAIT FOR ANYONE!
WHEN WAS THAT?
...COLLEGE?
UH-HUH. WELL.
HEY, NOT SO FAST!

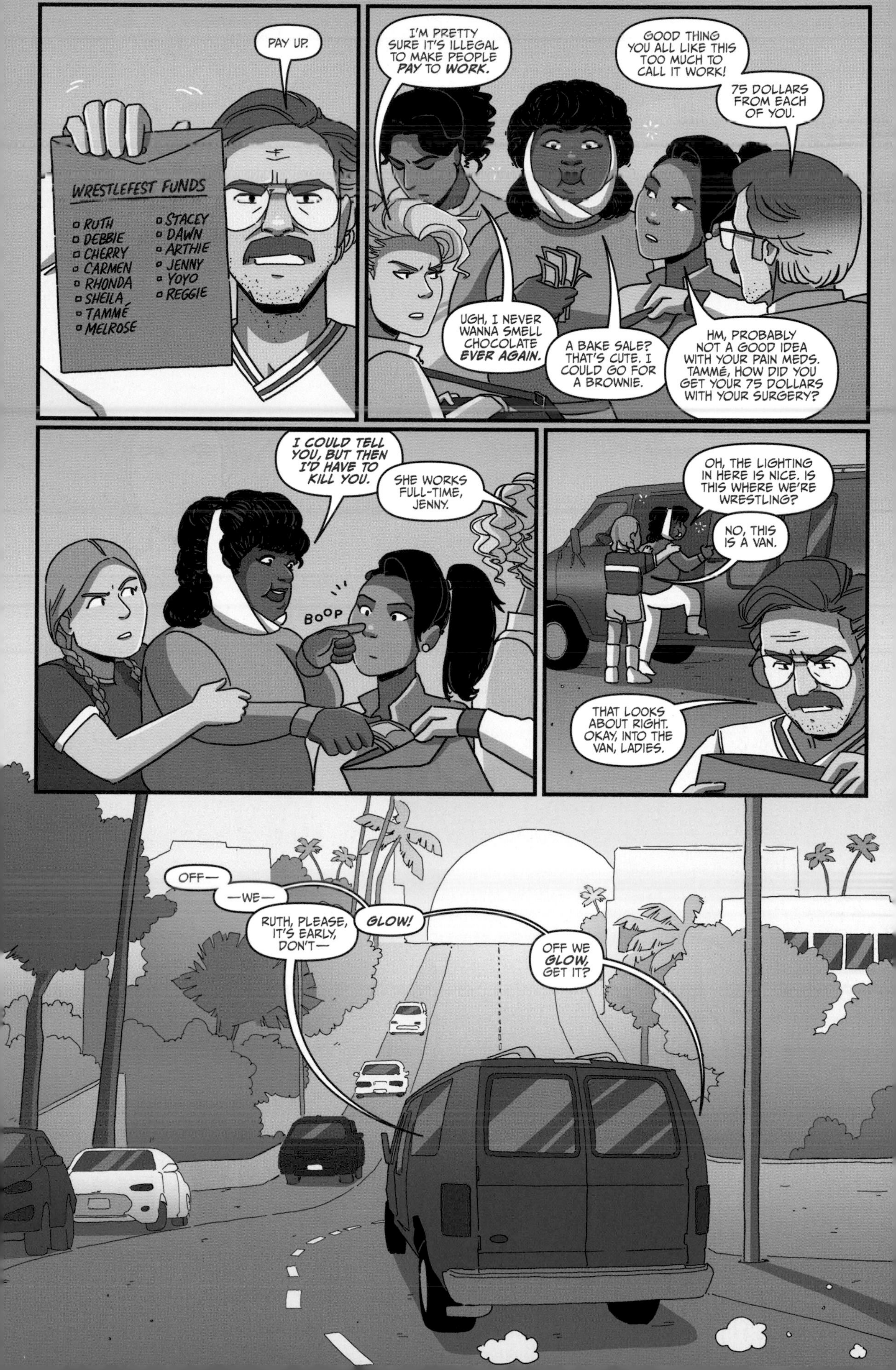
PAY UP.
WRESTLEFEST FUNDS
RUTH
DEBBIE
CHERRY
CARMEN
RHONDA
SHEILA
TAMMÉ
MELROSE
STACEY
DAWN
ARTHIE
JENNY
YOYO
REGGIE
I'M PRETTY SURE IT'S ILLEGAL TO MAKE PEOPLE PAY TO WORK.
GOOD THING YOU ALL LIKE THIS TOO MUCH TO CALL IT WORK!
75 DOLLARS FROM EACH OF YOU.
UGH, I NEVER WANNA SMELL CHOCOLATE EVER AGAIN.
A BAKE SALE? THAT'S CUTE. I COULD GO FOR A BROWNIE.
HM, PROBABLY NOT A GOOD IDEA WITH YOUR PAIN MEDS. TAMMÉ, HOW DID YOU GET YOUR 75 DOLLARS WITH YOUR SURGERY?
I COULD TELL YOU, BUT THEN I'D HAVE TO KILL YOU.
SHE WORKS FULL-TIME, JENNY.
BOOP
OH, THE LIGHTING IN HERE IS NICE. IS THIS WHERE WE'RE WRESTLING?
NO, THIS IS A VAN.
THAT LOOKS ABOUT RIGHT. OKAY, INTO THE VAN, LADIES.
OFF—
—WE—
GLOW!
RUTH, PLEASE, IT'S EARLY, DON'T—
OFF WE GLOW, GET IT?

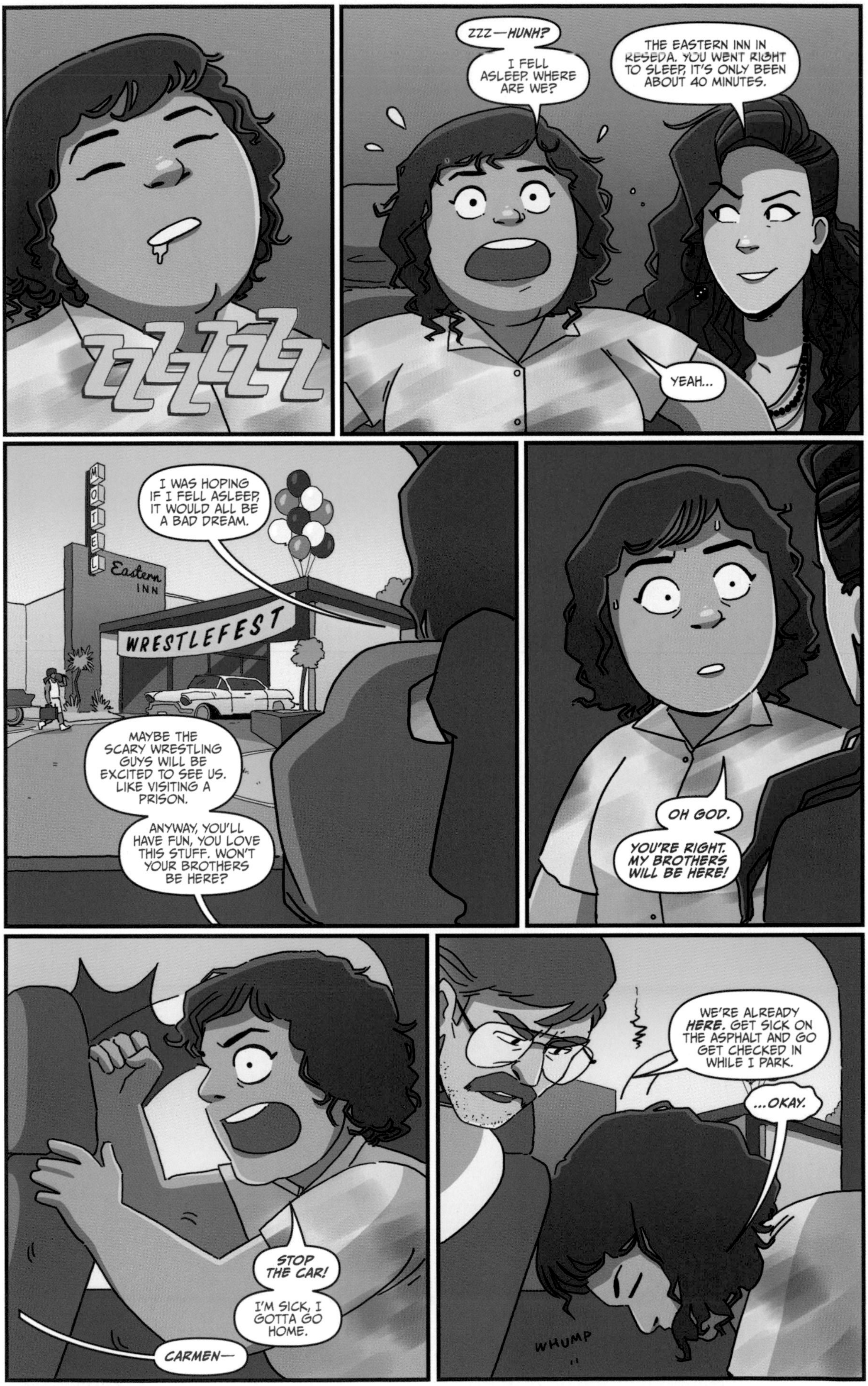
ZZZZZZZZ
ZZZ—HUNH?
I FELL ASLEEP. WHERE ARE WE?
THE EASTERN INN IN RESEDA. YOU WENT RIGHT TO SLEEP, IT'S ONLY BEEN ABOUT 40 MINUTES.
YEAH...
MOTEL
Eastern INN
WRESTLEFEST
I WAS HOPING IF I FELL ASLEEP, IT WOULD ALL BE A BAD DREAM.
MAYBE THE SCARY WRESTLING GUYS WILL BE EXCITED TO SEE US. LIKE VISITING A PRISON.
ANYWAY, YOU'LL HAVE FUN, YOU LOVE THIS STUFF. WON'T YOUR BROTHERS BE HERE?
OH GOD.
YOU'RE RIGHT. MY BROTHERS WILL BE HERE!
STOP THE CAR!
I'M SICK, I GOTTA GO HOME.
CARMEN—
WE'RE ALREADY HERE. GET SICK ON THE ASPHALT AND GO GET CHECKED IN WHILE I PARK.
...OKAY.
WHUMP

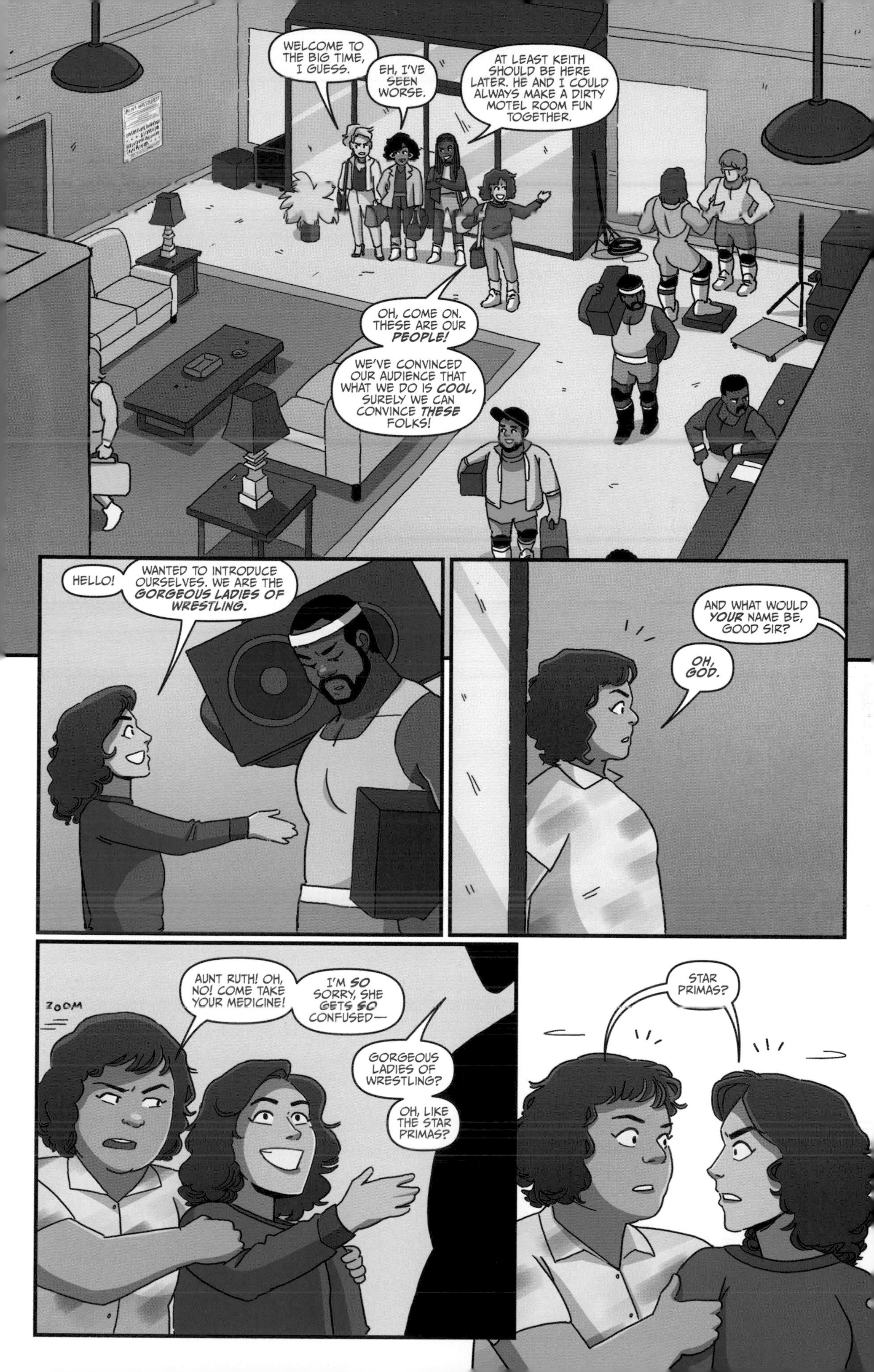
WELCOME TO THE BIG TIME, I GUESS.
EH, I'VE SEEN WORSE.
AT LEAST KEITH SHOULD BE HERE LATER. HE AND I COULD ALWAYS MAKE A DIRTY MOTEL ROOM FUN TOGETHER.
OH, COME ON. THESE ARE OUR *PEOPLE!*
WE'VE CONVINCED OUR AUDIENCE THAT WHAT WE DO IS **COOL**, SURELY WE CAN CONVINCE *THESE* FOLKS!
HELLO!
WANTED TO INTRODUCE OURSELVES. WE ARE THE *GORGEOUS LADIES OF WRESTLING.*
AND WHAT WOULD *YOUR* NAME BE, GOOD SIR?
OH, GOD.
ZOOM
AUNT RUTH! OH, NO! COME TAKE YOUR MEDICINE!
I'M *SO* SORRY, SHE GETS *SO* CONFUSED—
GORGEOUS LADIES OF WRESTLING?
OH, LIKE THE STAR PRIMAS?
STAR PRIMAS?

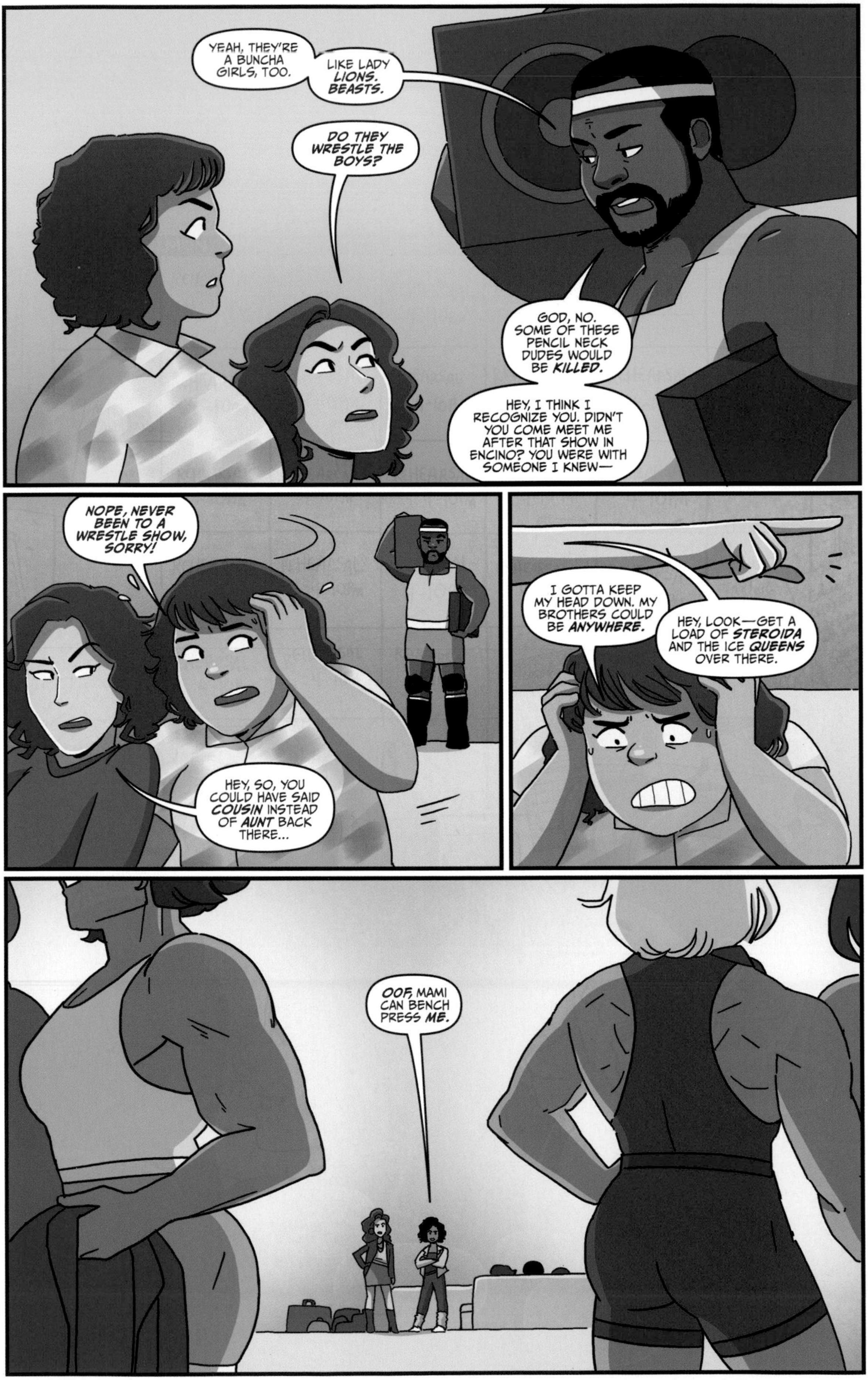
YEAH, THEY'RE A BUNCHA GIRLS, TOO.
LIKE LADY LIONS. BEASTS.
DO THEY WRESTLE THE BOYS?
GOD, NO. SOME OF THESE PENCIL NECK DUDES WOULD BE KILLED.
HEY, I THINK I RECOGNIZE YOU. DIDN'T YOU COME MEET ME AFTER THAT SHOW IN ENCINO? YOU WERE WITH SOMEONE I KNEW—
NOPE, NEVER BEEN TO A WRESTLE SHOW, SORRY!
HEY, SO, YOU COULD HAVE SAID COUSIN INSTEAD OF AUNT BACK THERE...
I GOTTA KEEP MY HEAD DOWN. MY BROTHERS COULD BE ANYWHERE.
HEY, LOOK—GET A LOAD OF STEROIDA AND THE ICE QUEENS OVER THERE.
OOF, MAMI CAN BENCH PRESS ME.

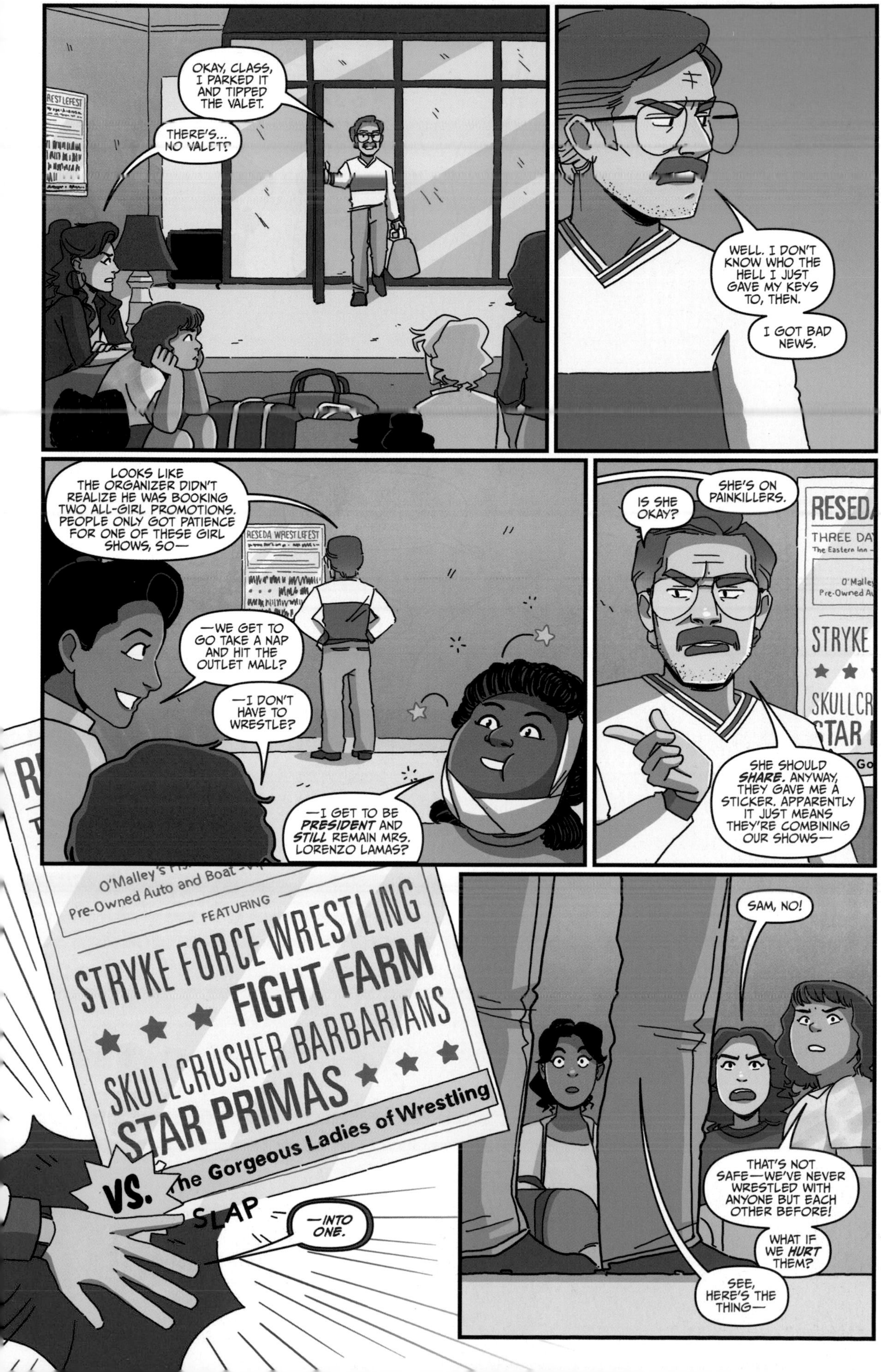

RESEDA WRESTLEFEST
OKAY, CLASS, I PARKED IT AND TIPPED THE VALET.
THERE'S... NO VALET?
WELL. I DON'T KNOW WHO THE HELL I JUST GAVE MY KEYS TO, THEN.
I GOT BAD NEWS.
LOOKS LIKE THE ORGANIZER DIDN'T REALIZE HE WAS BOOKING TWO ALL-GIRL PROMOTIONS. PEOPLE ONLY GOT PATIENCE FOR ONE OF THESE GIRL SHOWS, SO—
—WE GET TO GO TAKE A NAP AND HIT THE OUTLET MALL?
—I DON'T HAVE TO WRESTLE?
—I GET TO BE PRESIDENT AND STILL REMAIN MRS. LORENZO LAMAS?
IS SHE OKAY?
SHE'S ON PAINKILLERS.
SHE SHOULD SHARE. ANYWAY, THEY GAVE ME A STICKER. APPARENTLY IT JUST MEANS THEY'RE COMBINING OUR SHOWS—
O'Malley's
Pre-Owned Auto and Boat
FEATURING
STRYKE FORCE WRESTLING
FIGHT FARM
SKULLCRUSHER BARBARIANS
STAR PRIMAS
VS.
The Gorgeous Ladies of Wrestling
SLAP
—INTO ONE.
SAM, NO!
THAT'S NOT SAFE—WE'VE NEVER WRESTLED WITH ANYONE BUT EACH OTHER BEFORE!
WHAT IF WE HURT THEM?
SEE, HERE'S THE THING—

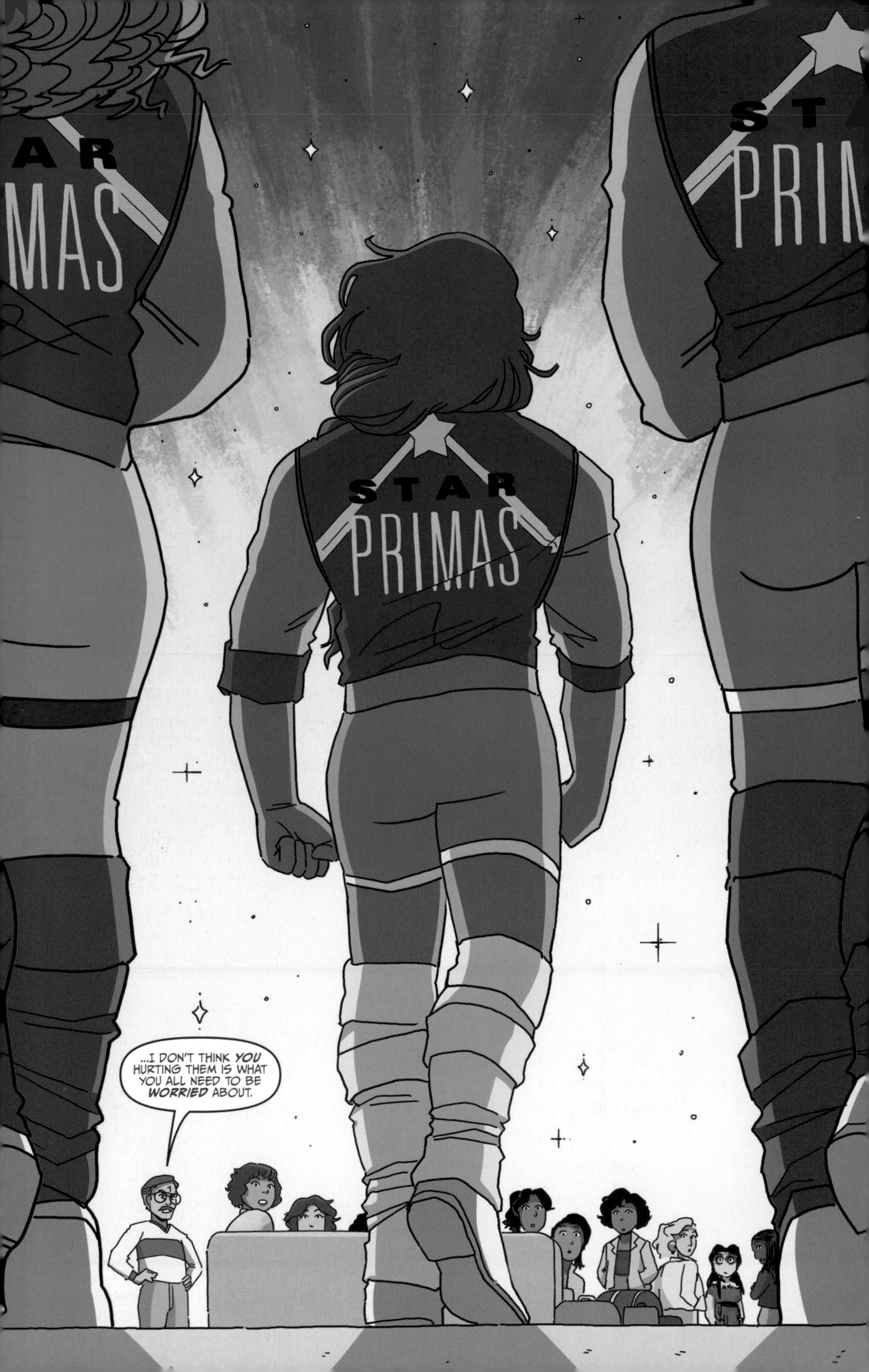
STAR
PRIMAS
...I DON'T THINK YOU HURTING THEM IS WHAT YOU ALL NEED TO BE WORRIED ABOUT.

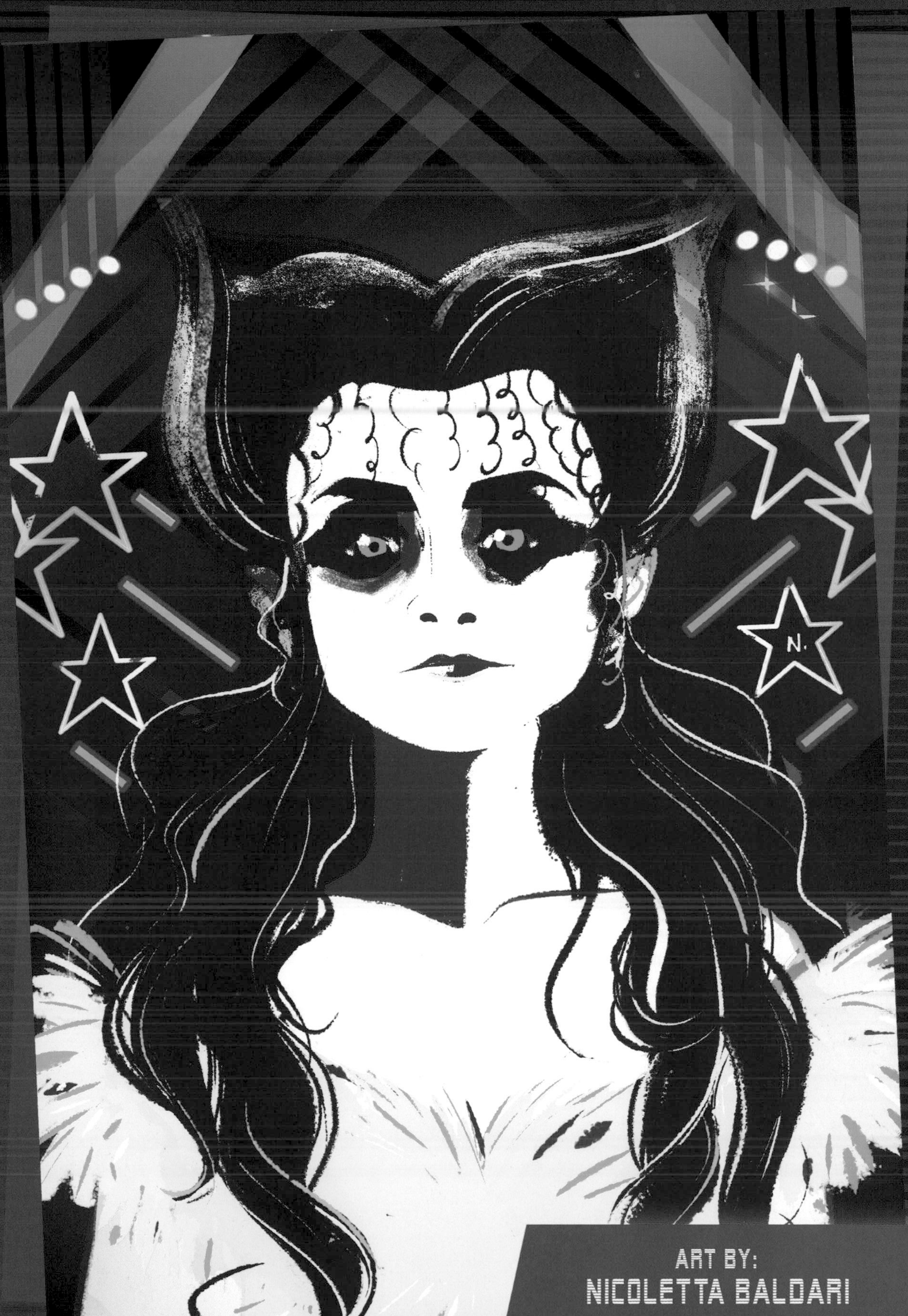
ART BY:
NICOLETTA BALDARI

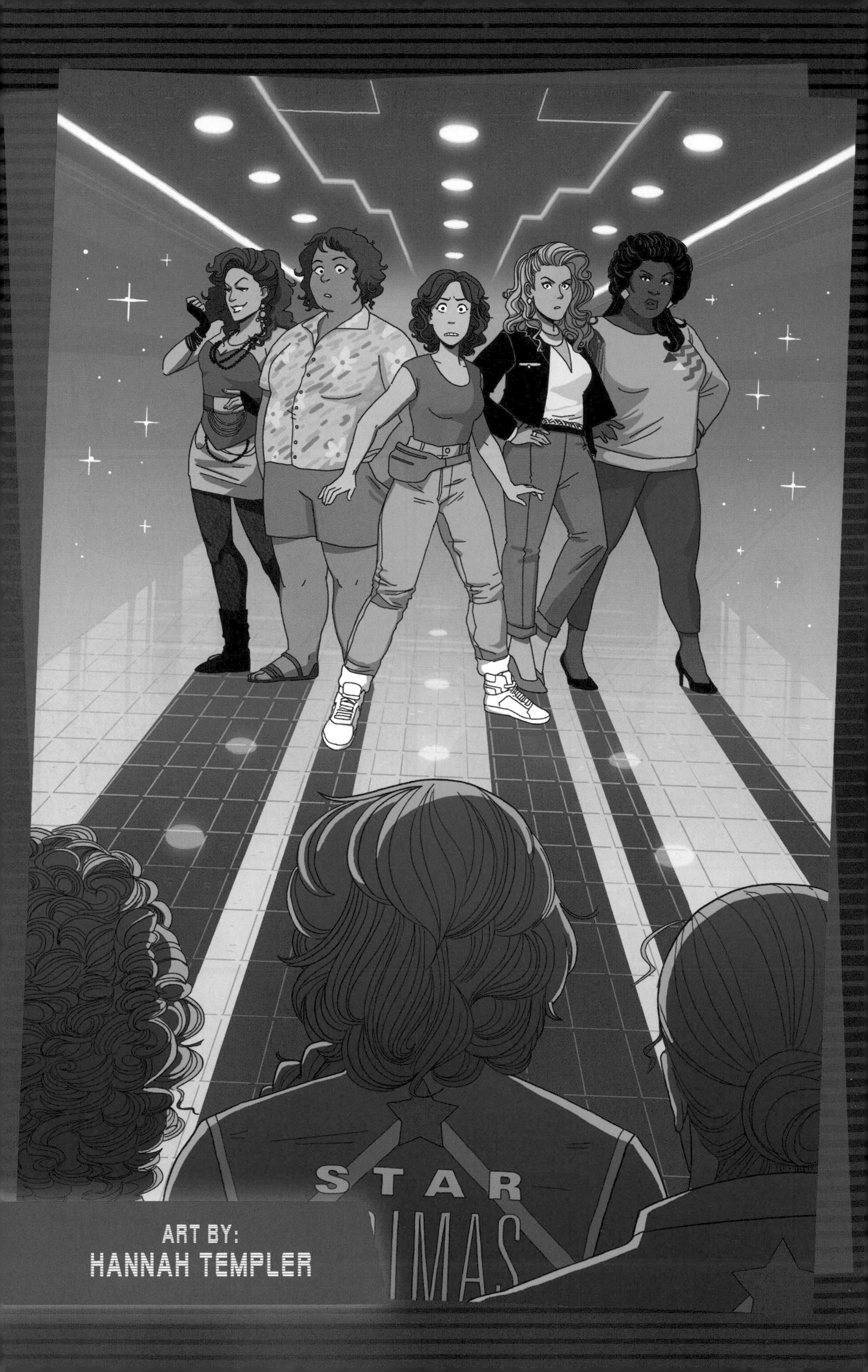
STAR
ART BY:
HANNAH TEMPLER

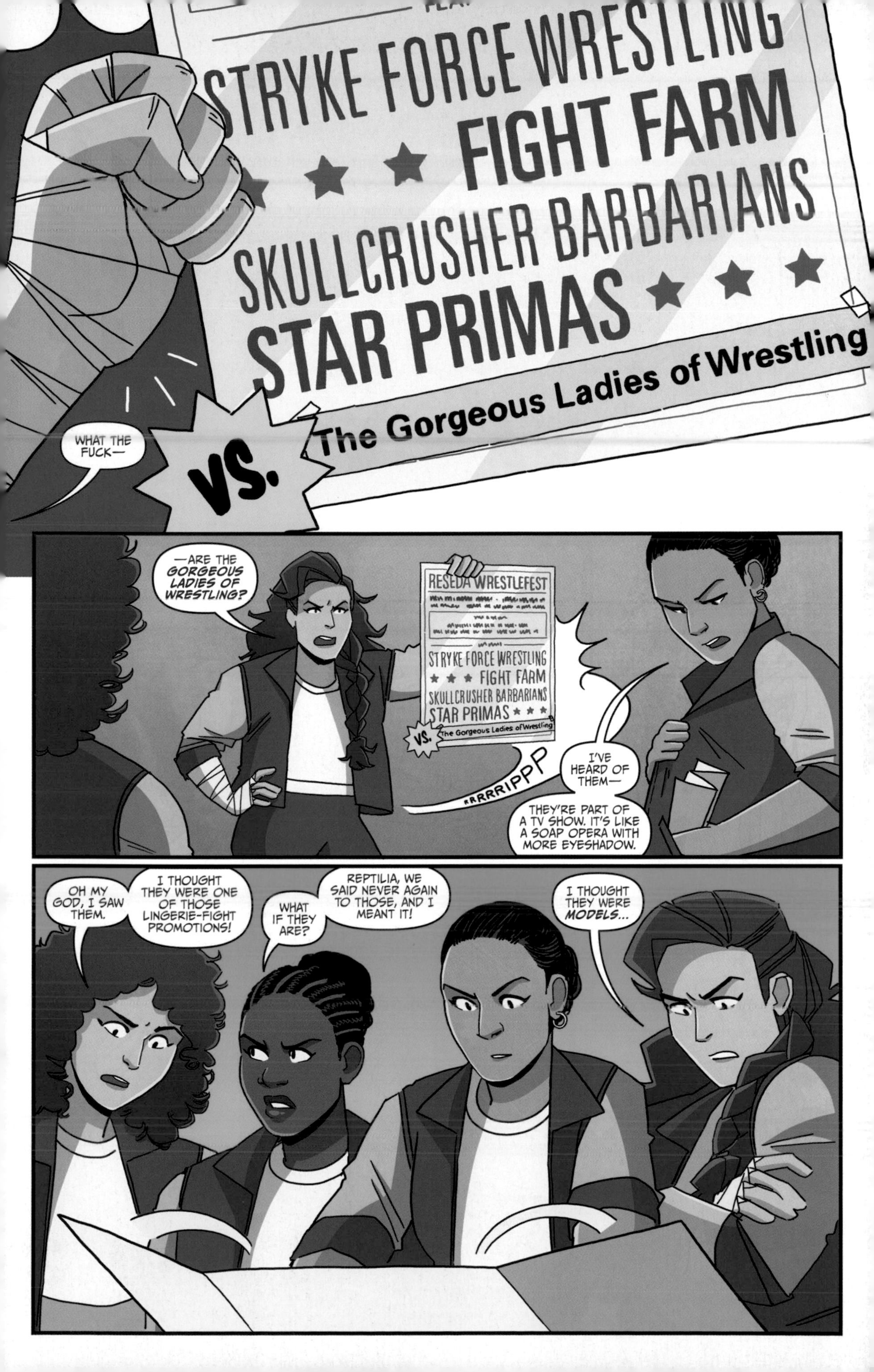
STRYKE FORCE WRESTLING
FIGHT FARM
SKULLCRUSHER BARBARIANS
STAR PRIMAS
The Gorgeous Ladies of Wrestling
VS.
WHAT THE FUCK—
—ARE THE GORGEOUS LADIES OF WRESTLING?
RESEDA WRESTLEFEST
STRYKE FORCE WRESTLING
FIGHT FARM
SKULLCRUSHER BARBARIANS
STAR PRIMAS
VS. The Gorgeous Ladies of Wrestling
RRRRIPPP
I'VE HEARD OF THEM—
THEY'RE PART OF A TV SHOW. IT'S LIKE A SOAP OPERA WITH MORE EYESHADOW.
OH MY GOD, I SAW THEM.
I THOUGHT THEY WERE ONE OF THOSE LINGERIE-FIGHT PROMOTIONS!
WHAT IF THEY ARE?
REPTILIA, WE SAID NEVER AGAIN TO THOSE, AND I MEANT IT!
I THOUGHT THEY WERE MODELS...

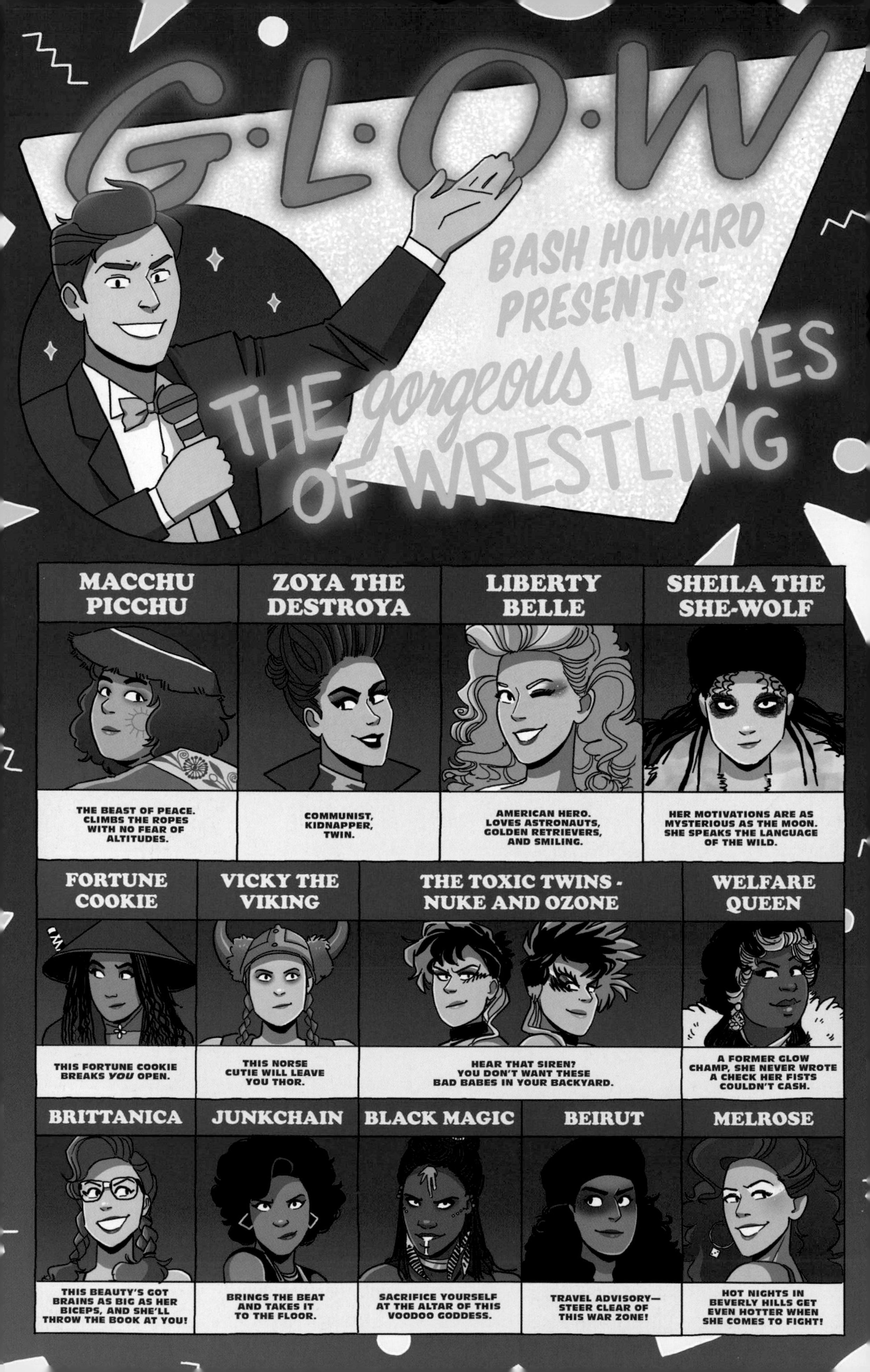
G·L·O·W
BASH HOWARD PRESENTS -
THE gorgeous LADIES OF WRESTLING
MACCHU PICCHU
THE BEAST OF PEACE. CLIMBS THE ROPES WITH NO FEAR OF ALTITUDES.
ZOYA THE DESTROYA
COMMUNIST, KIDNAPPER, TWIN.
LIBERTY BELLE
AMERICAN HERO. LOVES ASTRONAUTS, GOLDEN RETRIEVERS, AND SMILING.
SHEILA THE SHE-WOLF
HER MOTIVATIONS ARE AS MYSTERIOUS AS THE MOON. SHE SPEAKS THE LANGUAGE OF THE WILD.
FORTUNE COOKIE
THIS FORTUNE COOKIE BREAKS *YOU* OPEN.
VICKY THE VIKING
THIS NORSE CUTIE WILL LEAVE YOU THOR.
THE TOXIC TWINS - NUKE AND OZONE
HEAR THAT SIREN? YOU DON'T WANT THESE BAD BABES IN YOUR BACKYARD.
WELFARE QUEEN
A FORMER GLOW CHAMP, SHE NEVER WROTE A CHECK HER FISTS COULDN'T CASH.
BRITTANICA
THIS BEAUTY'S GOT BRAINS AS BIG AS HER BICEPS, AND SHE'LL THROW THE BOOK AT YOU!
JUNKCHAIN
BRINGS THE BEAT AND TAKES IT TO THE FLOOR.
BLACK MAGIC
SACRIFICE YOURSELF AT THE ALTAR OF THIS VOODOO GODDESS.
BEIRUT
TRAVEL ADVISORY— STEER CLEAR OF THIS WAR ZONE!
MELROSE
HOT NIGHTS IN BEVERLY HILLS GET EVEN HOTTER WHEN SHE COMES TO FIGHT!

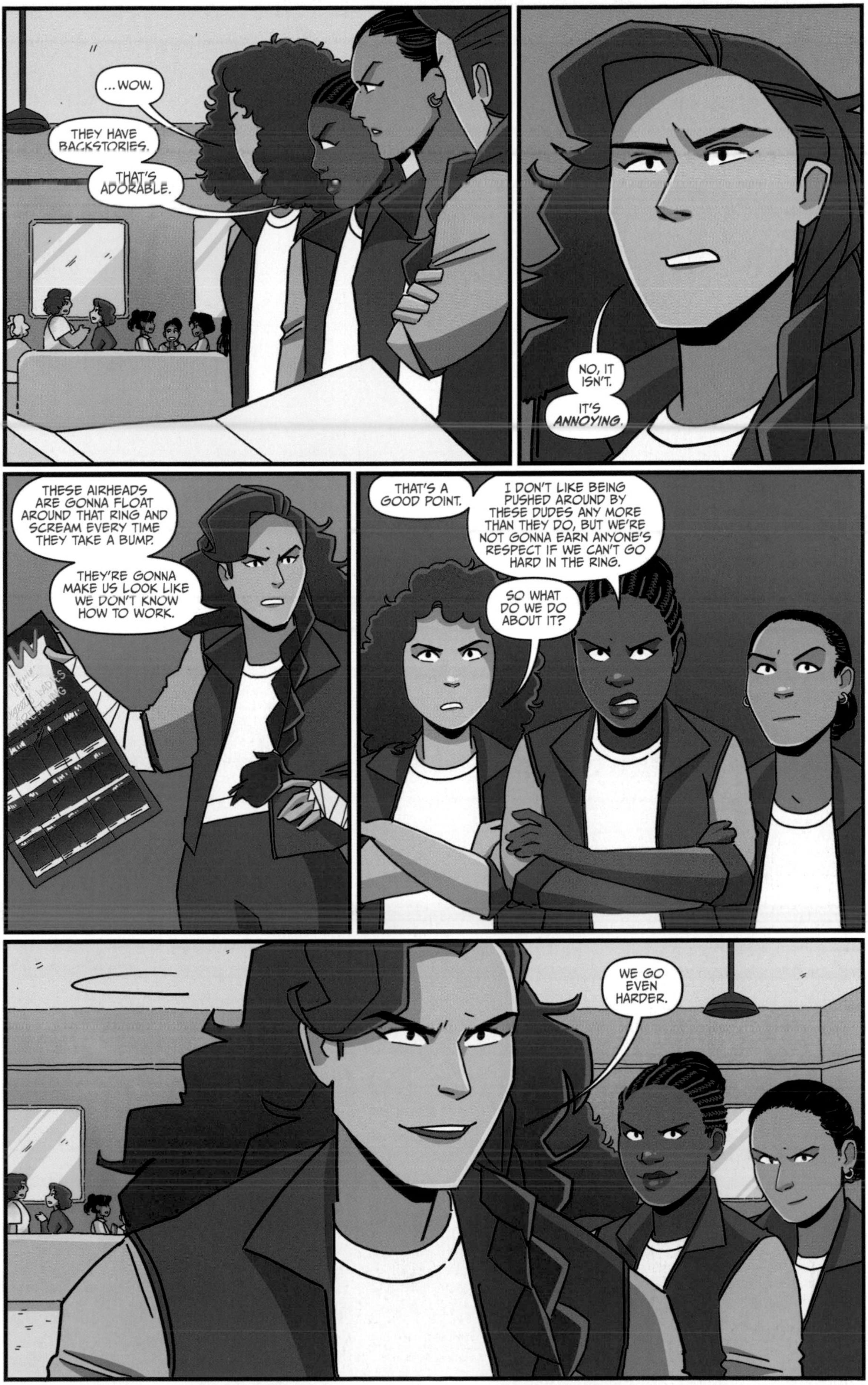
...WOW.
THEY HAVE BACKSTORIES.
THAT'S ADORABLE.
NO, IT ISN'T.
IT'S *ANNOYING*.
THESE AIRHEADS ARE GONNA FLOAT AROUND THAT RING AND SCREAM EVERY TIME THEY TAKE A BUMP.
THEY'RE GONNA MAKE US LOOK LIKE WE DON'T KNOW HOW TO WORK.
THAT'S A GOOD POINT.
I DON'T LIKE BEING PUSHED AROUND BY THESE DUDES ANY MORE THAN THEY DO, BUT WE'RE NOT GONNA EARN ANYONE'S RESPECT IF WE CAN'T GO HARD IN THE RING.
SO WHAT DO WE DO ABOUT IT?
WE GO EVEN HARDER.

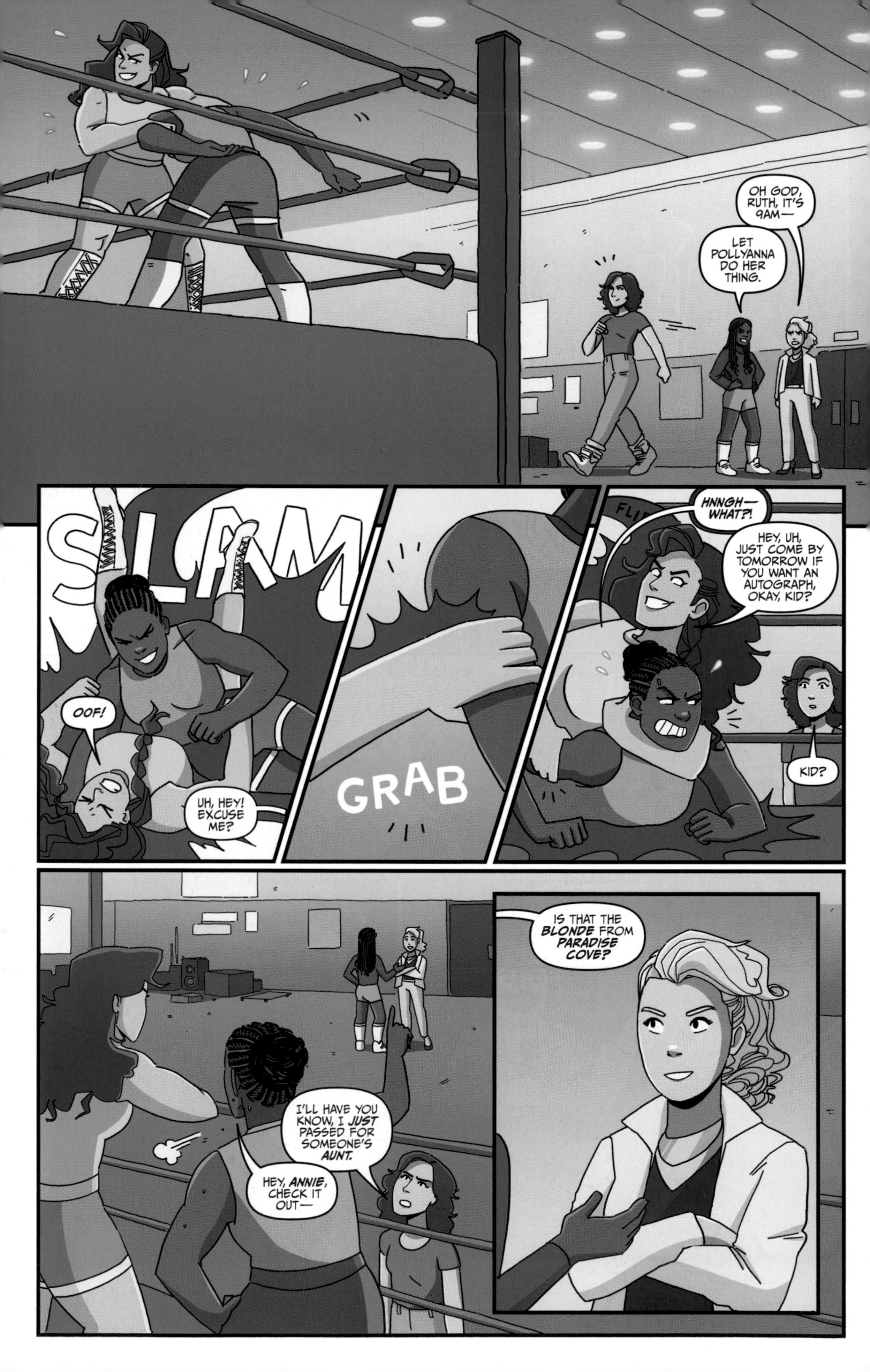
OH GOD, RUTH, IT'S 9AM—
LET POLLYANNA DO HER THING.
SLAM
OOF!
UH, HEY! EXCUSE ME?
GRAB
HNNGH— WHAT?!
HEY, UH, JUST COME BY TOMORROW IF YOU WANT AN AUTOGRAPH, OKAY, KID?
KID?
I'LL HAVE YOU KNOW, I JUST PASSED FOR SOMEONE'S AUNT.
HEY, ANNIE, CHECK IT OUT—
IS THAT THE BLONDE FROM PARADISE COVE?

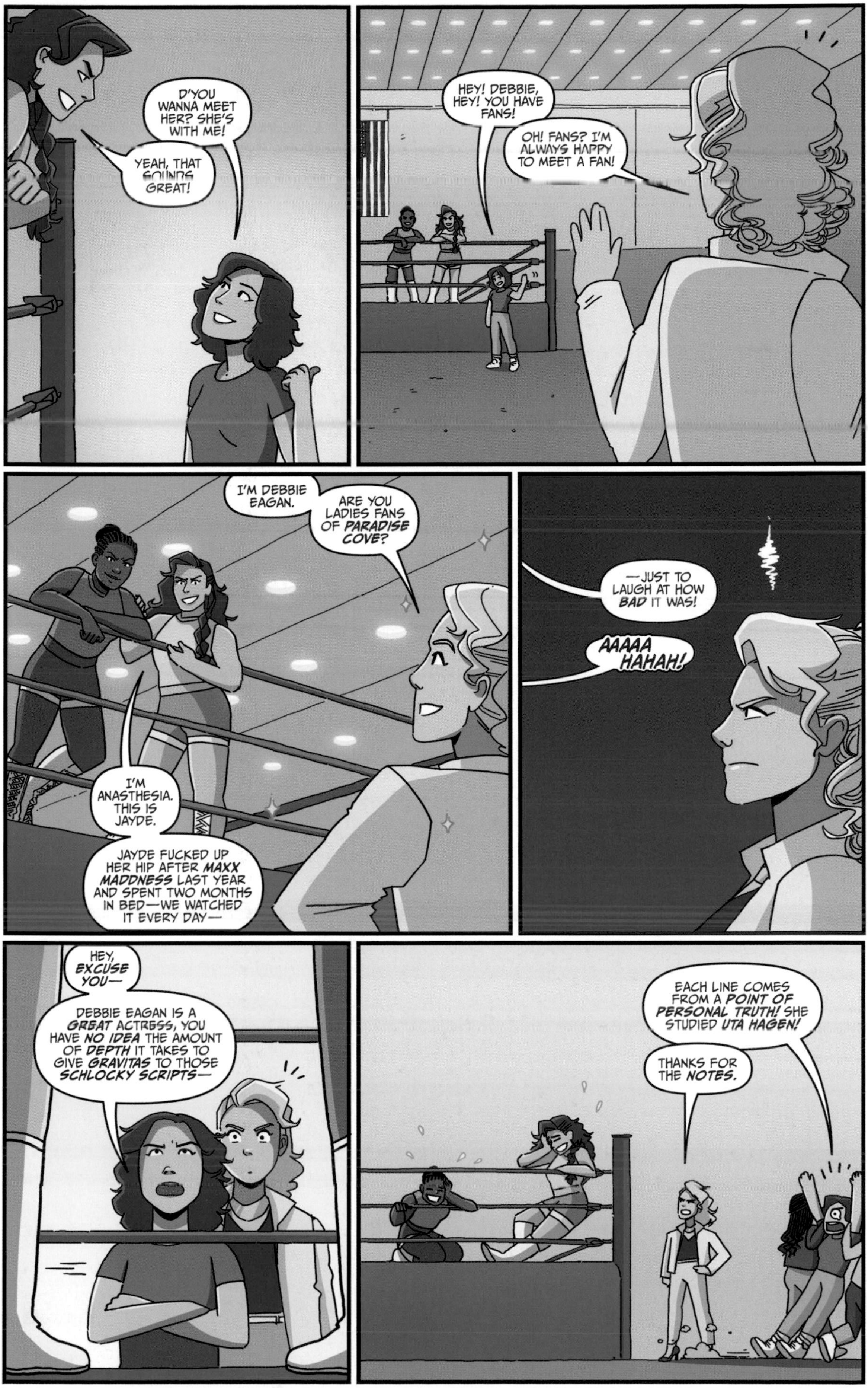
D'YOU WANNA MEET HER? SHE'S WITH ME!
YEAH, THAT SOUNDS GREAT!
HEY! DEBBIE, HEY! YOU HAVE FANS!
OH! FANS? I'M ALWAYS HAPPY TO MEET A FAN!
I'M DEBBIE EAGAN.
ARE YOU LADIES FANS OF *PARADISE COVE?*
I'M ANASTHESIA. THIS IS JAYDE.
JAYDE FUCKED UP HER HIP AFTER *MAXX MADDNESS* LAST YEAR AND SPENT TWO MONTHS IN BED—WE WATCHED IT EVERY DAY—
—JUST TO LAUGH AT HOW *BAD* IT WAS!
AAAAA HAHAH!
HEY, *EXCUSE YOU*—
DEBBIE EAGAN IS A *GREAT* ACTRESS, YOU HAVE *NO IDEA* THE AMOUNT OF *DEPTH* IT TAKES TO GIVE *GRAVITAS* TO THOSE *SCHLOCKY SCRIPTS*—
EACH LINE COMES FROM A *POINT OF PERSONAL TRUTH!* SHE STUDIED *UTA HAGEN!*
THANKS FOR THE *NOTES.*

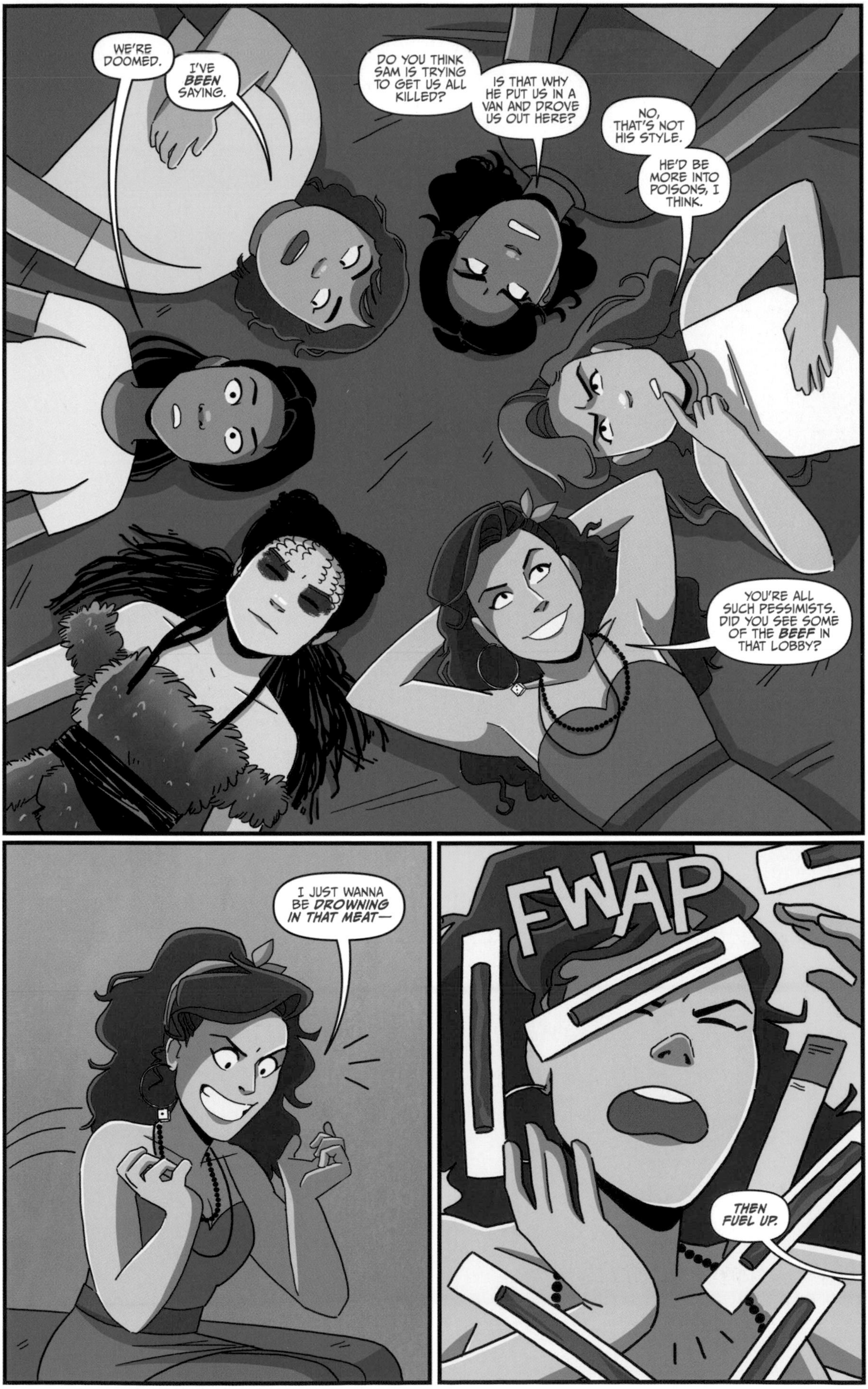
WE'RE DOOMED.
I'VE BEEN SAYING.
DO YOU THINK SAM IS TRYING TO GET US ALL KILLED?
IS THAT WHY HE PUT US IN A VAN AND DROVE US OUT HERE?
NO, THAT'S NOT HIS STYLE.
HE'D BE MORE INTO POISONS, I THINK.
YOU'RE ALL SUCH PESSIMISTS. DID YOU SEE SOME OF THE BEEF IN THAT LOBBY?
I JUST WANNA BE DROWNING IN THAT MEAT—
FWAP
THEN FUEL UP.

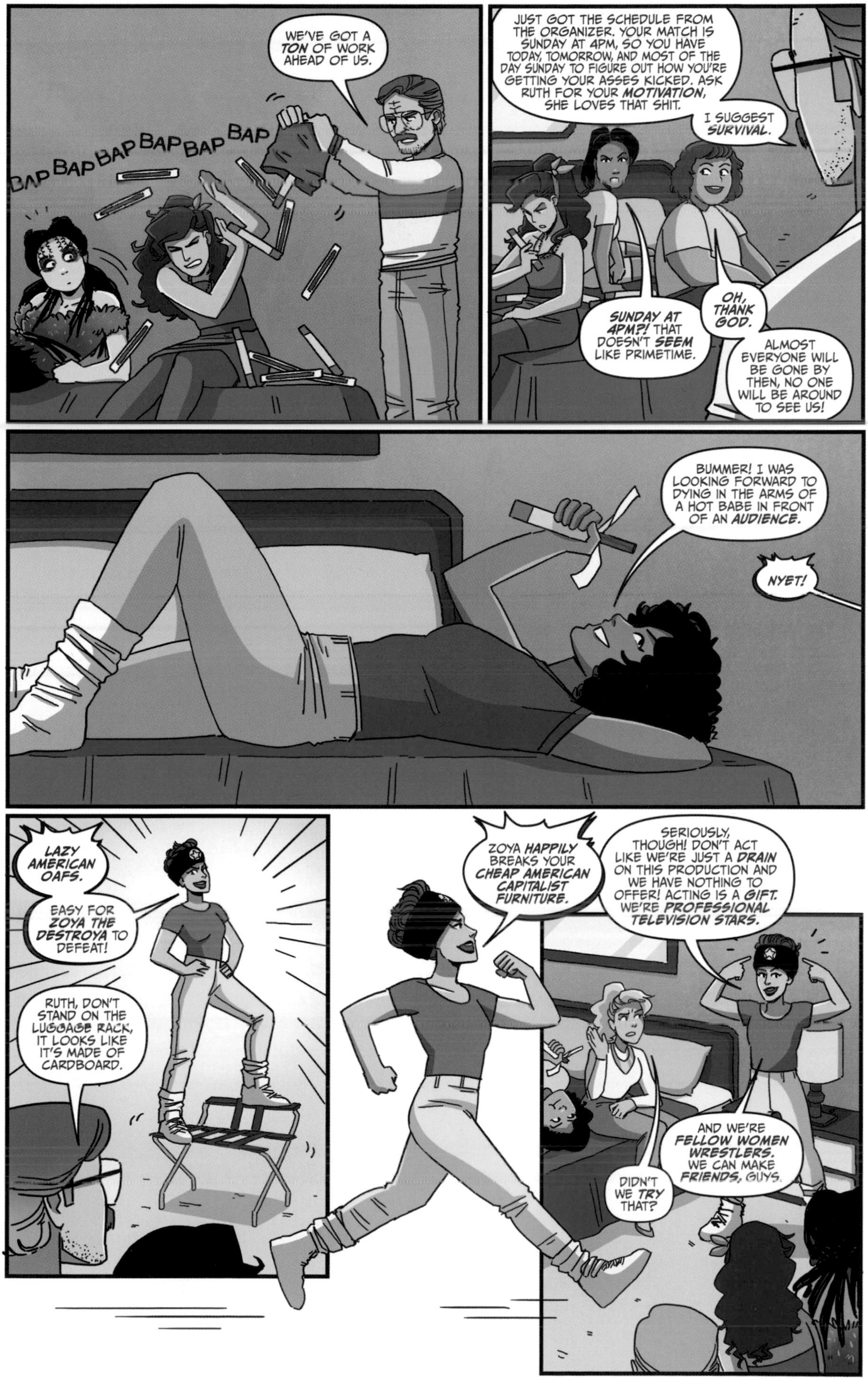
WE'VE GOT A TON OF WORK AHEAD OF US.
BAP BAP BAP BAP BAP BAP
JUST GOT THE SCHEDULE FROM THE ORGANIZER. YOUR MATCH IS SUNDAY AT 4PM, SO YOU HAVE TODAY, TOMORROW, AND MOST OF THE DAY SUNDAY TO FIGURE OUT HOW YOU'RE GETTING YOUR ASSES KICKED. ASK RUTH FOR YOUR MOTIVATION, SHE LOVES THAT SHIT.
I SUGGEST SURVIVAL.
SUNDAY AT 4PM?! THAT DOESN'T SEEM LIKE PRIMETIME.
OH, THANK GOD.
ALMOST EVERYONE WILL BE GONE BY THEN, NO ONE WILL BE AROUND TO SEE US!
BUMMER! I WAS LOOKING FORWARD TO DYING IN THE ARMS OF A HOT BABE IN FRONT OF AN AUDIENCE.
NYET!
LAZY AMERICAN OAFS.
EASY FOR ZOYA THE DESTROYA TO DEFEAT!
RUTH, DON'T STAND ON THE LUGGAGE RACK, IT LOOKS LIKE IT'S MADE OF CARDBOARD.
ZOYA HAPPILY BREAKS YOUR CHEAP AMERICAN CAPITALIST FURNITURE.
SERIOUSLY, THOUGH! DON'T ACT LIKE WE'RE JUST A DRAIN ON THIS PRODUCTION AND WE HAVE NOTHING TO OFFER! ACTING IS A GIFT. WE'RE PROFESSIONAL TELEVISION STARS.
AND WE'RE FELLOW WOMEN WRESTLERS. WE CAN MAKE FRIENDS, GUYS.
DIDN'T WE TRY THAT?

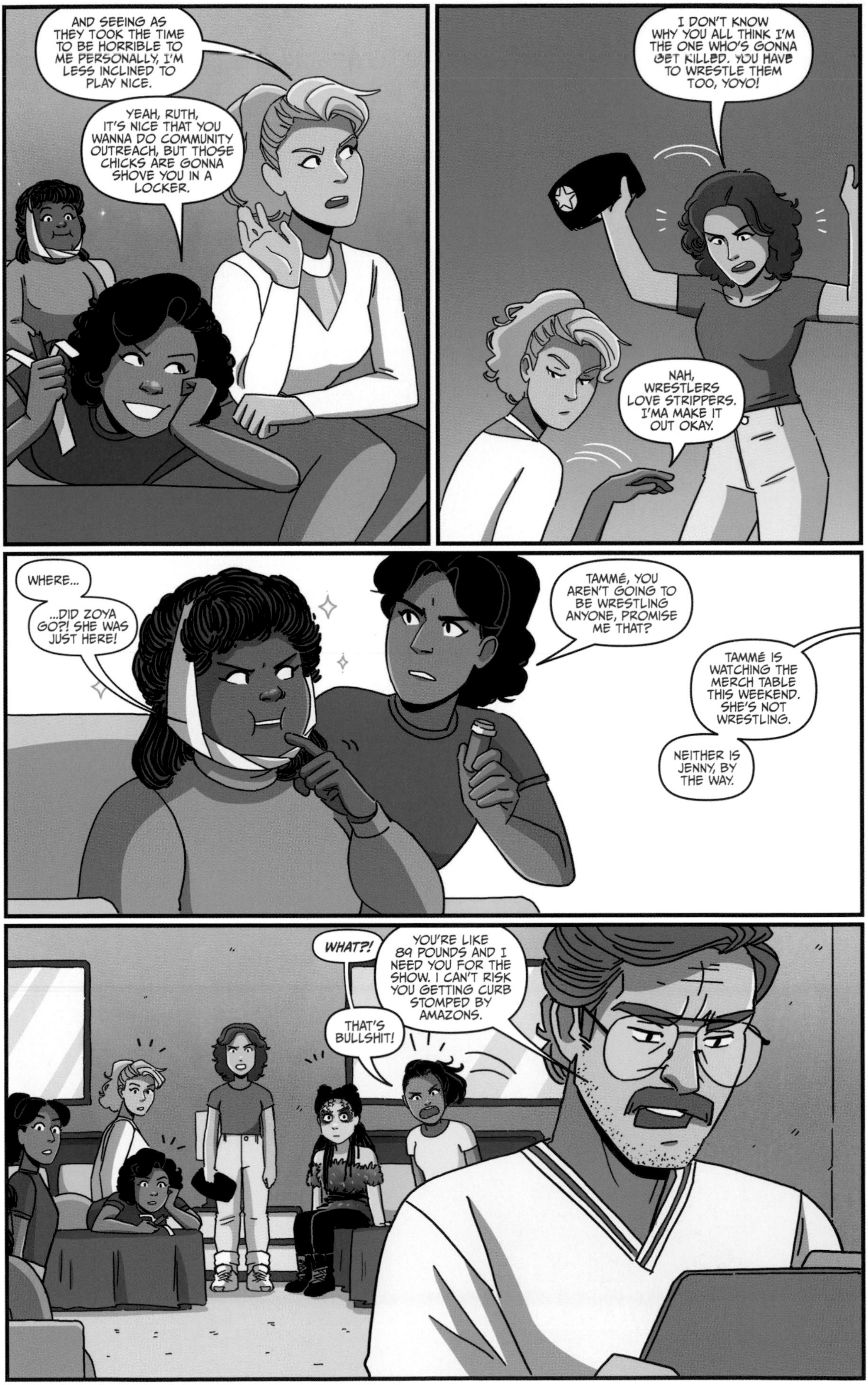
AND SEEING AS THEY TOOK THE TIME TO BE HORRIBLE TO ME PERSONALLY, I'M LESS INCLINED TO PLAY NICE.
YEAH, RUTH, IT'S NICE THAT YOU WANNA DO COMMUNITY OUTREACH, BUT THOSE CHICKS ARE GONNA SHOVE YOU IN A LOCKER.
I DON'T KNOW WHY YOU ALL THINK I'M THE ONE WHO'S GONNA GET KILLED. YOU HAVE TO WRESTLE THEM TOO, YOYO!
NAH, WRESTLERS LOVE STRIPPERS. I'MA MAKE IT OUT OKAY.
WHERE...
...DID ZOYA GO?! SHE WAS JUST HERE!
TAMMÉ, YOU AREN'T GOING TO BE WRESTLING ANYONE, PROMISE ME THAT?
TAMMÉ IS WATCHING THE MERCH TABLE THIS WEEKEND. SHE'S NOT WRESTLING.
NEITHER IS JENNY, BY THE WAY.
WHAT?!
YOU'RE LIKE 89 POUNDS AND I NEED YOU FOR THE SHOW. I CAN'T RISK YOU GETTING CURB STOMPED BY AMAZONS.
THAT'S BULLSHIT!

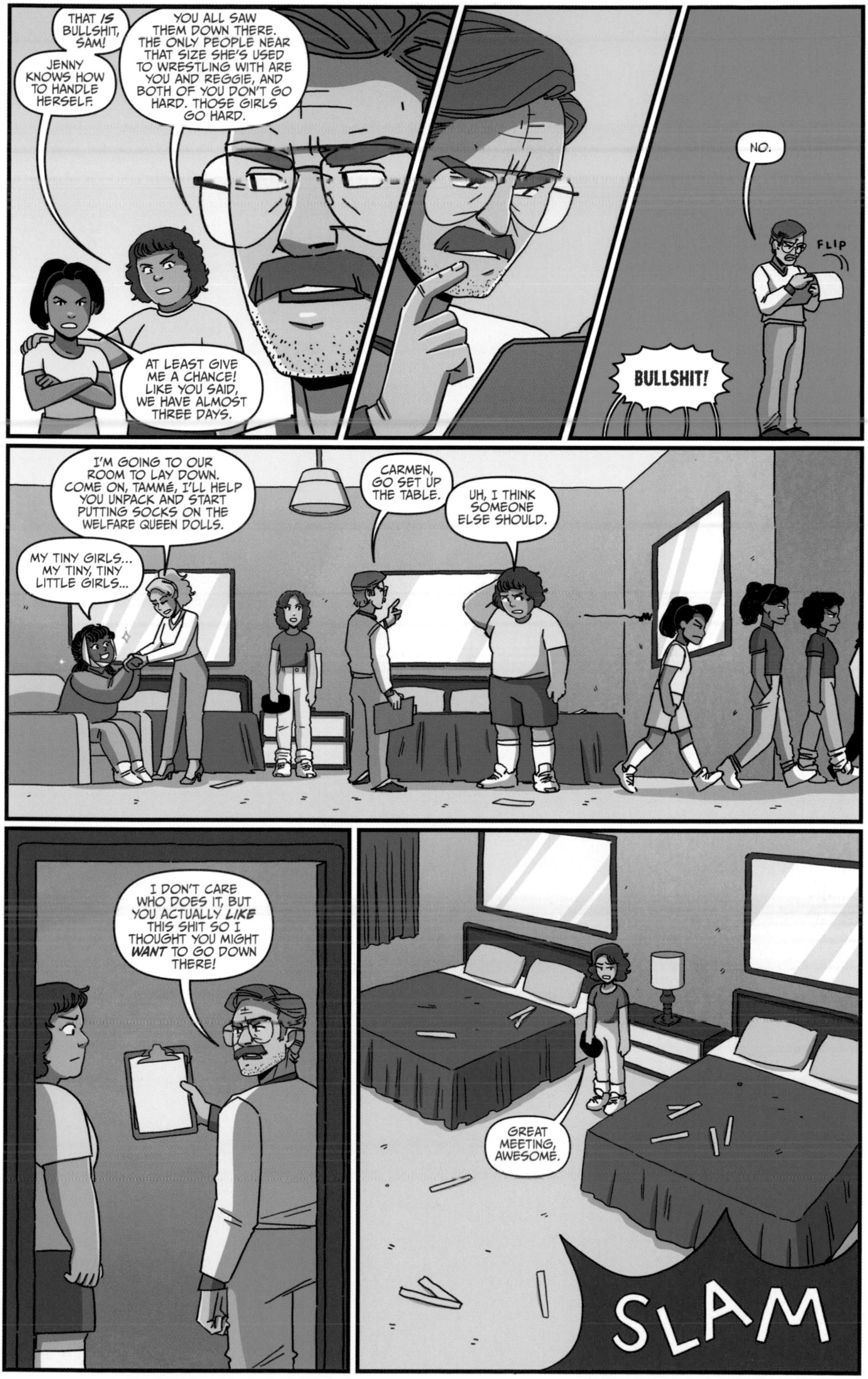

THAT *IS* BULLSHIT, SAM!
JENNY KNOWS HOW TO HANDLE HERSELF.
YOU ALL SAW THEM DOWN THERE. THE ONLY PEOPLE NEAR THAT SIZE SHE'S USED TO WRESTLING WITH ARE YOU AND REGGIE, AND BOTH OF YOU DON'T GO HARD. THOSE GIRLS GO HARD.
AT LEAST GIVE ME A CHANCE! LIKE YOU SAID, WE HAVE ALMOST THREE DAYS.
NO.
FLIP
BULLSHIT!
I'M GOING TO OUR ROOM TO LAY DOWN. COME ON, TAMMÉ, I'LL HELP YOU UNPACK AND START PUTTING SOCKS ON THE WELFARE QUEEN DOLLS.
MY TINY GIRLS... MY TINY, TINY LITTLE GIRLS...
CARMEN, GO SET UP THE TABLE.
UH, I THINK SOMEONE ELSE SHOULD.
I DON'T CARE WHO DOES IT, BUT YOU ACTUALLY *LIKE* THIS SHIT SO I THOUGHT YOU MIGHT ***WANT*** TO GO DOWN THERE!
GREAT MEETING, AWESOME.
SLAM

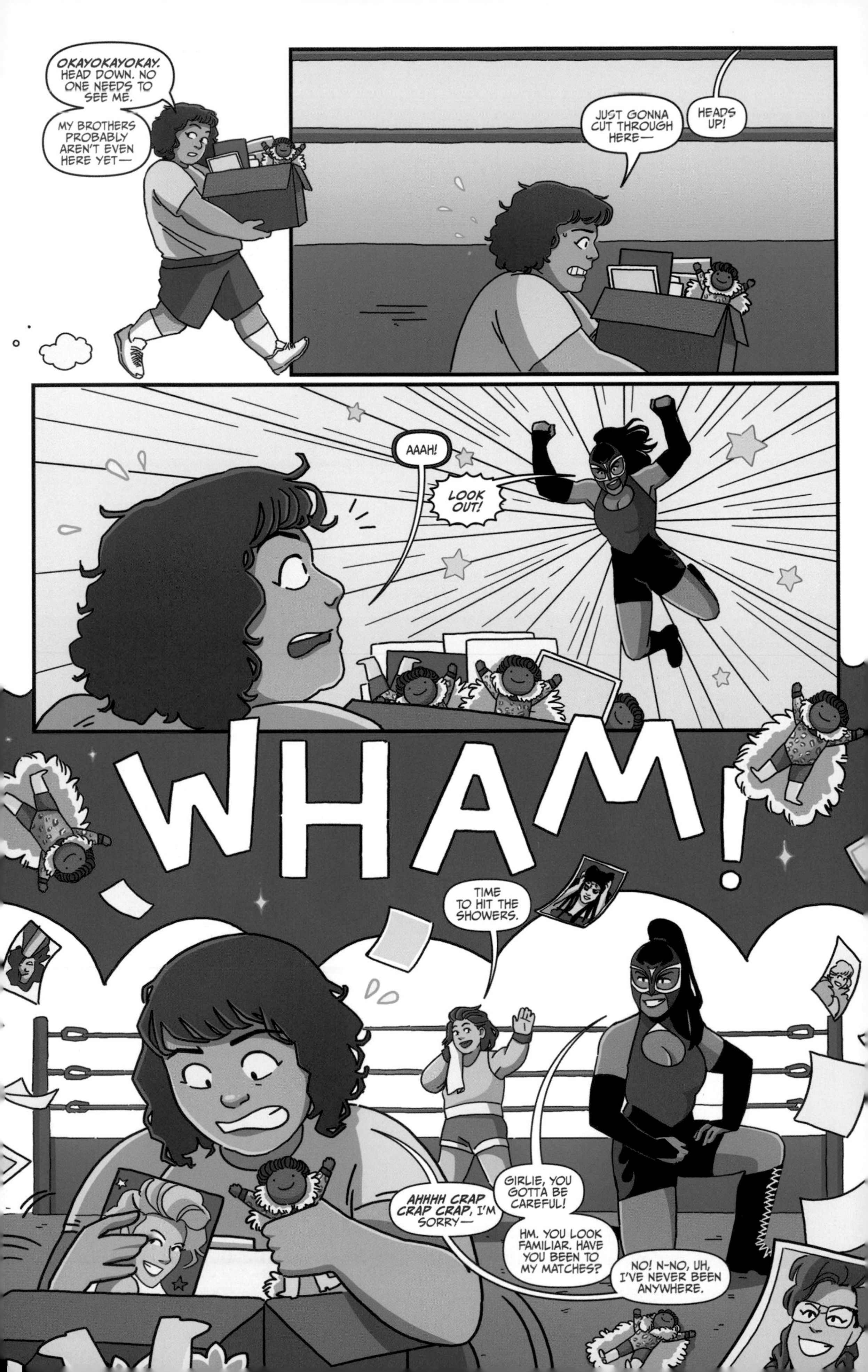

OKAYOKAYOKAY. HEAD DOWN. NO ONE NEEDS TO SEE ME.
MY BROTHERS PROBABLY AREN'T EVEN HERE YET—
JUST GONNA CUT THROUGH HERE—
HEADS UP!
AAAH!
LOOK OUT!
WHAM!
TIME TO HIT THE SHOWERS.
AHHHH CRAP CRAP CRAP, I'M SORRY—
GIRLIE, YOU GOTTA BE CAREFUL!
HM. YOU LOOK FAMILIAR. HAVE YOU BEEN TO MY MATCHES?
NO! N-NO, UH, I'VE NEVER BEEN ANYWHERE.

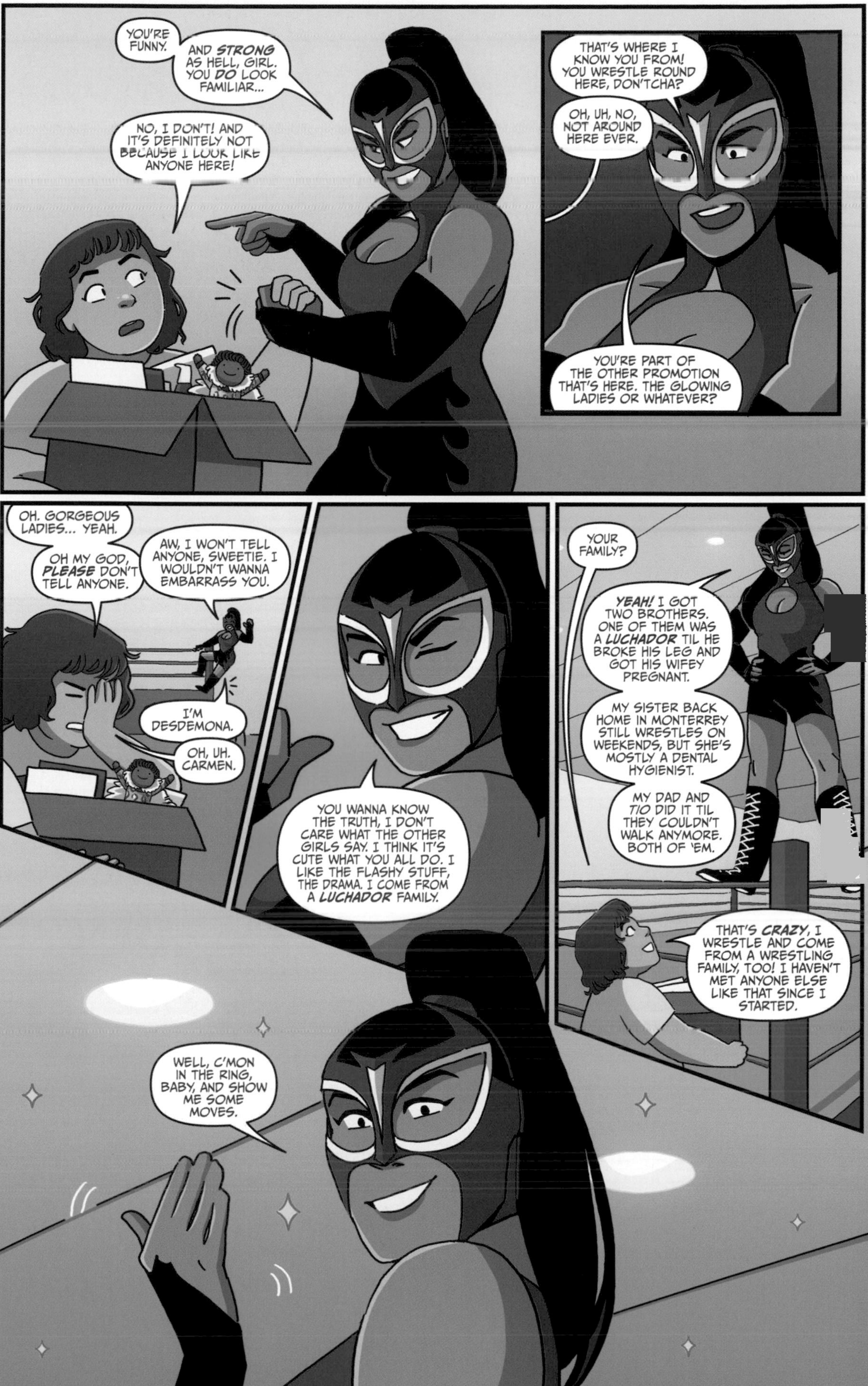
YOU'RE FUNNY.
AND STRONG AS HELL, GIRL. YOU DO LOOK FAMILIAR...
NO, I DON'T! AND IT'S DEFINITELY NOT BECAUSE I LOOK LIKE ANYONE HERE!
THAT'S WHERE I KNOW YOU FROM! YOU WRESTLE ROUND HERE, DON'TCHA?
OH, UH, NO, NOT AROUND HERE EVER.
YOU'RE PART OF THE OTHER PROMOTION THAT'S HERE. THE GLOWING LADIES OR WHATEVER?
OH. GORGEOUS LADIES... YEAH.
OH MY GOD, PLEASE DON'T TELL ANYONE.
AW, I WON'T TELL ANYONE, SWEETIE. I WOULDN'T WANNA EMBARRASS YOU.
I'M DESDEMONA.
OH, UH. CARMEN.
YOU WANNA KNOW THE TRUTH, I DON'T CARE WHAT THE OTHER GIRLS SAY. I THINK IT'S CUTE WHAT YOU ALL DO. I LIKE THE FLASHY STUFF, THE DRAMA. I COME FROM A LUCHADOR FAMILY.
YOUR FAMILY?
YEAH! I GOT TWO BROTHERS. ONE OF THEM WAS A LUCHADOR TIL HE BROKE HIS LEG AND GOT HIS WIFEY PREGNANT.
MY SISTER BACK HOME IN MONTERREY STILL WRESTLES ON WEEKENDS, BUT SHE'S MOSTLY A DENTAL HYGIENIST.
MY DAD AND TÍO DID IT TIL THEY COULDN'T WALK ANYMORE. BOTH OF 'EM.
THAT'S CRAZY, I WRESTLE AND COME FROM A WRESTLING FAMILY, TOO! I HAVEN'T MET ANYONE ELSE LIKE THAT SINCE I STARTED.
WELL, C'MON IN THE RING, BABY, AND SHOW ME SOME MOVES.

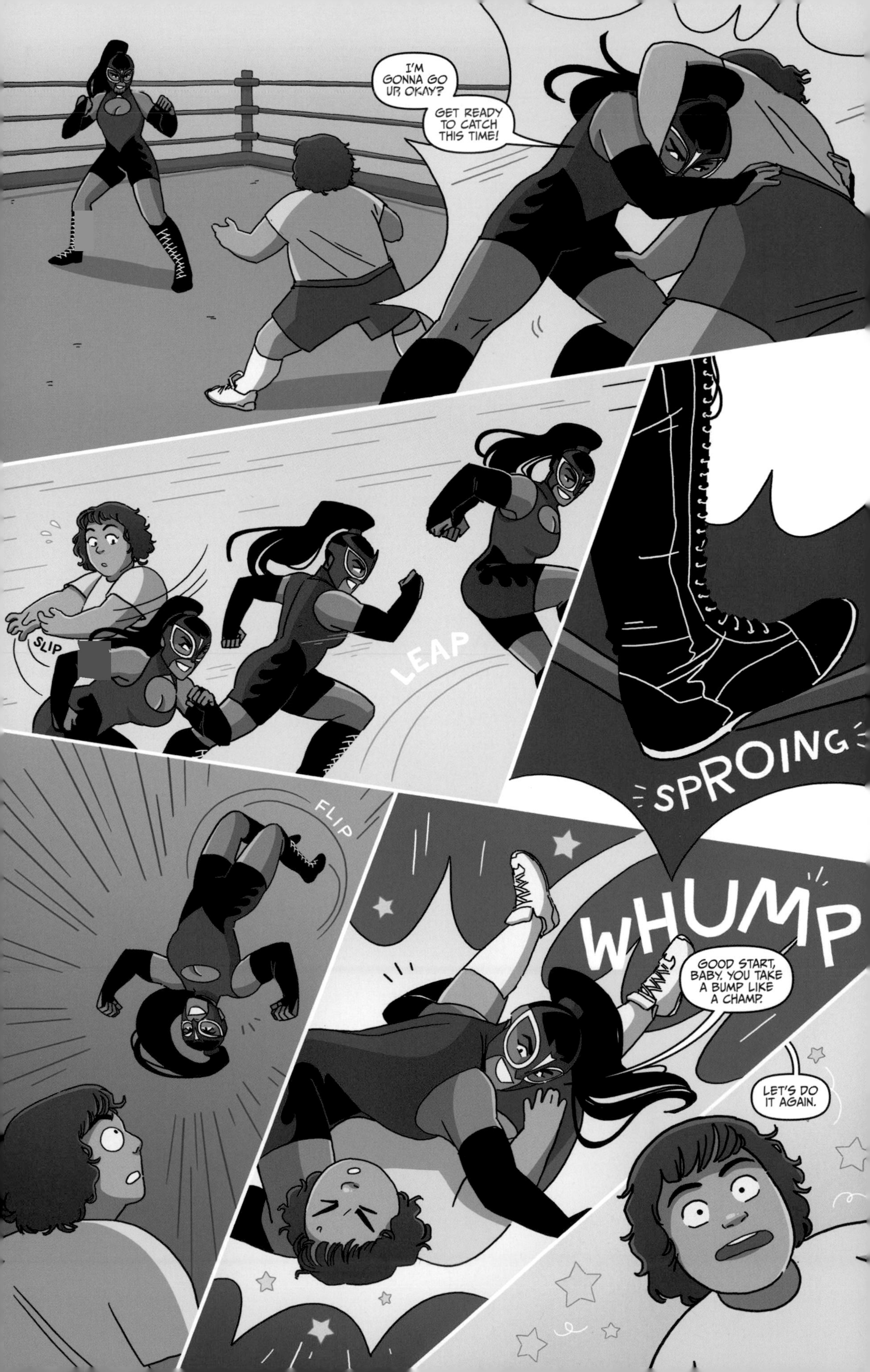
I'M GONNA GO UP, OKAY?
GET READY TO CATCH THIS TIME!
SLIP
LEAP
SPROING
FLIP
WHUMP
GOOD START, BABY. YOU TAKE A BUMP LIKE A CHAMP.
LET'S DO IT AGAIN.

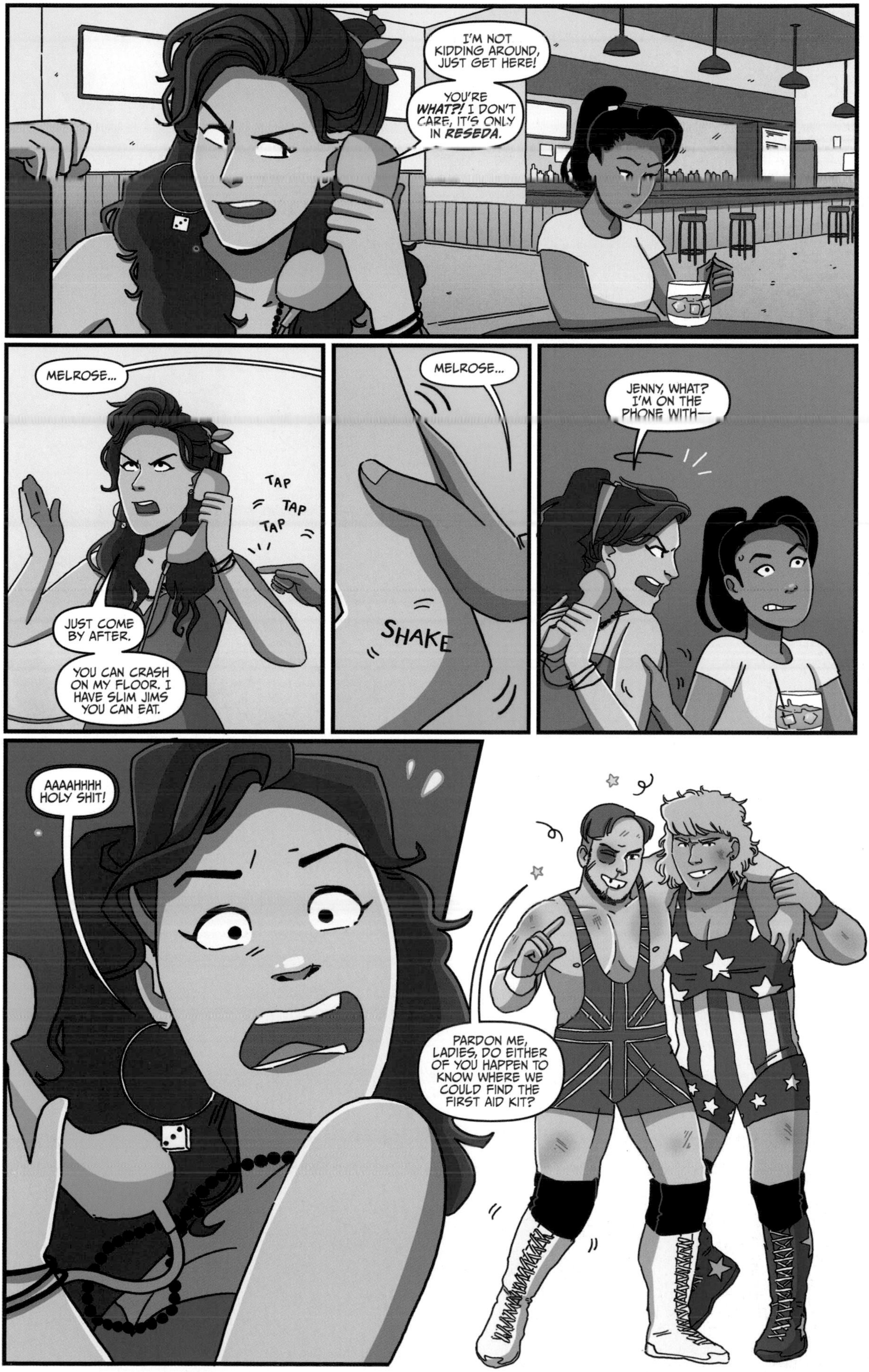
I'M NOT KIDDING AROUND, JUST GET HERE!
YOU'RE WHAT?! I DON'T CARE, IT'S ONLY IN RESEDA.
MELROSE...
TAP TAP TAP
JUST COME BY AFTER.
YOU CAN CRASH ON MY FLOOR. I HAVE SLIM JIMS YOU CAN EAT.
MELROSE...
SHAKE
JENNY, WHAT? I'M ON THE PHONE WITH—
AAAAHHHH HOLY SHIT!
PARDON ME, LADIES, DO EITHER OF YOU HAPPEN TO KNOW WHERE WE COULD FIND THE FIRST AID KIT?

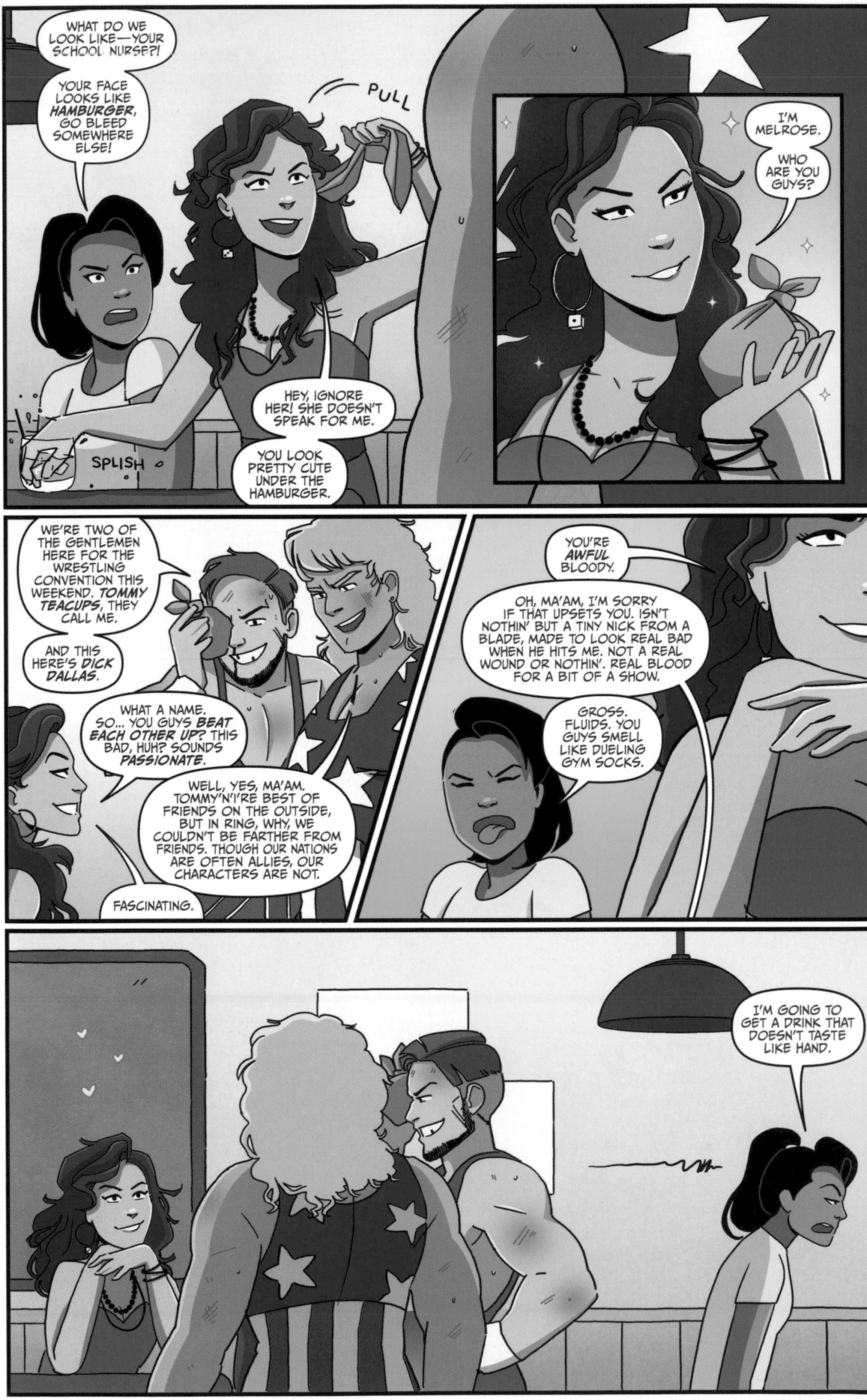
WHAT DO WE LOOK LIKE—YOUR SCHOOL NURSE?!
YOUR FACE LOOKS LIKE HAMBURGER, GO BLEED SOMEWHERE ELSE!
PULL
SPLISH
HEY, IGNORE HER! SHE DOESN'T SPEAK FOR ME.
YOU LOOK PRETTY CUTE UNDER THE HAMBURGER.
I'M MELROSE.
WHO ARE YOU GUYS?
WE'RE TWO OF THE GENTLEMEN HERE FOR THE WRESTLING CONVENTION THIS WEEKEND. TOMMY TEACUPS, THEY CALL ME.
AND THIS HERE'S DICK DALLAS.
WHAT A NAME. SO... YOU GUYS BEAT EACH OTHER UP? THIS BAD, HUH? SOUNDS PASSIONATE.
WELL, YES, MA'AM. TOMMY'N'I'RE BEST OF FRIENDS ON THE OUTSIDE, BUT IN RING, WHY, WE COULDN'T BE FARTHER FROM FRIENDS. THOUGH OUR NATIONS ARE OFTEN ALLIES, OUR CHARACTERS ARE NOT.
FASCINATING.
YOU'RE AWFUL BLOODY.
OH, MA'AM, I'M SORRY IF THAT UPSETS YOU. ISN'T NOTHIN' BUT A TINY NICK FROM A BLADE, MADE TO LOOK REAL BAD WHEN HE HITS ME. NOT A REAL WOUND OR NOTHIN'. REAL BLOOD FOR A BIT OF A SHOW.
GROSS. FLUIDS. YOU GUYS SMELL LIKE DUELING GYM SOCKS.
I'M GOING TO GET A DRINK THAT DOESN'T TASTE LIKE HAND.

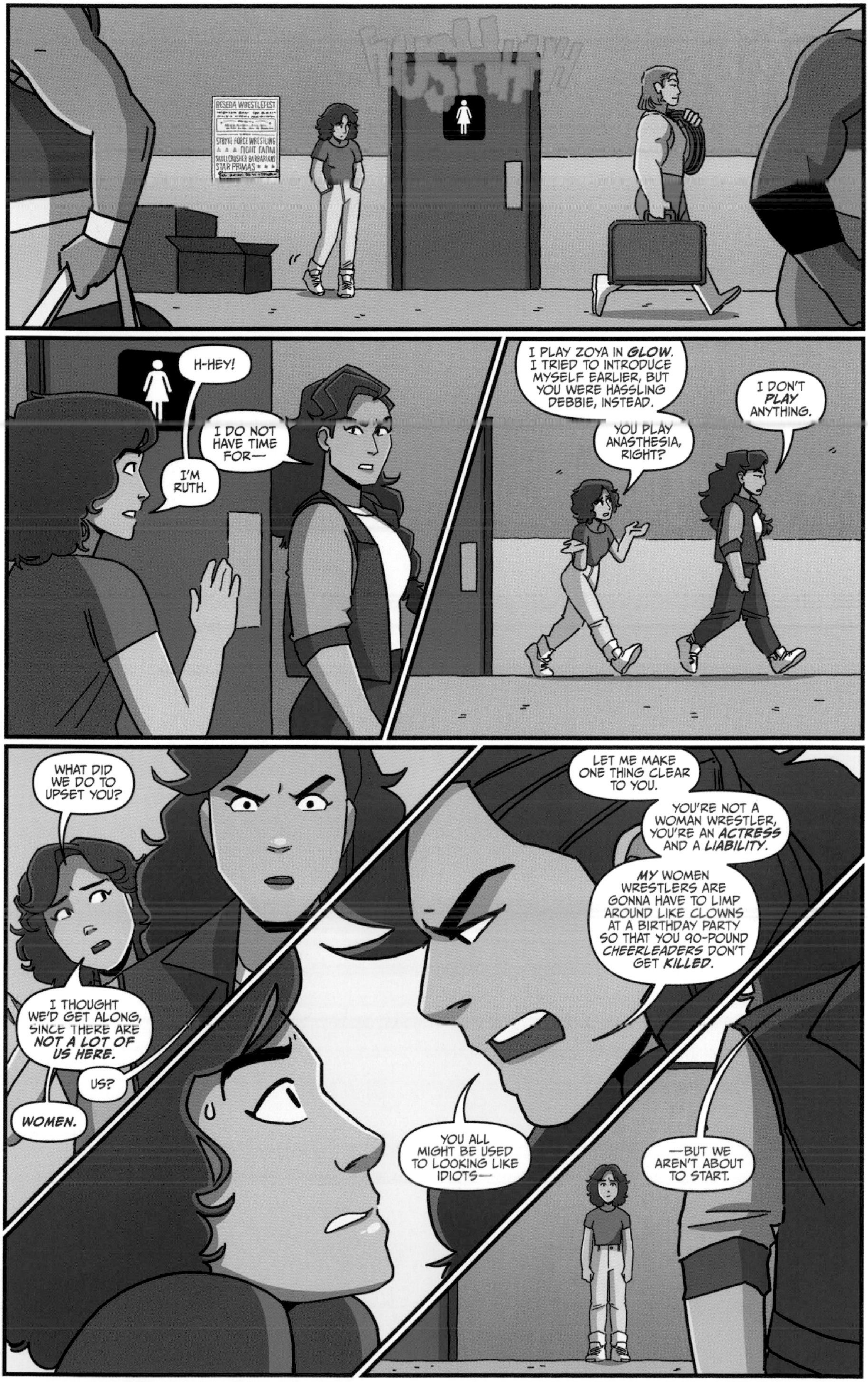

RESEDA WRESTLEFEST
STRYKE FORCE WRESTLING
SKULLCRUSHER BARBARIANS
STAR PRIMAS
H-HEY!
I'M RUTH.
I DO NOT HAVE TIME FOR—
I PLAY ZOYA IN *GLOW*. I TRIED TO INTRODUCE MYSELF EARLIER, BUT YOU WERE HASSLING DEBBIE, INSTEAD.
YOU PLAY ANASTHESIA, RIGHT?
I DON'T *PLAY* ANYTHING.
WHAT DID WE DO TO UPSET YOU?
I THOUGHT WE'D GET ALONG, SINCE THERE ARE ***NOT A LOT OF US HERE.***
US?
WOMEN.
LET ME MAKE ONE THING CLEAR TO YOU.
YOU'RE NOT A WOMAN WRESTLER, YOU'RE AN ***ACTRESS*** AND A ***LIABILITY***.
MY WOMEN WRESTLERS ARE GONNA HAVE TO LIMP AROUND LIKE CLOWNS AT A BIRTHDAY PARTY SO THAT YOU 90-POUND *CHEERLEADERS* DON'T GET ***KILLED***.
YOU ALL MIGHT BE USED TO LOOKING LIKE IDIOTS—
—BUT WE AREN'T ABOUT TO START.

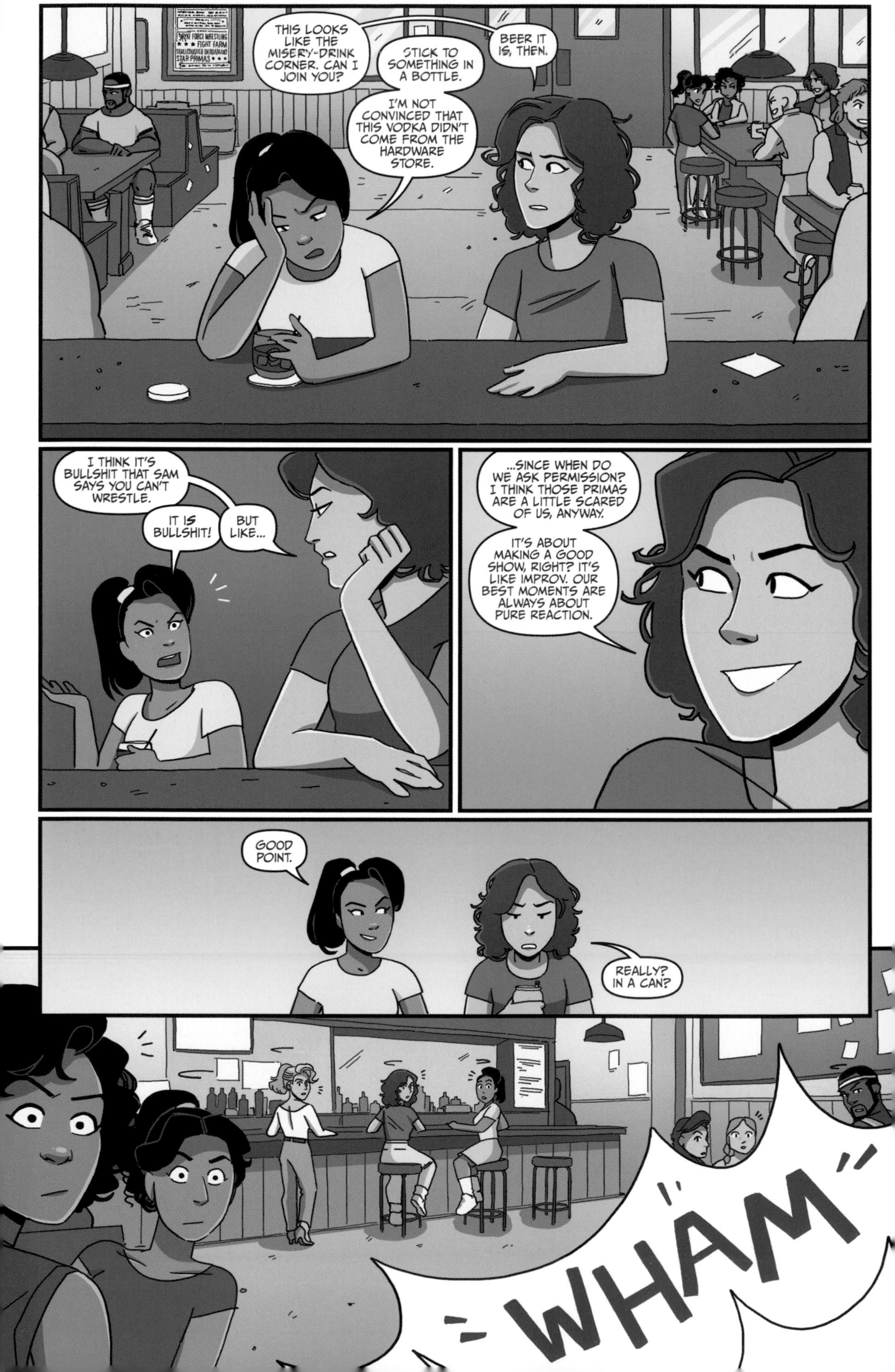
FORCE WRESTLING
FIGHT FARM
STAR PRIMAS
THIS LOOKS LIKE THE MISERY-DRINK CORNER. CAN I JOIN YOU?
STICK TO SOMETHING IN A BOTTLE.
I'M NOT CONVINCED THAT THIS VODKA DIDN'T COME FROM THE HARDWARE STORE.
BEER IT IS, THEN.
I THINK IT'S BULLSHIT THAT SAM SAYS YOU CAN'T WRESTLE.
IT *IS* BULLSHIT!
BUT LIKE...
...SINCE WHEN DO WE ASK PERMISSION? I THINK THOSE PRIMAS ARE A LITTLE SCARED OF US, ANYWAY.
IT'S ABOUT MAKING A GOOD SHOW, RIGHT? IT'S LIKE IMPROV. OUR BEST MOMENTS ARE ALWAYS ABOUT PURE REACTION.
GOOD POINT.
REALLY? IN A CAN?
WHAM

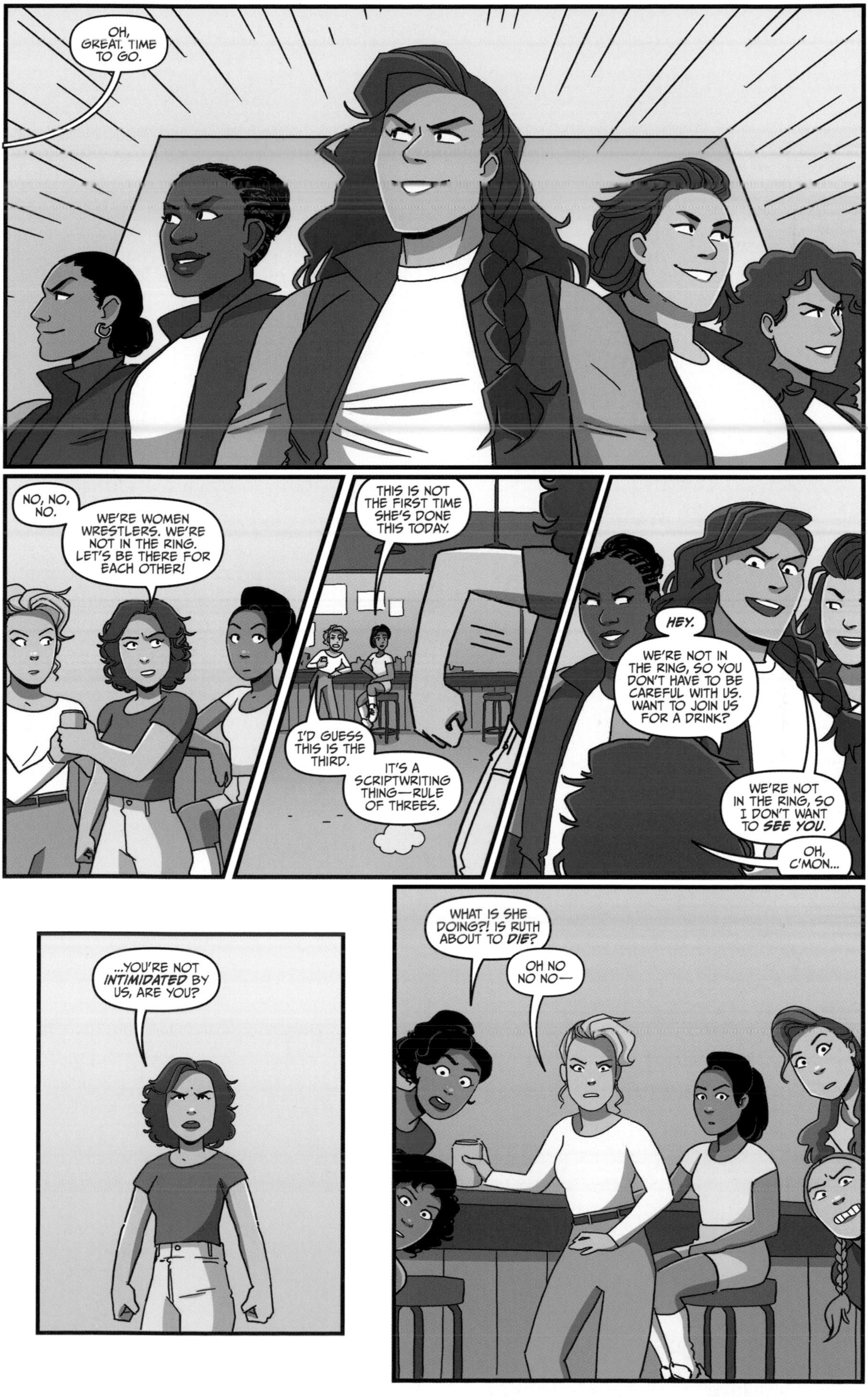
OH, GREAT. TIME TO GO.
NO, NO, NO.
WE'RE WOMEN WRESTLERS. WE'RE NOT IN THE RING. LET'S BE THERE FOR EACH OTHER!
THIS IS NOT THE FIRST TIME SHE'S DONE THIS TODAY.
I'D GUESS THIS IS THE THIRD.
IT'S A SCRIPTWRITING THING—RULE OF THREES.
HEY.
WE'RE NOT IN THE RING, SO YOU DON'T HAVE TO BE CAREFUL WITH US. WANT TO JOIN US FOR A DRINK?
WE'RE NOT IN THE RING, SO I DON'T WANT TO SEE YOU.
OH, C'MON...
...YOU'RE NOT INTIMIDATED BY US, ARE YOU?
WHAT IS SHE DOING?! IS RUTH ABOUT TO DIE?
OH NO NO NO—

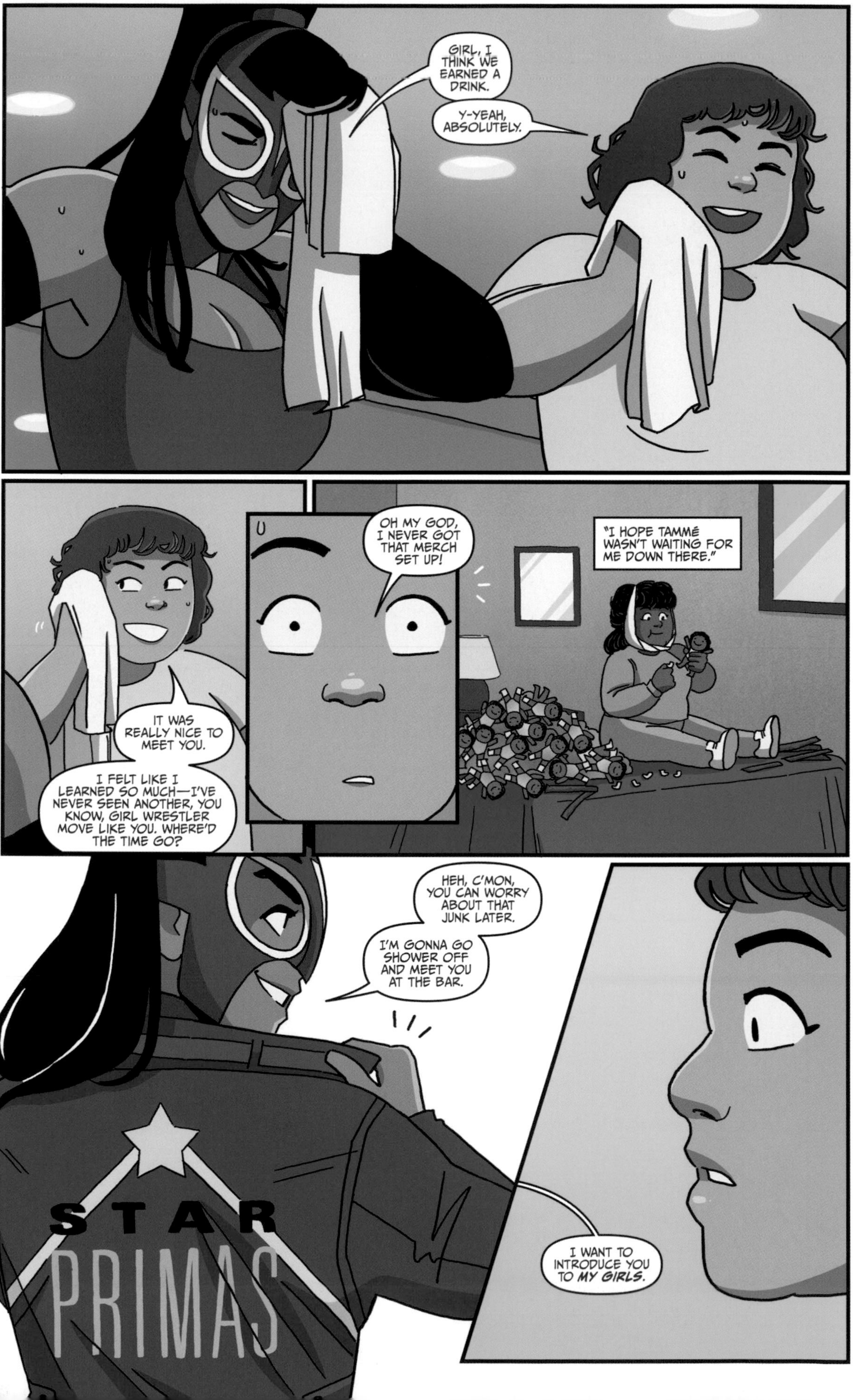
GIRL, I THINK WE EARNED A DRINK.
Y-YEAH, ABSOLUTELY.
IT WAS REALLY NICE TO MEET YOU.
I FELT LIKE I LEARNED SO MUCH—I'VE NEVER SEEN ANOTHER, YOU KNOW, GIRL WRESTLER MOVE LIKE YOU. WHERE'D THE TIME GO?
OH MY GOD, I NEVER GOT THAT MERCH SET UP!
"I HOPE TAMMÉ WASN'T WAITING FOR ME DOWN THERE."
HEH, C'MON, YOU CAN WORRY ABOUT THAT JUNK LATER.
I'M GONNA GO SHOWER OFF AND MEET YOU AT THE BAR.
STAR
PRIMAS
I WANT TO INTRODUCE YOU TO *MY GIRLS*.

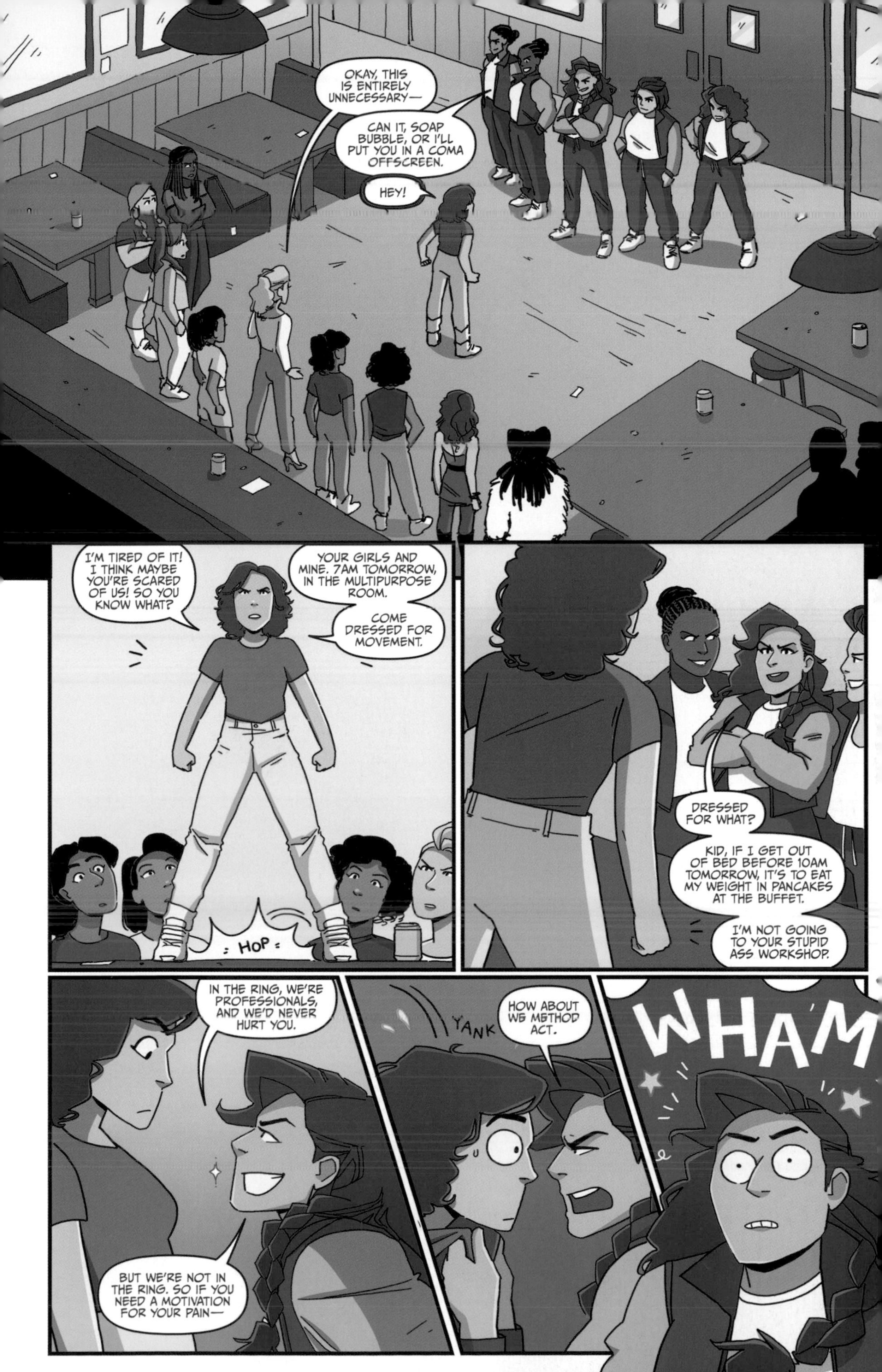

OKAY, THIS IS ENTIRELY UNNECESSARY—
CAN IT, SOAP BUBBLE, OR I'LL PUT YOU IN A COMA OFFSCREEN.
HEY!
I'M TIRED OF IT! I THINK MAYBE YOU'RE SCARED OF US! SO YOU KNOW WHAT?
YOUR GIRLS AND MINE. 7AM TOMORROW, IN THE MULTIPURPOSE ROOM.
COME DRESSED FOR MOVEMENT.
HOP
DRESSED FOR WHAT?
KID, IF I GET OUT OF BED BEFORE 10AM TOMORROW, IT'S TO EAT MY WEIGHT IN PANCAKES AT THE BUFFET.
I'M NOT GOING TO YOUR STUPID ASS WORKSHOP.
IN THE RING, WE'RE PROFESSIONALS, AND WE'D NEVER HURT YOU.
BUT WE'RE NOT IN THE RING. SO IF YOU NEED A MOTIVATION FOR YOUR PAIN—
YANK
HOW ABOUT WE METHOD ACT.
WHAM

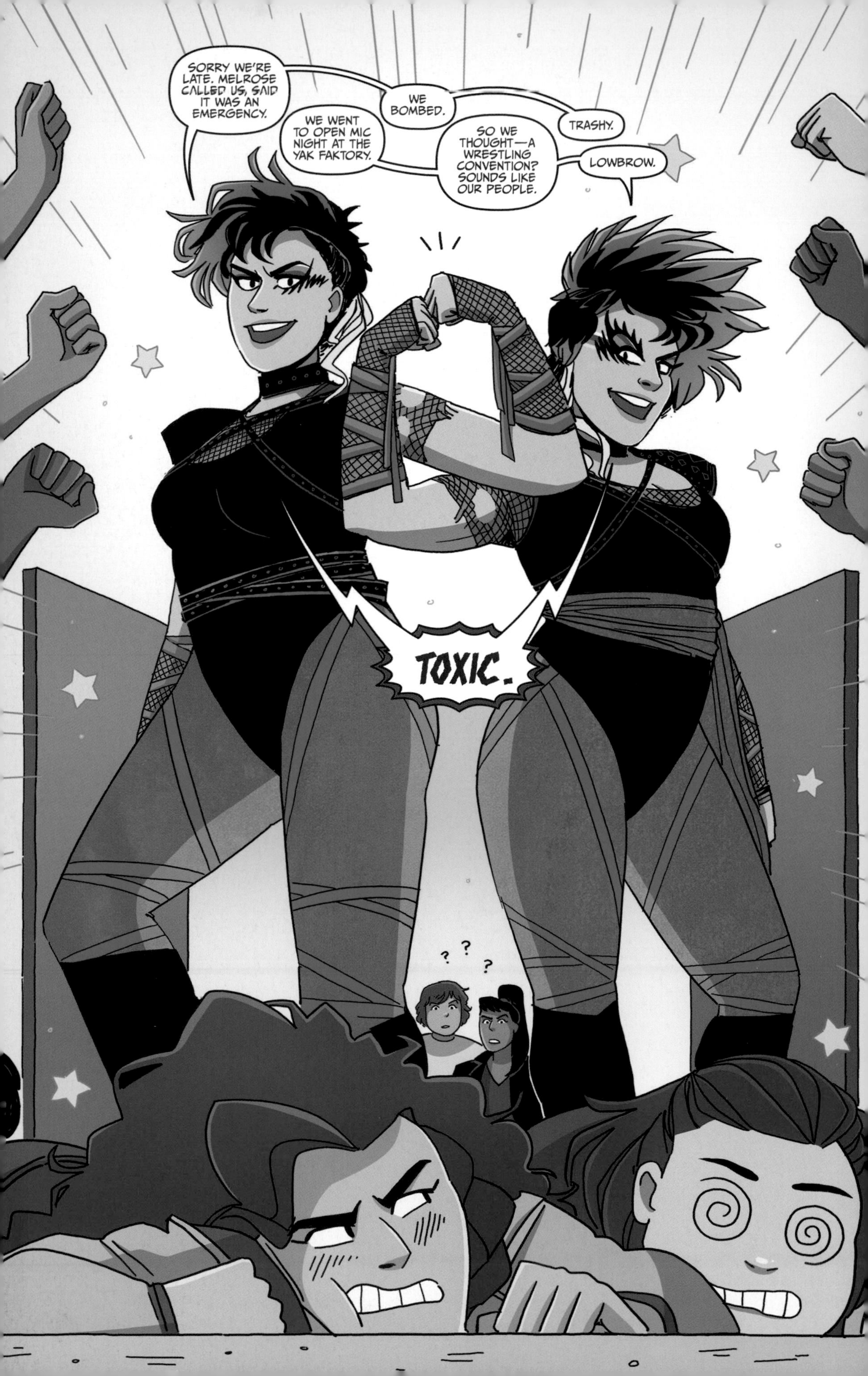
SORRY WE'RE LATE. MELROSE CALLED US, SAID IT WAS AN EMERGENCY.
WE WENT TO OPEN MIC NIGHT AT THE YAK FAKTORY.
WE BOMBED.
SO WE THOUGHT—A WRESTLING CONVENTION? SOUNDS LIKE OUR PEOPLE.
TRASHY.
LOWBROW.
TOXIC.
? ? ?

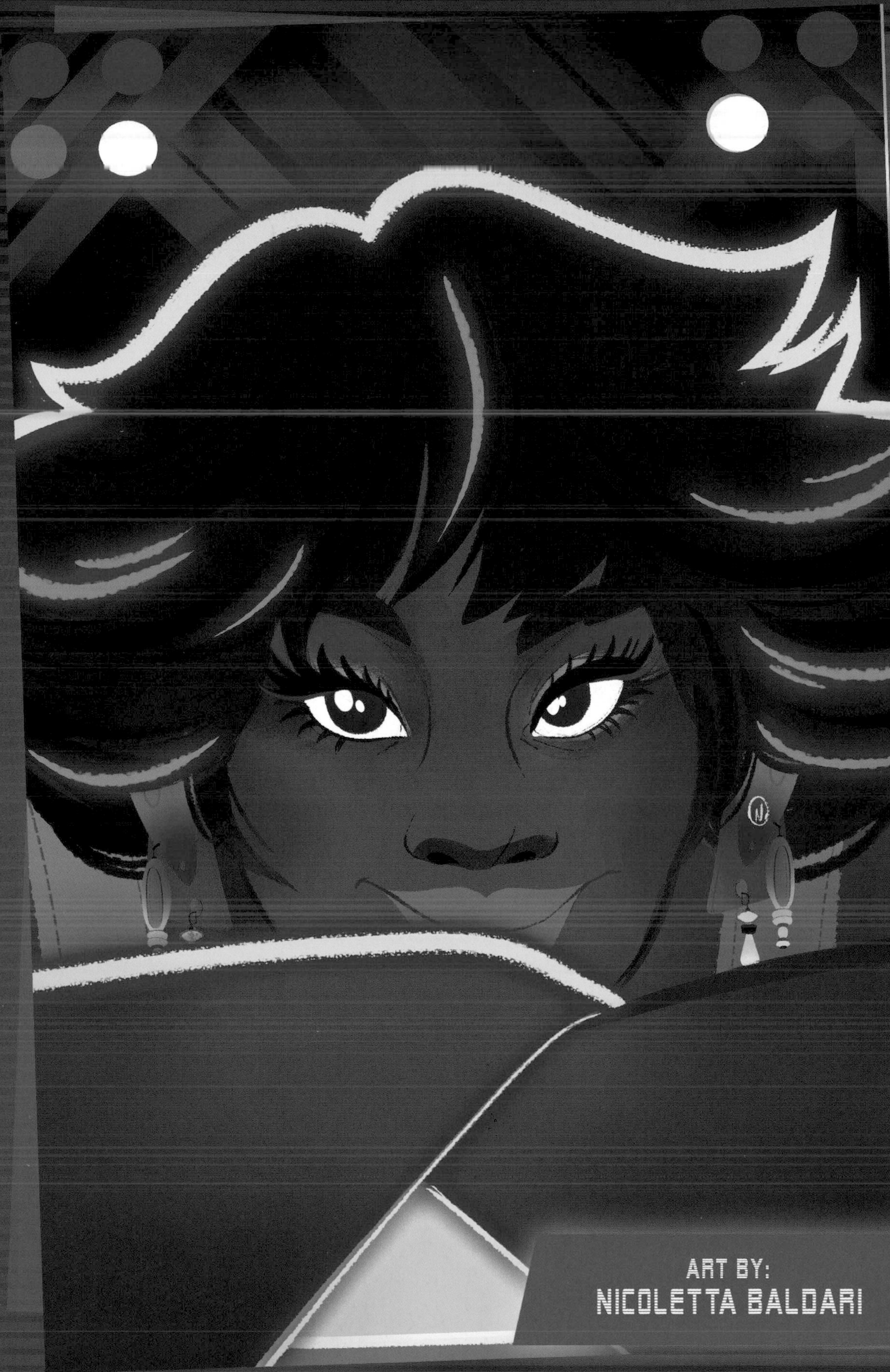
ART BY:
NICOLETTA BALDARI

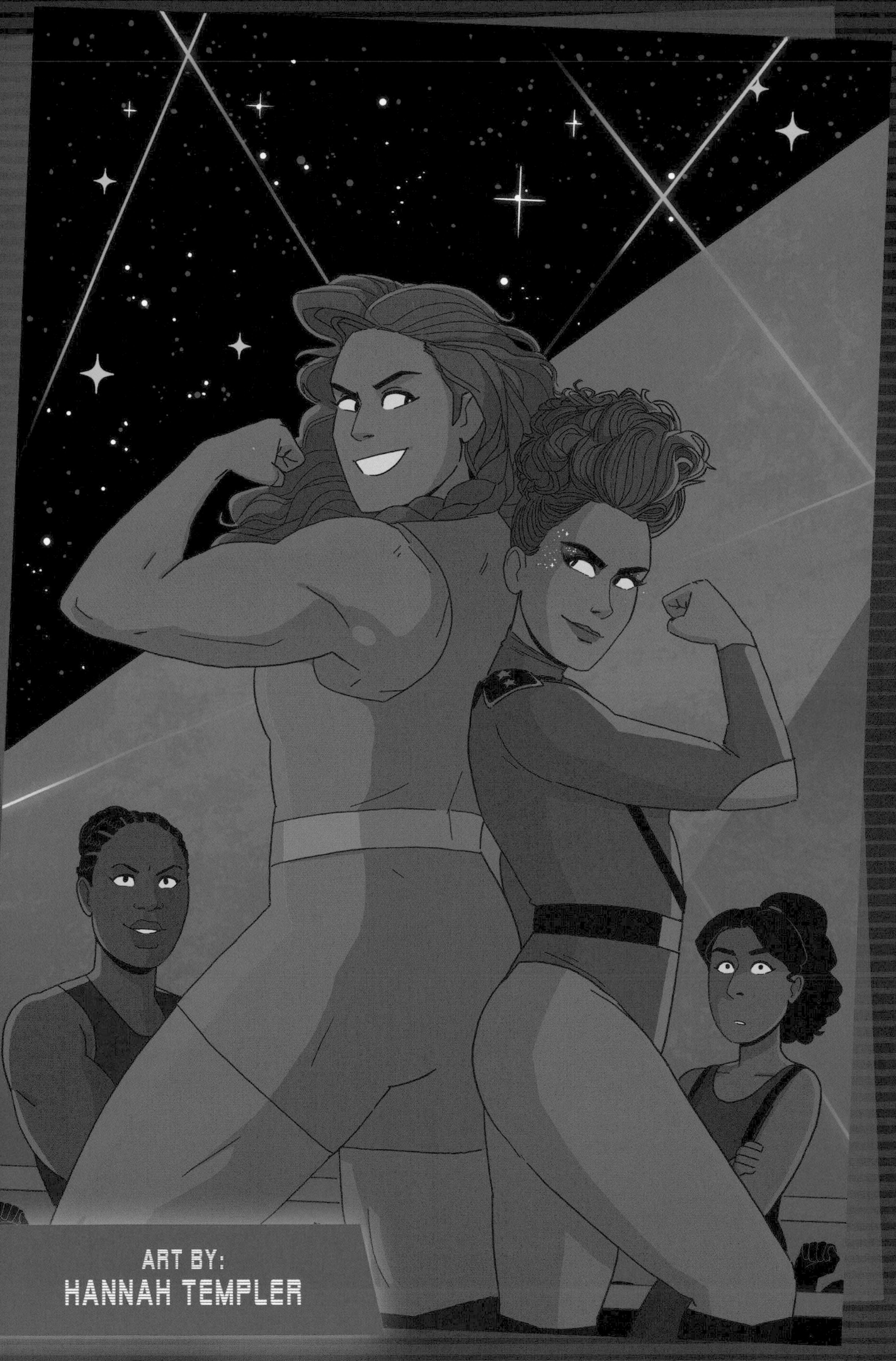

ART BY:
HANNAH TEMPLER

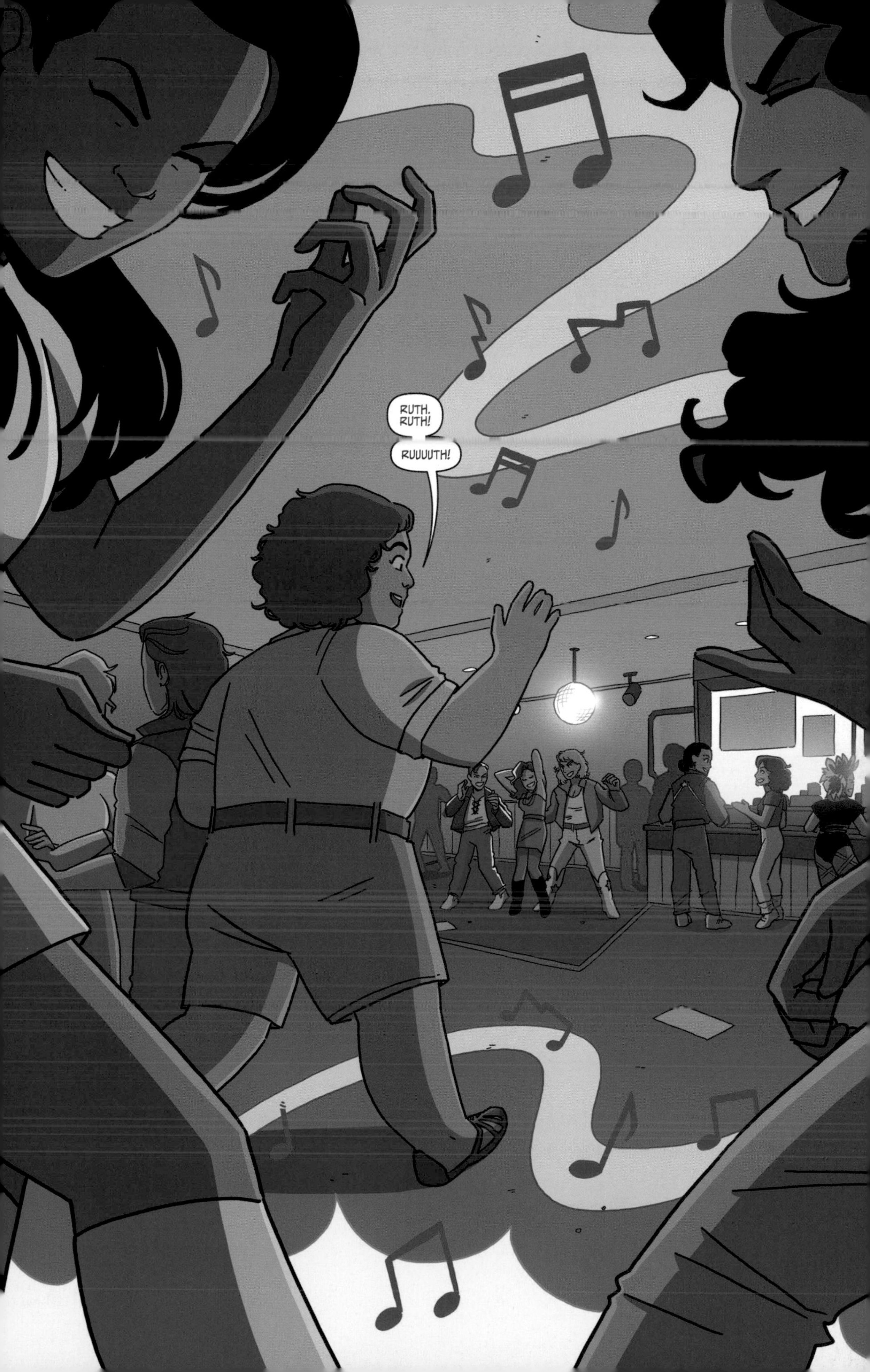
RUTH. RUTH!
RUUUUTH!

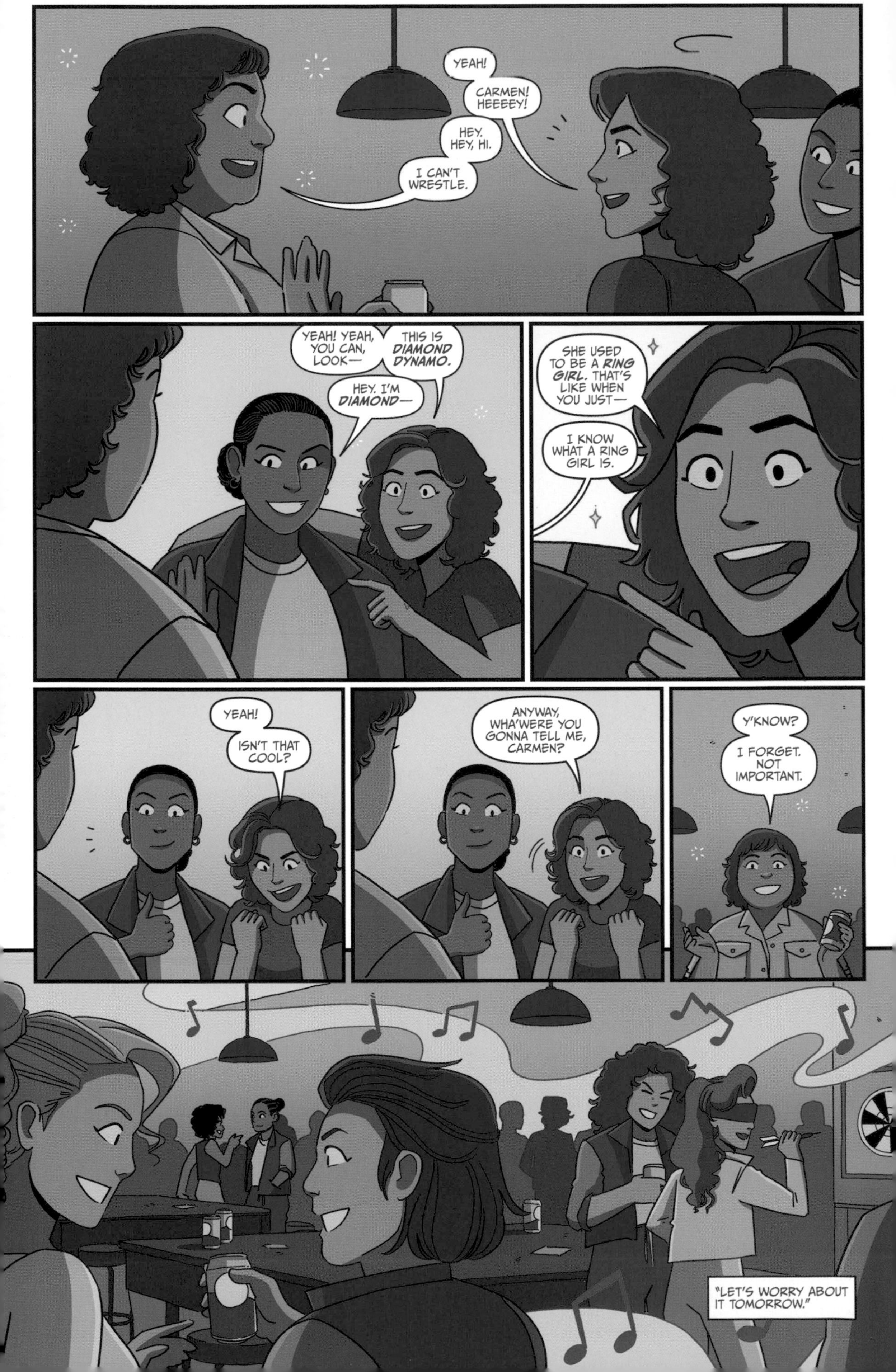
YEAH!
CARMEN! HEEEEY!
HEY. HEY, HI.
I CAN'T WRESTLE.
YEAH! YEAH, YOU CAN, LOOK—
THIS IS DIAMOND DYNAMO.
HEY. I'M DIAMOND—
SHE USED TO BE A RING GIRL. THAT'S LIKE WHEN YOU JUST—
I KNOW WHAT A RING GIRL IS.
YEAH!
ISN'T THAT COOL?
ANYWAY, WHA'WERE YOU GONNA TELL ME, CARMEN?
Y'KNOW?
I FORGET. NOT IMPORTANT.
"LET'S WORRY ABOUT IT TOMORROW."

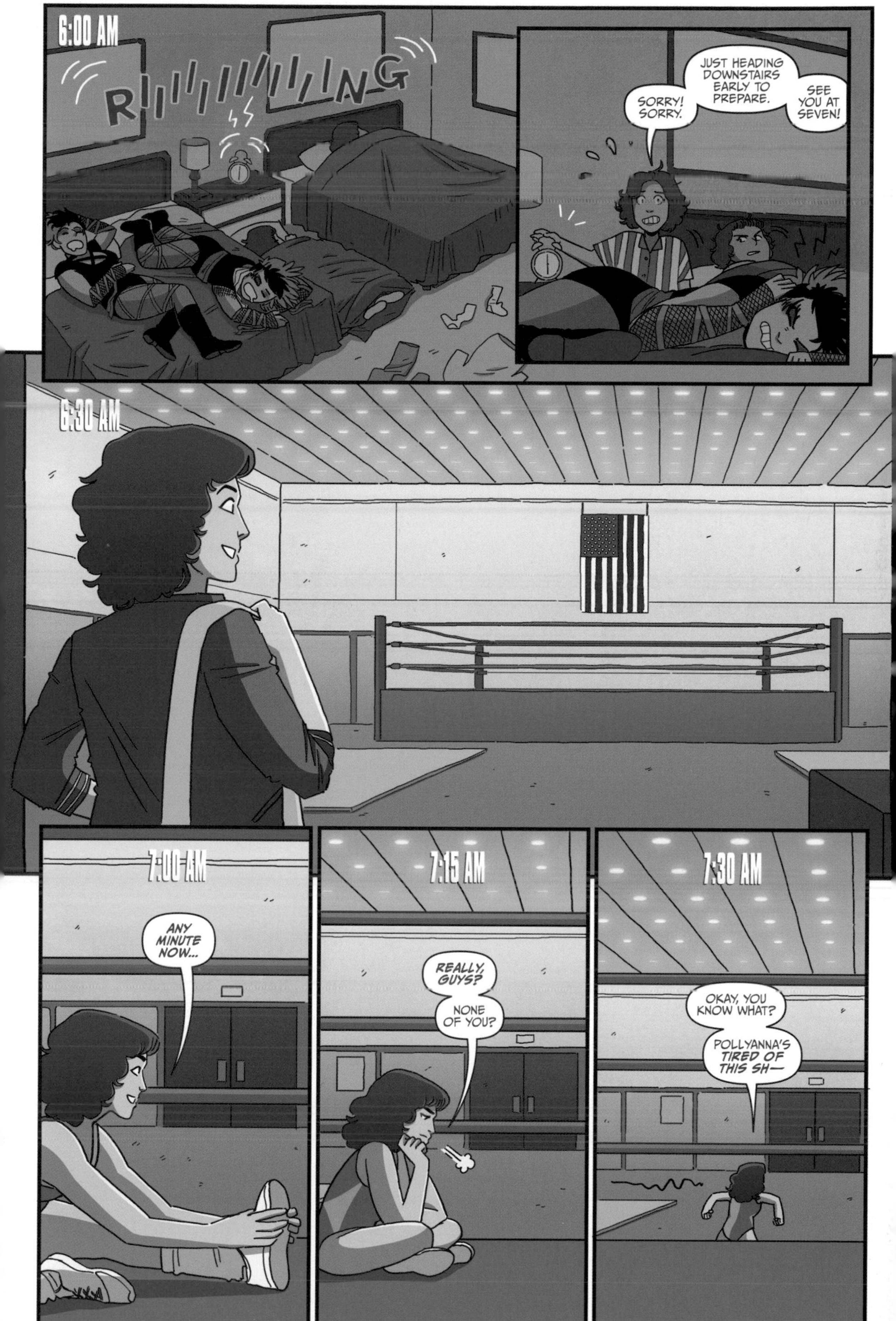
6:00 AM
RIIIIIIIIIING
SORRY! SORRY.
JUST HEADING DOWNSTAIRS EARLY TO PREPARE.
SEE YOU AT SEVEN!
6:30 AM
7:00 AM
ANY MINUTE NOW...
7:15 AM
REALLY, GUYS?
NONE OF YOU?
7:30 AM
OKAY, YOU KNOW WHAT?
POLLYANNA'S TIRED OF THIS SH—

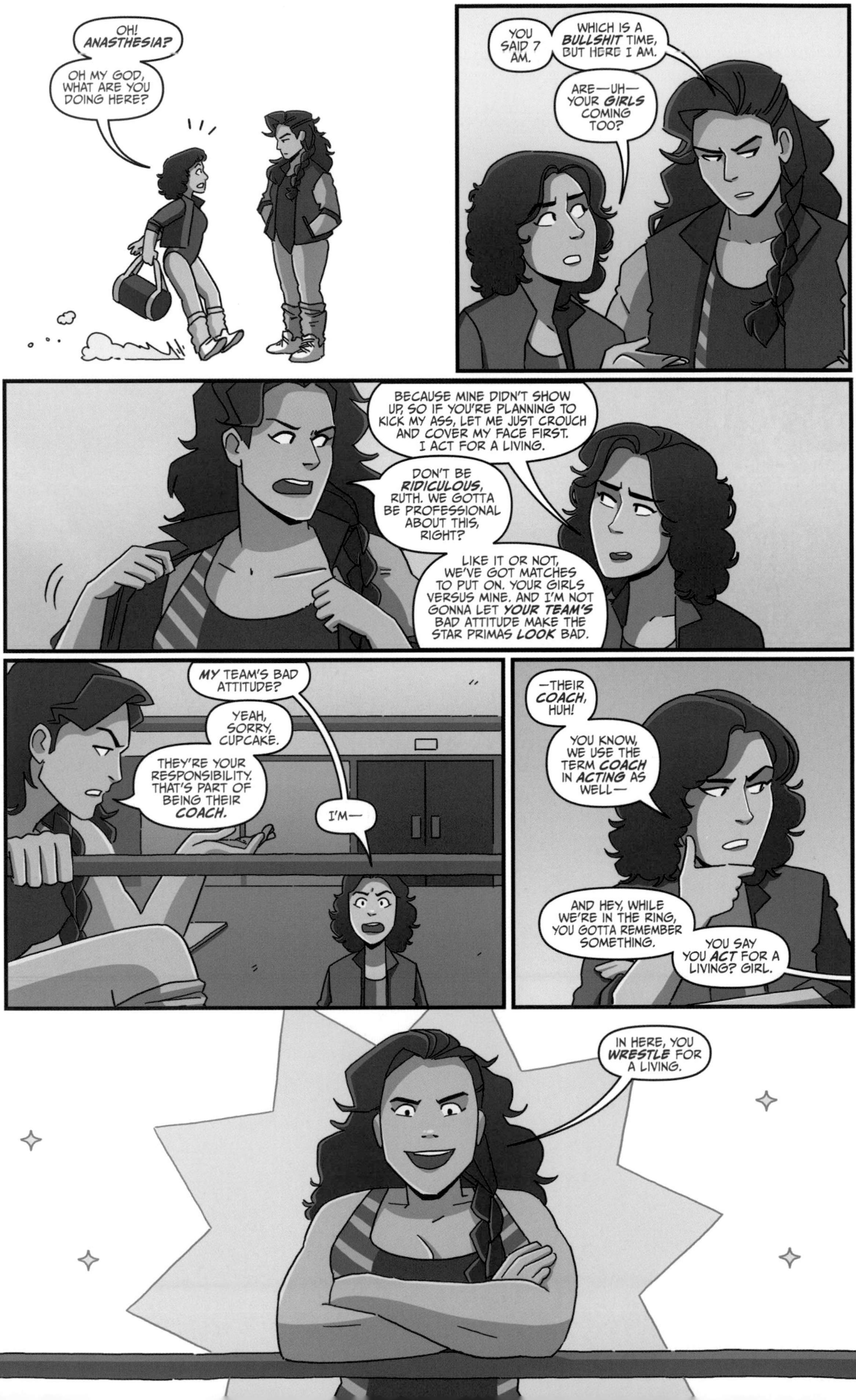

OH! ANASTHESIA?
OH MY GOD, WHAT ARE YOU DOING HERE?
YOU SAID 7 AM.
WHICH IS A BULLSHIT TIME, BUT HERE I AM.
ARE—UH— YOUR GIRLS COMING TOO?
BECAUSE MINE DIDN'T SHOW UP, SO IF YOU'RE PLANNING TO KICK MY ASS, LET ME JUST CROUCH AND COVER MY FACE FIRST. I ACT FOR A LIVING.
DON'T BE RIDICULOUS, RUTH. WE GOTTA BE PROFESSIONAL ABOUT THIS, RIGHT?
LIKE IT OR NOT, WE'VE GOT MATCHES TO PUT ON. YOUR GIRLS VERSUS MINE. AND I'M NOT GONNA LET YOUR TEAM'S BAD ATTITUDE MAKE THE STAR PRIMAS LOOK BAD.
MY TEAM'S BAD ATTITUDE?
YEAH, SORRY, CUPCAKE.
THEY'RE YOUR RESPONSIBILITY. THAT'S PART OF BEING THEIR COACH.
I'M—
—THEIR COACH, HUH!
YOU KNOW, WE USE THE TERM COACH IN ACTING AS WELL—
AND HEY, WHILE WE'RE IN THE RING, YOU GOTTA REMEMBER SOMETHING.
YOU SAY YOU ACT FOR A LIVING? GIRL.
IN HERE, YOU WRESTLE FOR A LIVING.

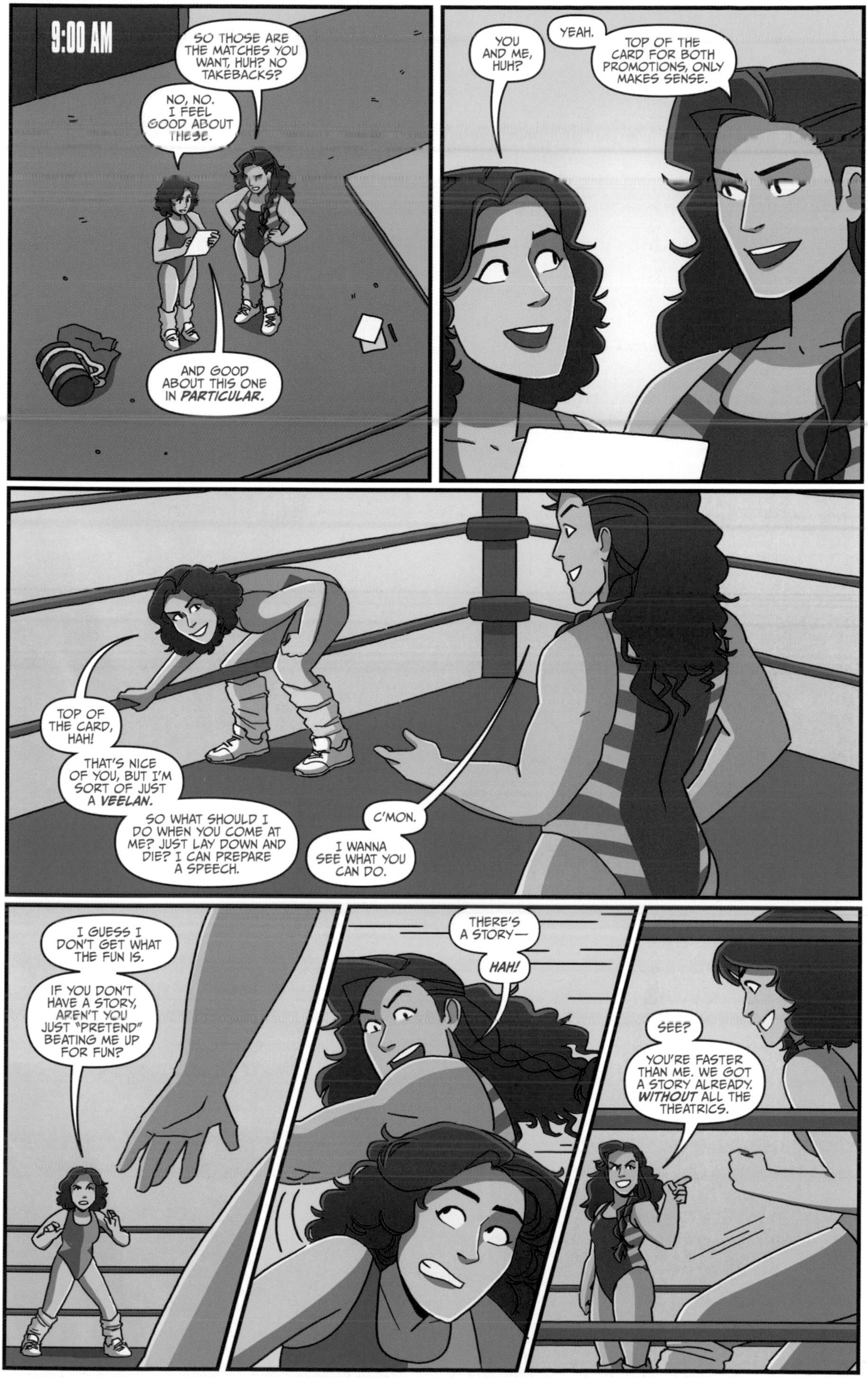
9:00 AM
SO THOSE ARE THE MATCHES YOU WANT, HUH? NO TAKEBACKS?
NO, NO. I FEEL GOOD ABOUT THESE.
AND GOOD ABOUT THIS ONE IN *PARTICULAR.*
YOU AND ME, HUH?
YEAH.
TOP OF THE CARD FOR BOTH PROMOTIONS, ONLY MAKES SENSE.
TOP OF THE CARD, HAH!
THAT'S NICE OF YOU, BUT I'M SORT OF JUST A *VEELAN.*
SO WHAT SHOULD I DO WHEN YOU COME AT ME? JUST LAY DOWN AND DIE? I CAN PREPARE A SPEECH.
C'MON.
I WANNA SEE WHAT YOU CAN DO.
I GUESS I DON'T GET WHAT THE FUN IS.
IF YOU DON'T HAVE A STORY, AREN'T YOU JUST "PRETEND" BEATING ME UP FOR FUN?
THERE'S A STORY—
HAH!
SEE?
YOU'RE FASTER THAN ME. WE GOT A STORY ALREADY. *WITHOUT* ALL THE THEATRICS.

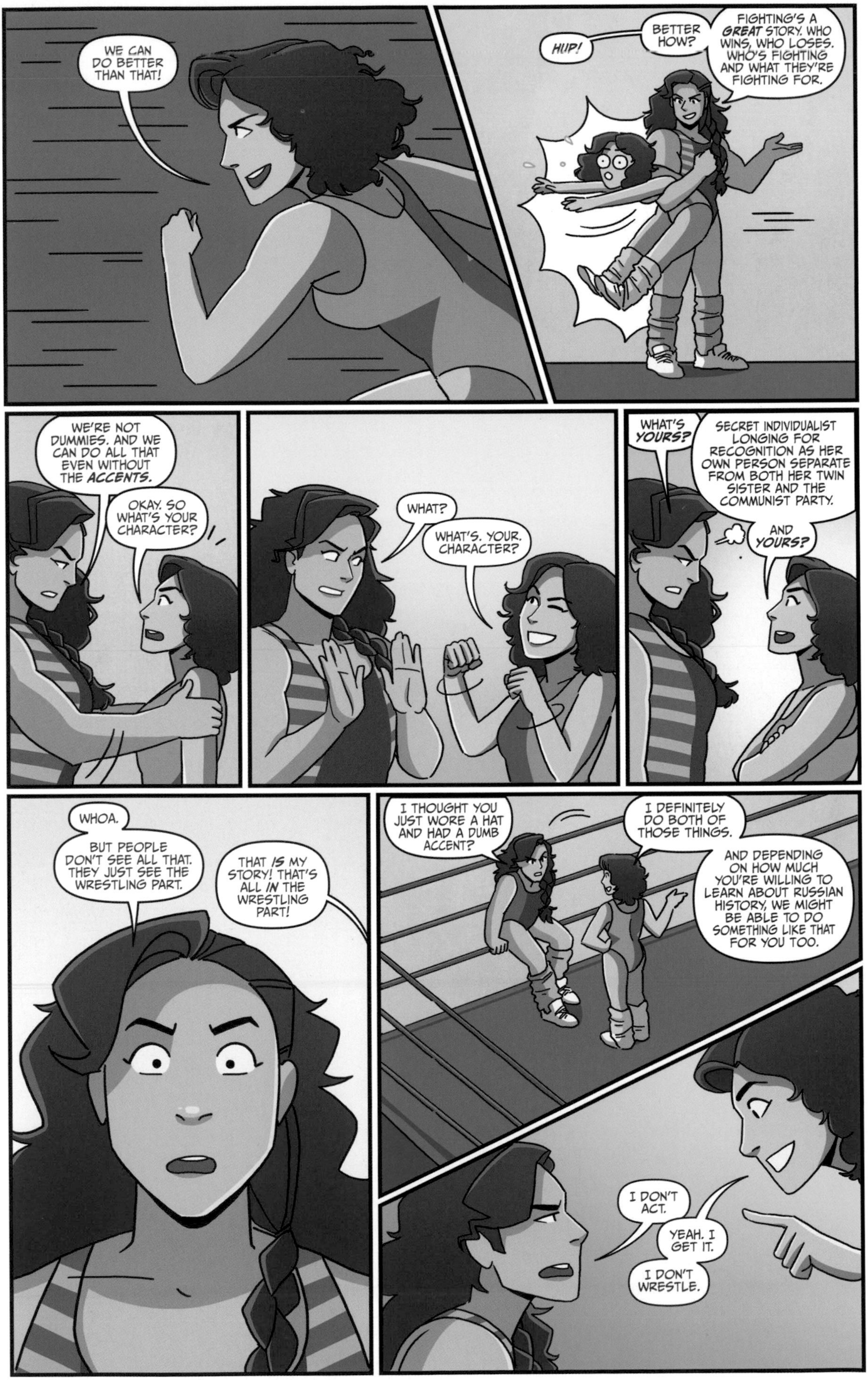
WE CAN DO BETTER THAN THAT!
HUP!
BETTER HOW?
FIGHTING'S A GREAT STORY. WHO WINS, WHO LOSES. WHO'S FIGHTING AND WHAT THEY'RE FIGHTING FOR.
WE'RE NOT DUMMIES. AND WE CAN DO ALL THAT EVEN WITHOUT THE ACCENTS.
OKAY. SO WHAT'S YOUR CHARACTER?
WHAT?
WHAT'S. YOUR. CHARACTER?
WHAT'S YOURS?
SECRET INDIVIDUALIST LONGING FOR RECOGNITION AS HER OWN PERSON SEPARATE FROM BOTH HER TWIN SISTER AND THE COMMUNIST PARTY.
AND YOURS?
WHOA.
BUT PEOPLE DON'T SEE ALL THAT. THEY JUST SEE THE WRESTLING PART.
THAT IS MY STORY! THAT'S ALL IN THE WRESTLING PART!
I THOUGHT YOU JUST WORE A HAT AND HAD A DUMB ACCENT?
I DEFINITELY DO BOTH OF THOSE THINGS.
AND DEPENDING ON HOW MUCH YOU'RE WILLING TO LEARN ABOUT RUSSIAN HISTORY, WE MIGHT BE ABLE TO DO SOMETHING LIKE THAT FOR YOU TOO.
I DON'T ACT.
YEAH. I GET IT.
I DON'T WRESTLE.

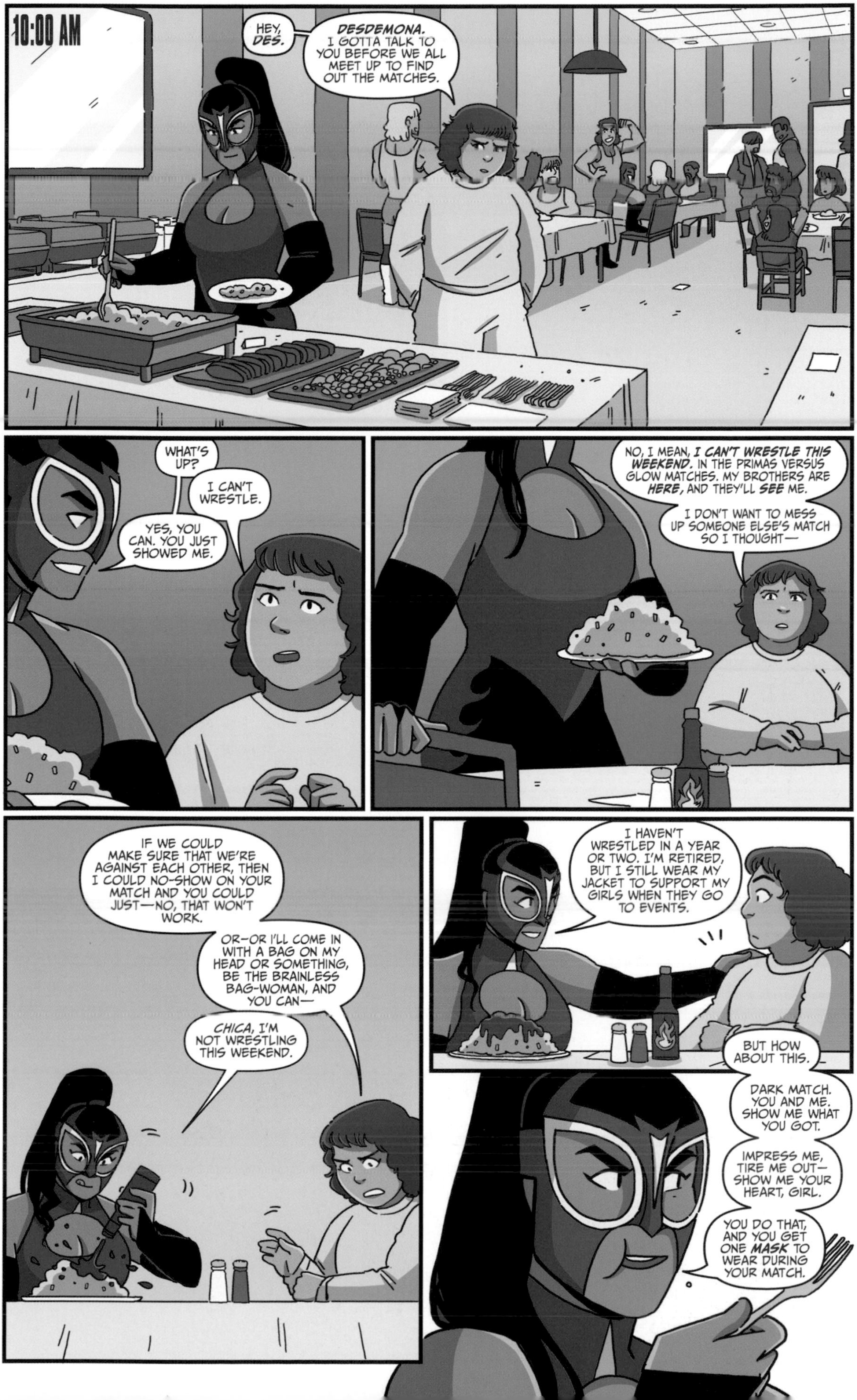
10:00 AM
HEY, DES.
DESDEMONA. I GOTTA TALK TO YOU BEFORE WE ALL MEET UP TO FIND OUT THE MATCHES.
WHAT'S UP?
I CAN'T WRESTLE.
YES, YOU CAN. YOU JUST SHOWED ME.
NO, I MEAN, I CAN'T WRESTLE THIS WEEKEND. IN THE PRIMAS VERSUS GLOW MATCHES. MY BROTHERS ARE HERE, AND THEY'LL SEE ME.
I DON'T WANT TO MESS UP SOMEONE ELSE'S MATCH SO I THOUGHT—
IF WE COULD MAKE SURE THAT WE'RE AGAINST EACH OTHER, THEN I COULD NO-SHOW ON YOUR MATCH AND YOU COULD JUST—NO, THAT WON'T WORK.
OR—OR I'LL COME IN WITH A BAG ON MY HEAD OR SOMETHING, BE THE BRAINLESS BAG-WOMAN, AND YOU CAN—
CHICA, I'M NOT WRESTLING THIS WEEKEND.
I HAVEN'T WRESTLED IN A YEAR OR TWO. I'M RETIRED, BUT I STILL WEAR MY JACKET TO SUPPORT MY GIRLS WHEN THEY GO TO EVENTS.
BUT HOW ABOUT THIS.
DARK MATCH. YOU AND ME. SHOW ME WHAT YOU GOT.
IMPRESS ME, TIRE ME OUT— SHOW ME YOUR HEART, GIRL.
YOU DO THAT, AND YOU GET ONE MASK TO WEAR DURING YOUR MATCH.

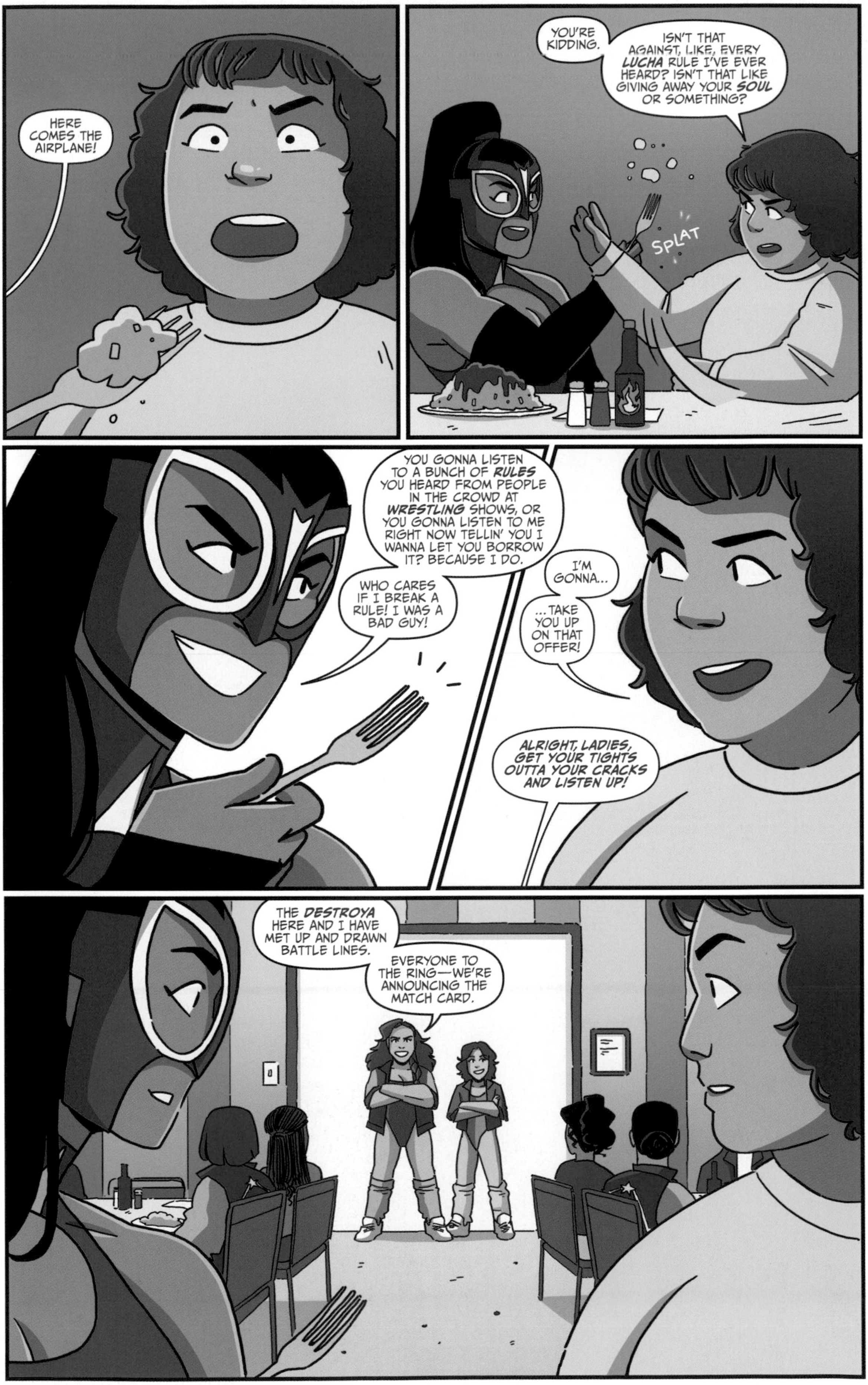
HERE COMES THE AIRPLANE!
YOU'RE KIDDING.
ISN'T THAT AGAINST, LIKE, EVERY LUCHA RULE I'VE EVER HEARD? ISN'T THAT LIKE GIVING AWAY YOUR SOUL OR SOMETHING?
SPLAT
YOU GONNA LISTEN TO A BUNCH OF RULES YOU HEARD FROM PEOPLE IN THE CROWD AT WRESTLING SHOWS, OR YOU GONNA LISTEN TO ME RIGHT NOW TELLIN' YOU I WANNA LET YOU BORROW IT? BECAUSE I DO.
WHO CARES IF I BREAK A RULE! I WAS A BAD GUY!
I'M GONNA...
...TAKE YOU UP ON THAT OFFER!
ALRIGHT, LADIES, GET YOUR TIGHTS OUTTA YOUR CRACKS AND LISTEN UP!
THE DESTROYA HERE AND I HAVE MET UP AND DRAWN BATTLE LINES.
EVERYONE TO THE RING—WE'RE ANNOUNCING THE MATCH CARD.

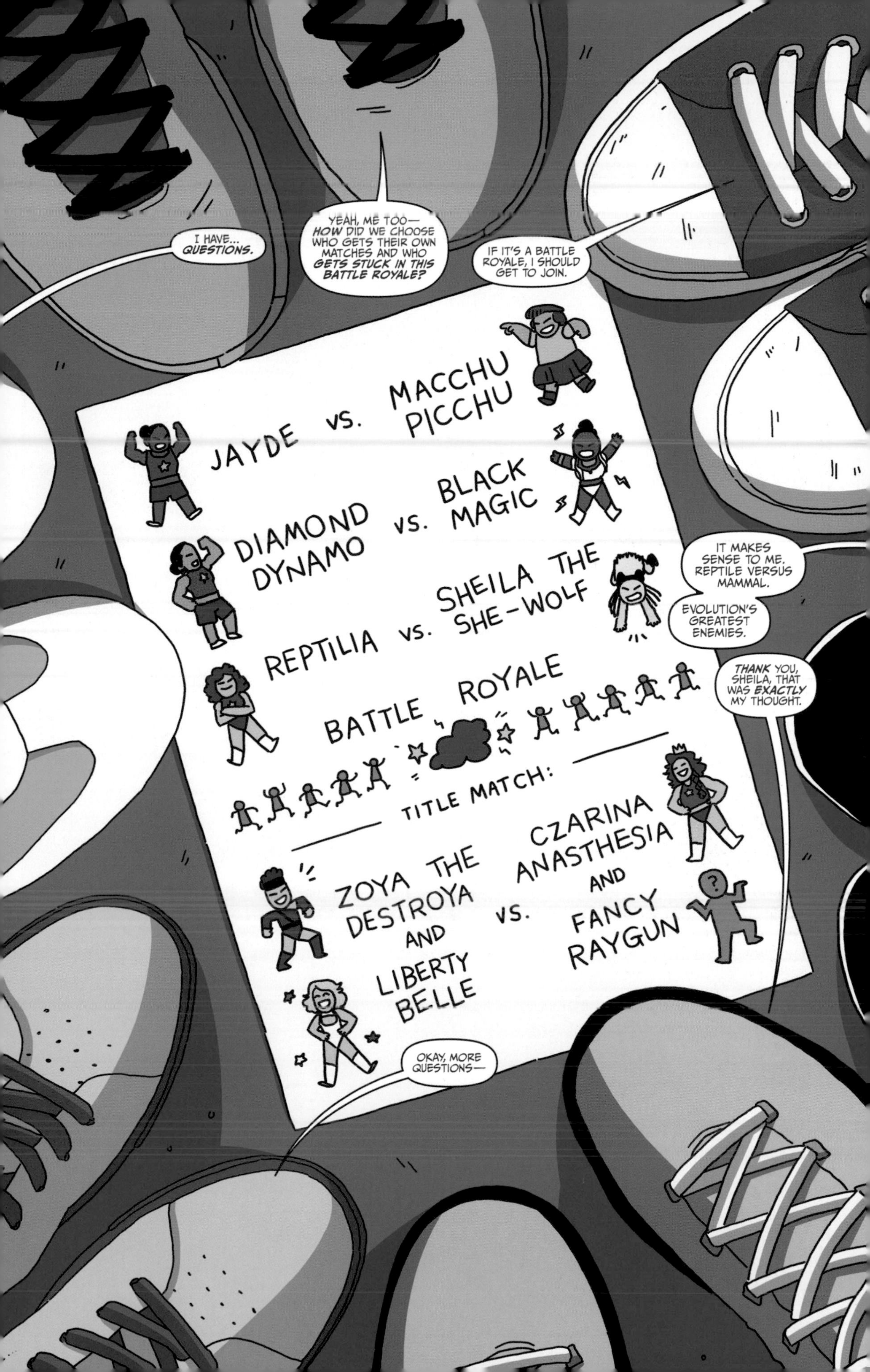
I HAVE... QUESTIONS.
YEAH, ME TOO— HOW DID WE CHOOSE WHO GETS THEIR OWN MATCHES AND WHO GETS STUCK IN THIS BATTLE ROYALE?
IF IT'S A BATTLE ROYALE, I SHOULD GET TO JOIN.
JAYDE VS. MACCHU PICCHU
DIAMOND DYNAMO VS. BLACK MAGIC
REPTILIA VS. SHEILA THE SHE-WOLF
BATTLE ROYALE
TITLE MATCH:
ZOYA THE DESTROYA AND LIBERTY BELLE VS. CZARINA ANASTHESIA AND FANCY RAYGUN
IT MAKES SENSE TO ME. REPTILE VERSUS MAMMAL.
EVOLUTION'S GREATEST ENEMIES.
THANK YOU, SHEILA, THAT WAS EXACTLY MY THOUGHT.
OKAY, MORE QUESTIONS—

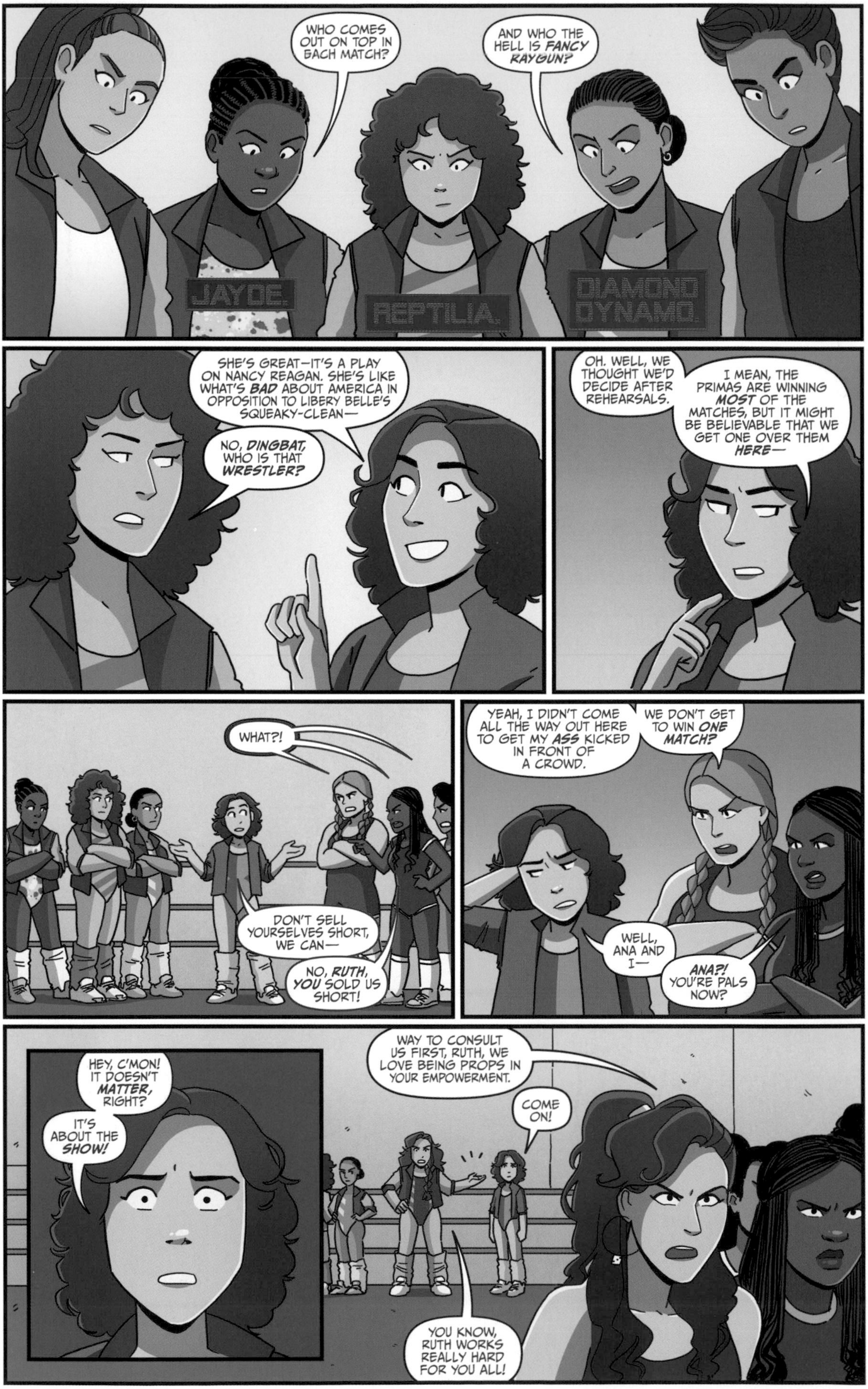
WHO COMES OUT ON TOP IN EACH MATCH?
AND WHO THE HELL IS FANCY RAYGUN?
JAYDE.
REPTILIA.
DIAMOND DYNAMO.
SHE'S GREAT—IT'S A PLAY ON NANCY REAGAN. SHE'S LIKE WHAT'S BAD ABOUT AMERICA IN OPPOSITION TO LIBERY BELLE'S SQUEAKY-CLEAN—
NO, DINGBAT, WHO IS THAT WRESTLER?
OH. WELL, WE THOUGHT WE'D DECIDE AFTER REHEARSALS.
I MEAN, THE PRIMAS ARE WINNING MOST OF THE MATCHES, BUT IT MIGHT BE BELIEVABLE THAT WE GET ONE OVER THEM HERE—
WHAT?!
DON'T SELL YOURSELVES SHORT, WE CAN—
NO, RUTH, YOU SOLD US SHORT!
YEAH, I DIDN'T COME ALL THE WAY OUT HERE TO GET MY ASS KICKED IN FRONT OF A CROWD.
WE DON'T GET TO WIN ONE MATCH?
WELL, ANA AND I—
ANA?! YOU'RE PALS NOW?
HEY, C'MON! IT DOESN'T MATTER, RIGHT?
IT'S ABOUT THE SHOW!
WAY TO CONSULT US FIRST, RUTH, WE LOVE BEING PROPS IN YOUR EMPOWERMENT.
COME ON!
YOU KNOW, RUTH WORKS REALLY HARD FOR YOU ALL!

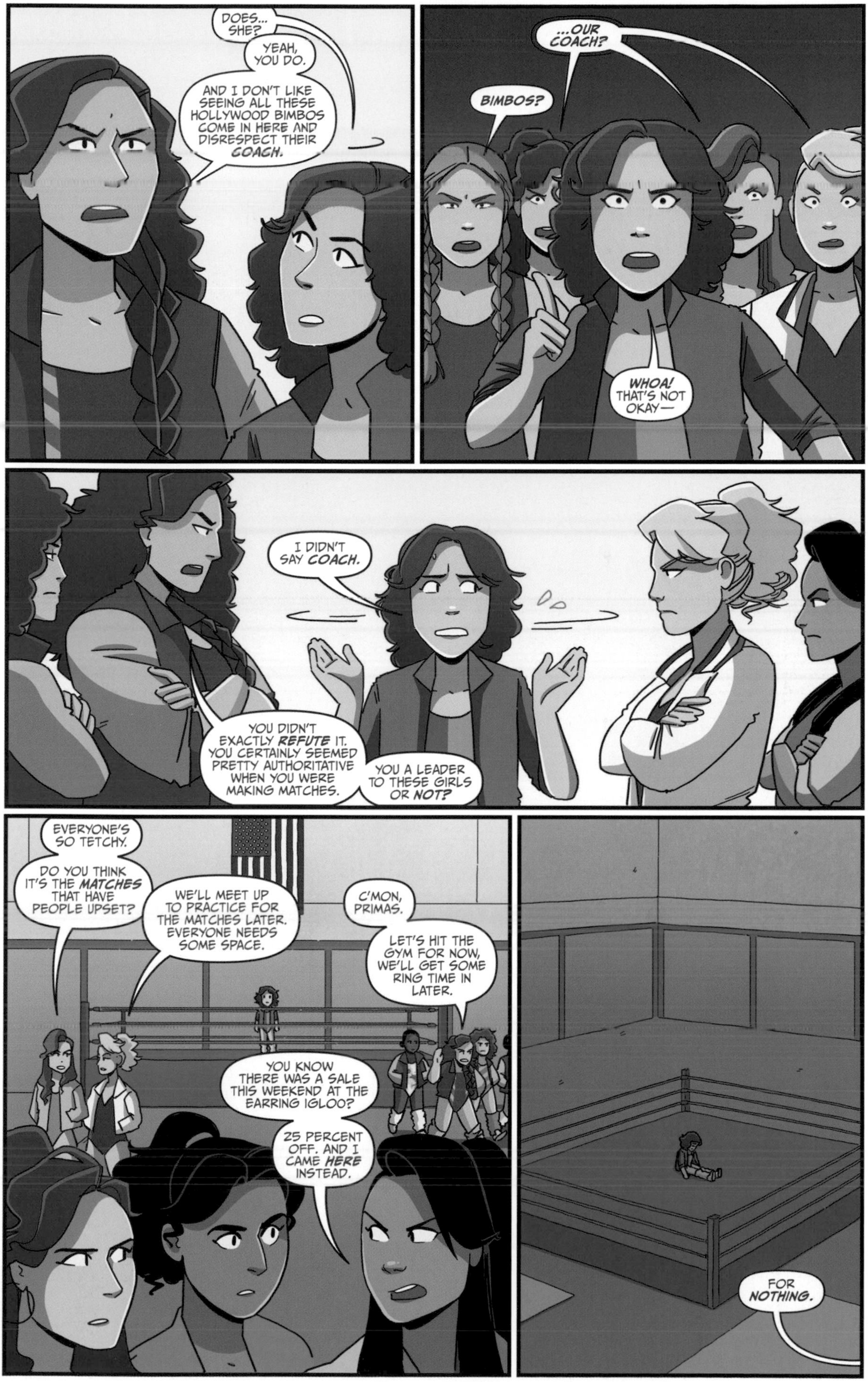
DOES... SHE?
YEAH, YOU DO.
AND I DON'T LIKE SEEING ALL THESE HOLLYWOOD BIMBOS COME IN HERE AND DISRESPECT THEIR COACH.
...OUR COACH?
BIMBOS?
WHOA! THAT'S NOT OKAY—
I DIDN'T SAY COACH.
YOU DIDN'T EXACTLY REFUTE IT. YOU CERTAINLY SEEMED PRETTY AUTHORITATIVE WHEN YOU WERE MAKING MATCHES.
YOU A LEADER TO THESE GIRLS OR NOT?
EVERYONE'S SO TETCHY.
DO YOU THINK IT'S THE MATCHES THAT HAVE PEOPLE UPSET?
WE'LL MEET UP TO PRACTICE FOR THE MATCHES LATER. EVERYONE NEEDS SOME SPACE.
C'MON, PRIMAS.
LET'S HIT THE GYM FOR NOW, WE'LL GET SOME RING TIME IN LATER.
YOU KNOW THERE WAS A SALE THIS WEEKEND AT THE EARRING IGLOO?
25 PERCENT OFF. AND I CAME HERE INSTEAD.
FOR NOTHING.

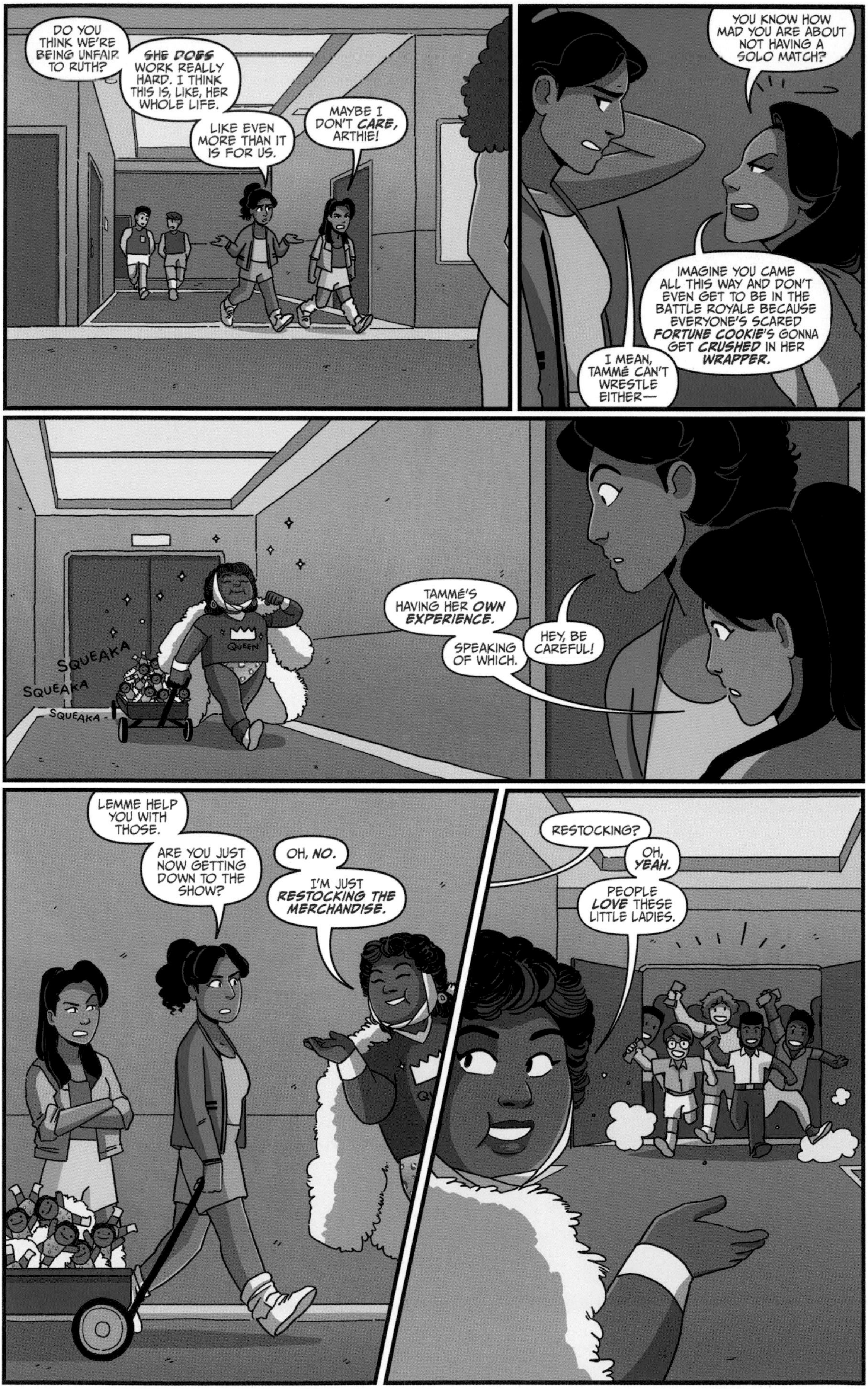
DO YOU THINK WE'RE BEING UNFAIR TO RUTH?
SHE DOES WORK REALLY HARD. I THINK THIS IS, LIKE, HER WHOLE LIFE.
LIKE EVEN MORE THAN IT IS FOR US.
MAYBE I DON'T CARE, ARTHIE!
YOU KNOW HOW MAD YOU ARE ABOUT NOT HAVING A SOLO MATCH?
IMAGINE YOU CAME ALL THIS WAY AND DON'T EVEN GET TO BE IN THE BATTLE ROYALE BECAUSE EVERYONE'S SCARED FORTUNE COOKIE'S GONNA GET CRUSHED IN HER WRAPPER.
I MEAN, TAMMÉ CAN'T WRESTLE EITHER—
QUEEN
SQUEAKA
SQUEAKA
SQUEAKA
TAMMÉ'S HAVING HER OWN EXPERIENCE.
SPEAKING OF WHICH.
HEY, BE CAREFUL!
LEMME HELP YOU WITH THOSE.
ARE YOU JUST NOW GETTING DOWN TO THE SHOW?
OH, NO.
I'M JUST RESTOCKING THE MERCHANDISE.
RESTOCKING?
OH, YEAH.
PEOPLE LOVE THESE LITTLE LADIES.

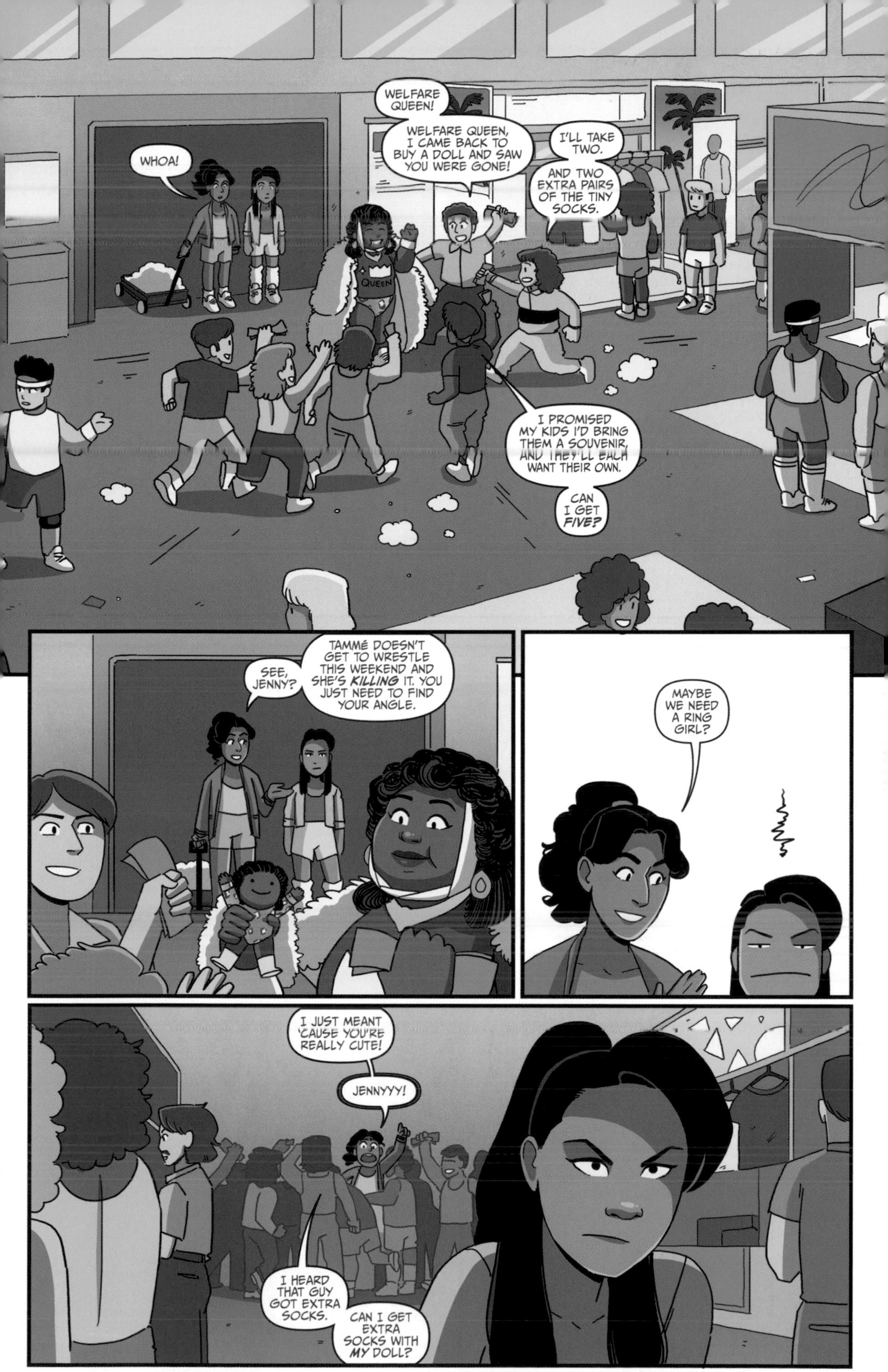
WHOA!
WELFARE QUEEN!
WELFARE QUEEN, I CAME BACK TO BUY A DOLL AND SAW YOU WERE GONE!
QUEEN
I'LL TAKE TWO.
AND TWO EXTRA PAIRS OF THE TINY SOCKS.
I PROMISED MY KIDS I'D BRING THEM A SOUVENIR, AND THEY'LL EACH WANT THEIR OWN.
CAN I GET *FIVE?*
SEE, JENNY?
TAMMÉ DOESN'T GET TO WRESTLE THIS WEEKEND AND SHE'S *KILLING* IT. YOU JUST NEED TO FIND YOUR ANGLE.
MAYBE WE NEED A RING GIRL?
I JUST MEANT 'CAUSE YOU'RE REALLY CUTE!
JENNYYY!
I HEARD THAT GUY GOT EXTRA SOCKS.
CAN I GET EXTRA SOCKS WITH *MY* DOLL?

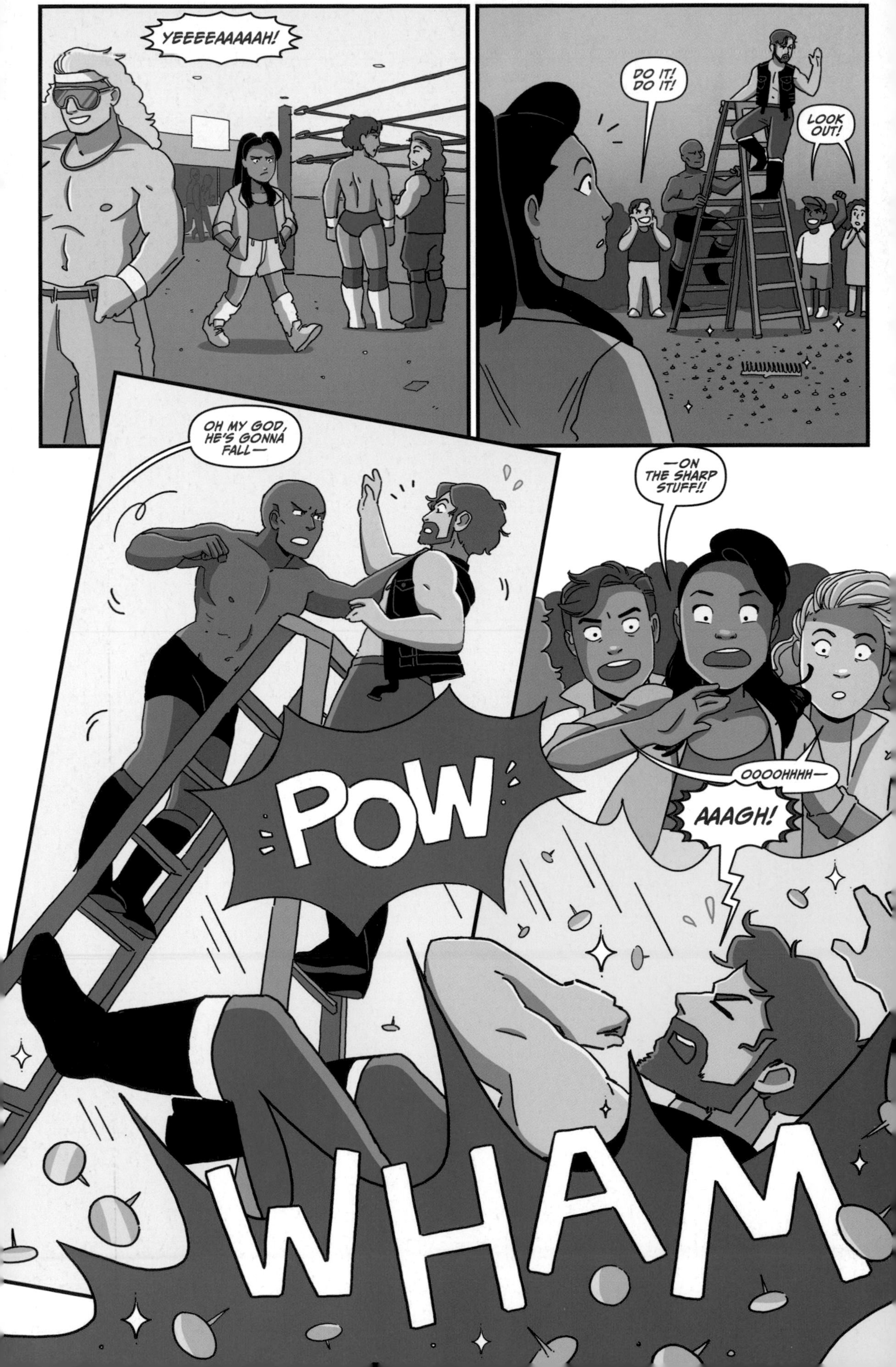
YEEEEAAAAAH!
DO IT! DO IT!
LOOK OUT!
OH MY GOD, HE'S GONNA FALL—
—ON THE SHARP STUFF!!
POW
OOOOHHHH—
AAAGH!
WHAM

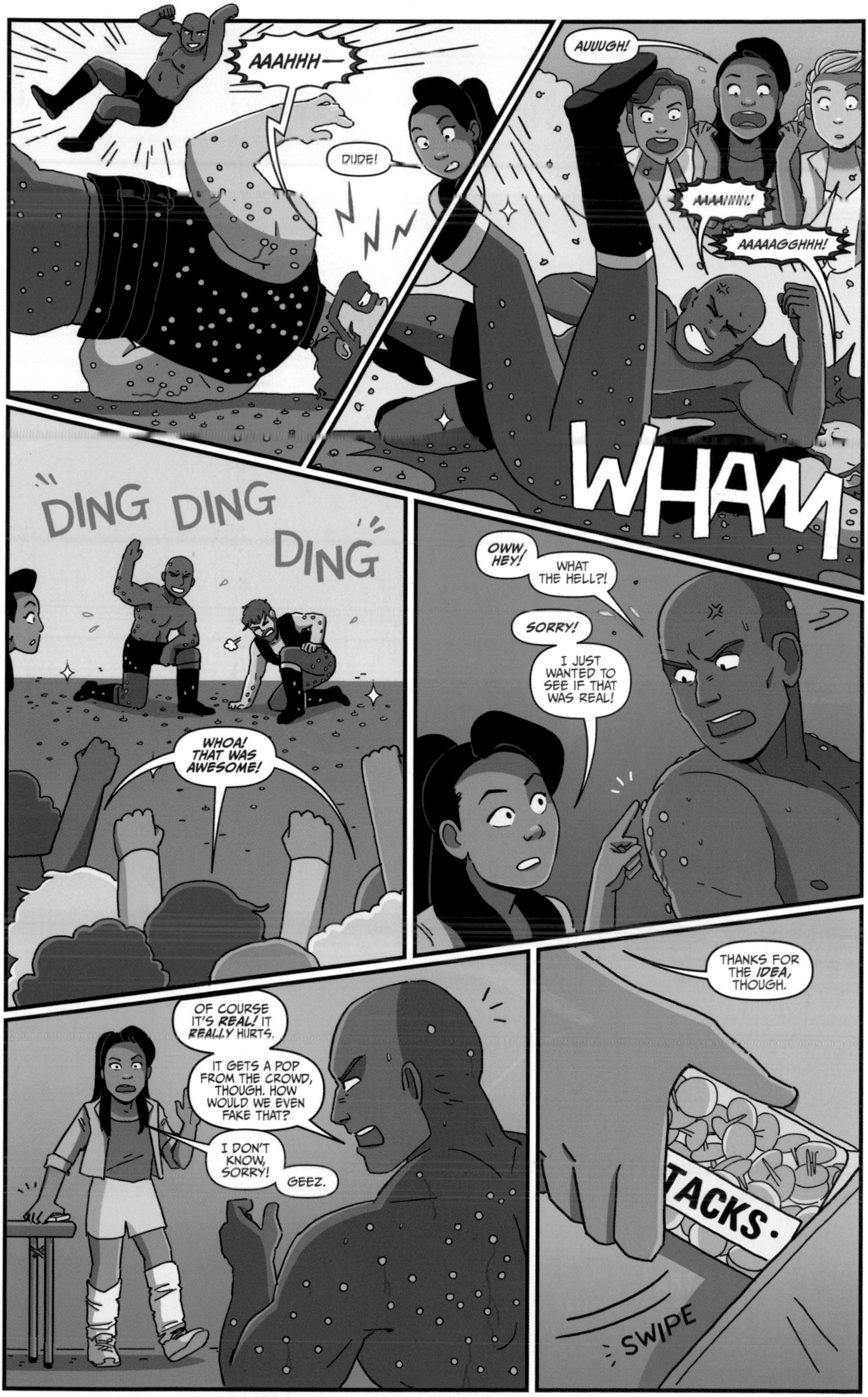
AAAHHH—
DUDE!
AUUUGH!
AAAAHHH!
AAAAAGGHHH!
WHAM
DING DING DING
WHOA! THAT WAS AWESOME!
OWW, HEY!
WHAT THE HELL?!
SORRY!
I JUST WANTED TO SEE IF THAT WAS REAL!
OF COURSE IT'S REAL! IT REALLY HURTS.
IT GETS A POP FROM THE CROWD, THOUGH. HOW WOULD WE EVEN FAKE THAT?
I DON'T KNOW, SORRY!
GEEZ.
THANKS FOR THE IDEA, THOUGH.
TACKS.
SWIPE

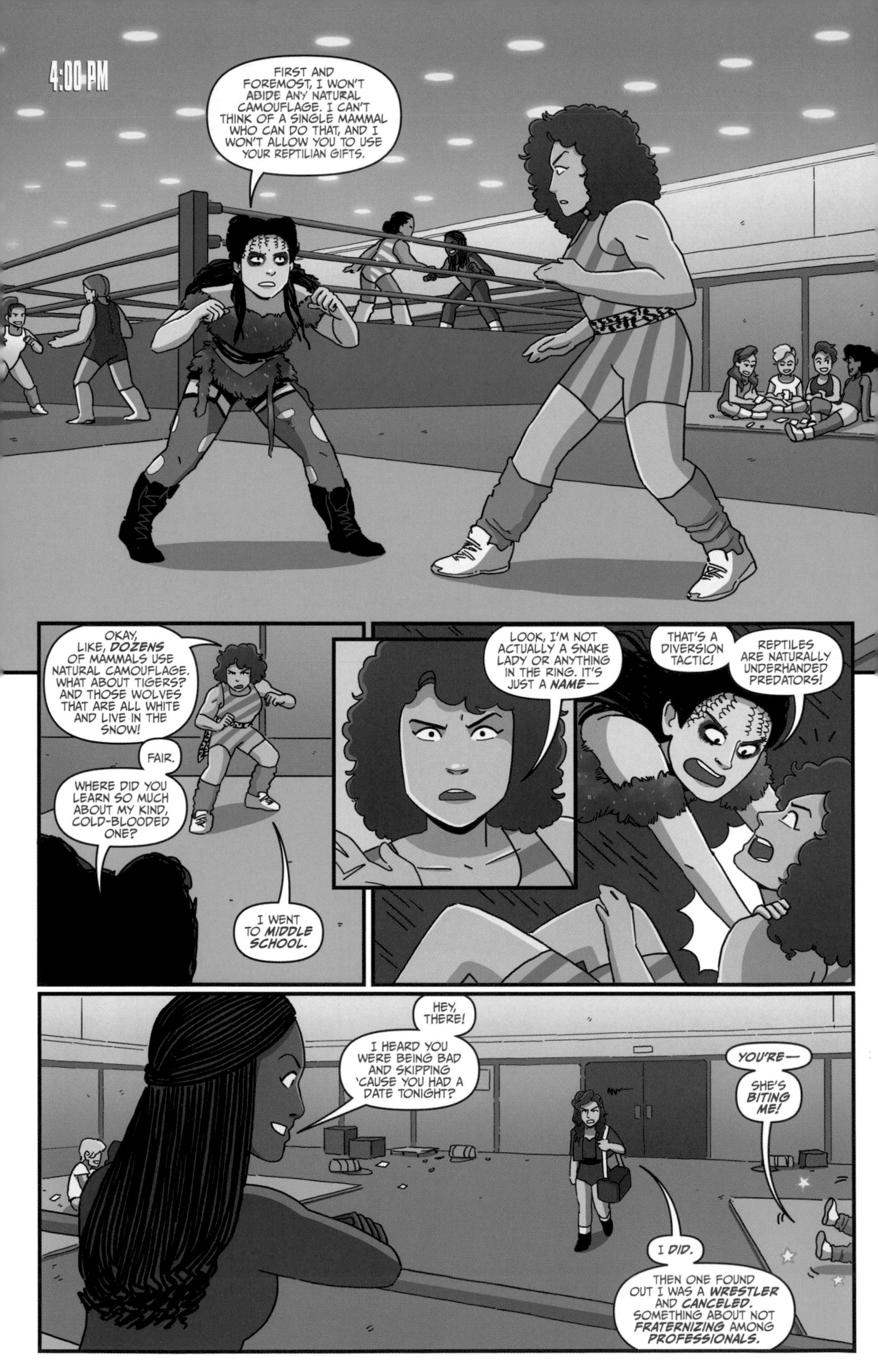
4:00 PM
FIRST AND FOREMOST, I WON'T ABIDE ANY NATURAL CAMOUFLAGE. I CAN'T THINK OF A SINGLE MAMMAL WHO CAN DO THAT, AND I WON'T ALLOW YOU TO USE YOUR REPTILIAN GIFTS.
OKAY, LIKE, DOZENS OF MAMMALS USE NATURAL CAMOUFLAGE. WHAT ABOUT TIGERS? AND THOSE WOLVES THAT ARE ALL WHITE AND LIVE IN THE SNOW!
FAIR.
WHERE DID YOU LEARN SO MUCH ABOUT MY KIND, COLD-BLOODED ONE?
I WENT TO MIDDLE SCHOOL.
LOOK, I'M NOT ACTUALLY A SNAKE LADY OR ANYTHING IN THE RING. IT'S JUST A NAME—
THAT'S A DIVERSION TACTIC!
REPTILES ARE NATURALLY UNDERHANDED PREDATORS!
HEY, THERE!
I HEARD YOU WERE BEING BAD AND SKIPPING 'CAUSE YOU HAD A DATE TONIGHT?
YOU'RE—
SHE'S BITING ME!
I DID.
THEN ONE FOUND OUT I WAS A WRESTLER AND CANCELED. SOMETHING ABOUT NOT FRATERNIZING AMONG PROFESSIONALS.

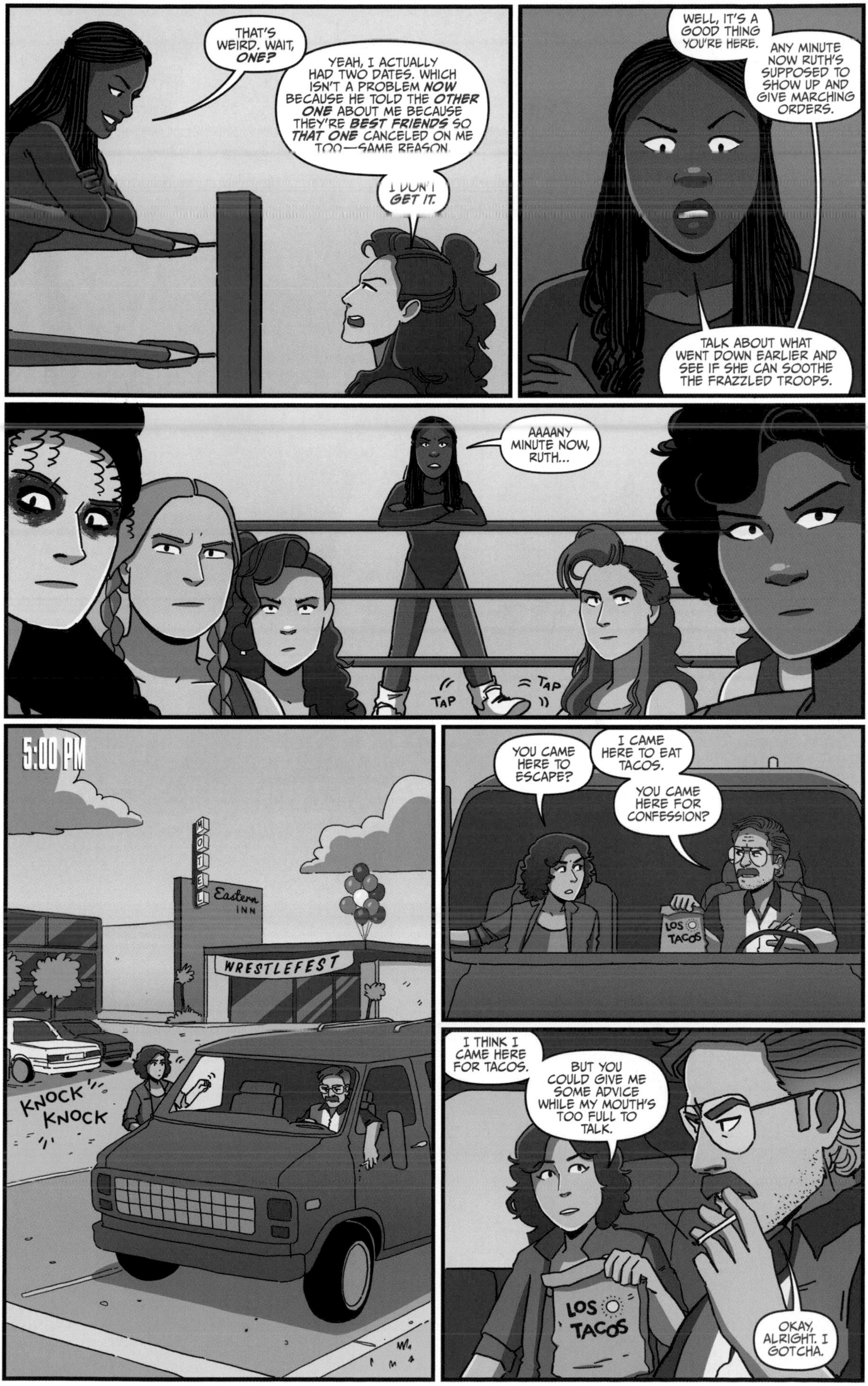
THAT'S WEIRD. WAIT, ONE?
YEAH, I ACTUALLY HAD TWO DATES. WHICH ISN'T A PROBLEM NOW BECAUSE HE TOLD THE OTHER ONE ABOUT ME BECAUSE THEY'RE BEST FRIENDS SO THAT ONE CANCELED ON ME TOO—SAME REASON.
I DON'T GET IT.
WELL, IT'S A GOOD THING YOU'RE HERE.
ANY MINUTE NOW RUTH'S SUPPOSED TO SHOW UP AND GIVE MARCHING ORDERS.
TALK ABOUT WHAT WENT DOWN EARLIER AND SEE IF SHE CAN SOOTHE THE FRAZZLED TROOPS.
AAAANY MINUTE NOW, RUTH...
TAP
TAP
5:00 PM
MOTEL
Eastern INN
WRESTLEFEST
KNOCK KNOCK
YOU CAME HERE TO ESCAPE?
I CAME HERE TO EAT TACOS.
YOU CAME HERE FOR CONFESSION?
LOS TACOS
I THINK I CAME HERE FOR TACOS.
BUT YOU COULD GIVE ME SOME ADVICE WHILE MY MOUTH'S TOO FULL TO TALK.
LOS TACOS
OKAY, ALRIGHT. I GOTCHA.

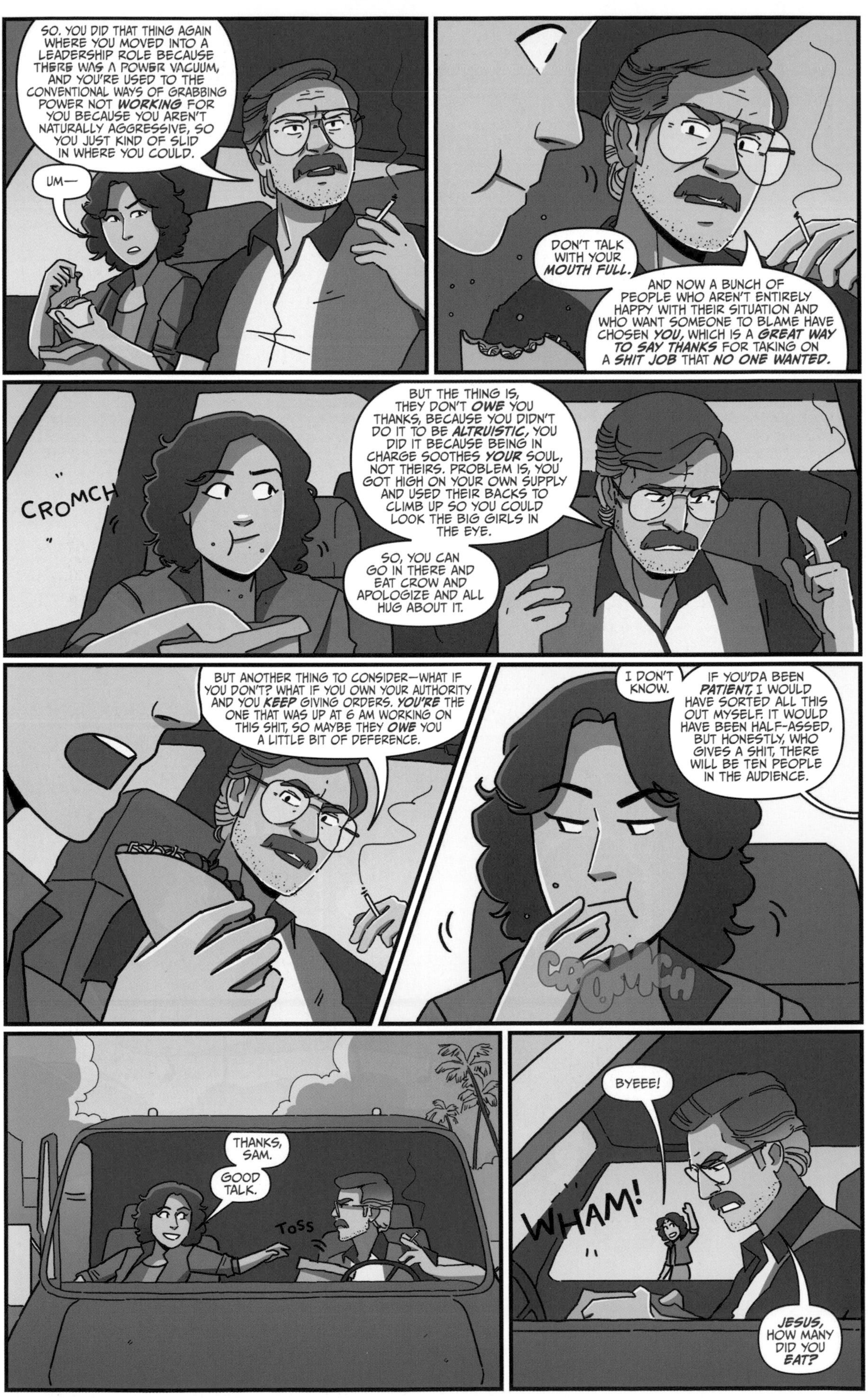
SO. YOU DID THAT THING AGAIN WHERE YOU MOVED INTO A LEADERSHIP ROLE BECAUSE THERE WAS A POWER VACUUM, AND YOU'RE USED TO THE CONVENTIONAL WAYS OF GRABBING POWER NOT WORKING FOR YOU BECAUSE YOU AREN'T NATURALLY AGGRESSIVE, SO YOU JUST KIND OF SLID IN WHERE YOU COULD.
UM—
DON'T TALK WITH YOUR MOUTH FULL.
AND NOW A BUNCH OF PEOPLE WHO AREN'T ENTIRELY HAPPY WITH THEIR SITUATION AND WHO WANT SOMEONE TO BLAME HAVE CHOSEN YOU, WHICH IS A GREAT WAY TO SAY THANKS FOR TAKING ON A SHIT JOB THAT NO ONE WANTED.
CROMCH
BUT THE THING IS, THEY DON'T OWE YOU THANKS, BECAUSE YOU DIDN'T DO IT TO BE ALTRUISTIC, YOU DID IT BECAUSE BEING IN CHARGE SOOTHES YOUR SOUL, NOT THEIRS. PROBLEM IS, YOU GOT HIGH ON YOUR OWN SUPPLY AND USED THEIR BACKS TO CLIMB UP SO YOU COULD LOOK THE BIG GIRLS IN THE EYE.
SO, YOU CAN GO IN THERE AND EAT CROW AND APOLOGIZE AND ALL HUG ABOUT IT.
BUT ANOTHER THING TO CONSIDER—WHAT IF YOU DON'T? WHAT IF YOU OWN YOUR AUTHORITY AND YOU KEEP GIVING ORDERS. YOU'RE THE ONE THAT WAS UP AT 6 AM WORKING ON THIS SHIT, SO MAYBE THEY OWE YOU A LITTLE BIT OF DEFERENCE.
I DON'T KNOW.
IF YOU'DA BEEN PATIENT, I WOULD HAVE SORTED ALL THIS OUT MYSELF. IT WOULD HAVE BEEN HALF-ASSED, BUT HONESTLY, WHO GIVES A SHIT, THERE WILL BE TEN PEOPLE IN THE AUDIENCE.
CROMCH
THANKS, SAM.
GOOD TALK.
TOSS
BYEEE!
WHAM!
JESUS, HOW MANY DID YOU EAT?

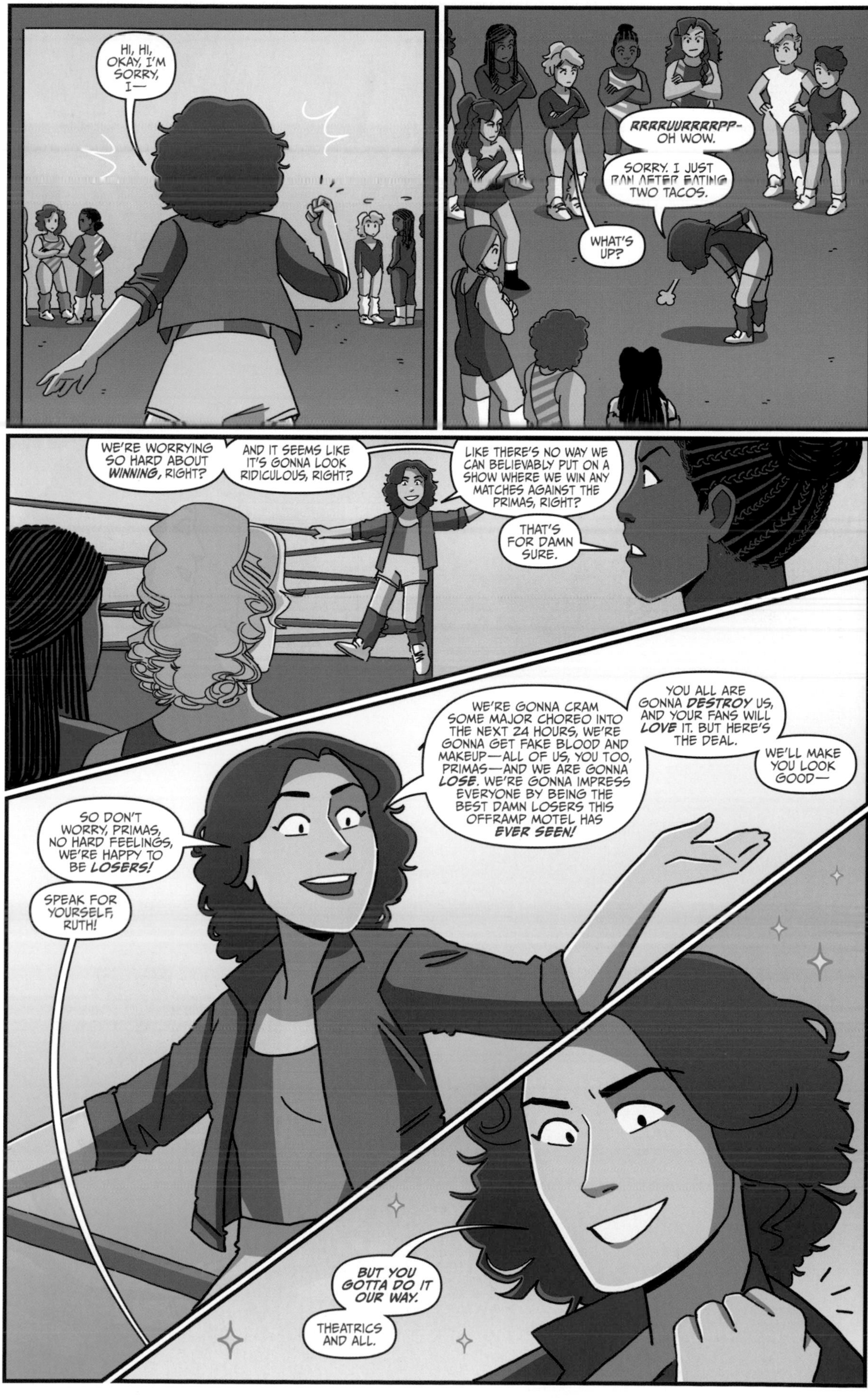
HI, HI, OKAY, I'M SORRY, I—
RRRRUURRRRPP- OH WOW.
SORRY. I JUST RAN AFTER EATING TWO TACOS.
WHAT'S UP?
WE'RE WORRYING SO HARD ABOUT WINNING, RIGHT?
AND IT SEEMS LIKE IT'S GONNA LOOK RIDICULOUS, RIGHT?
LIKE THERE'S NO WAY WE CAN BELIEVABLY PUT ON A SHOW WHERE WE WIN ANY MATCHES AGAINST THE PRIMAS, RIGHT?
THAT'S FOR DAMN SURE.
WE'RE GONNA CRAM SOME MAJOR CHOREO INTO THE NEXT 24 HOURS, WE'RE GONNA GET FAKE BLOOD AND MAKEUP—ALL OF US, YOU TOO, PRIMAS—AND WE ARE GONNA LOSE. WE'RE GONNA IMPRESS EVERYONE BY BEING THE BEST DAMN LOSERS THIS OFFRAMP MOTEL HAS EVER SEEN!
SO DON'T WORRY, PRIMAS, NO HARD FEELINGS, WE'RE HAPPY TO BE LOSERS!
SPEAK FOR YOURSELF, RUTH!
YOU ALL ARE GONNA DESTROY US, AND YOUR FANS WILL LOVE IT. BUT HERE'S THE DEAL.
WE'LL MAKE YOU LOOK GOOD—
BUT YOU GOTTA DO IT OUR WAY.
THEATRICS AND ALL.

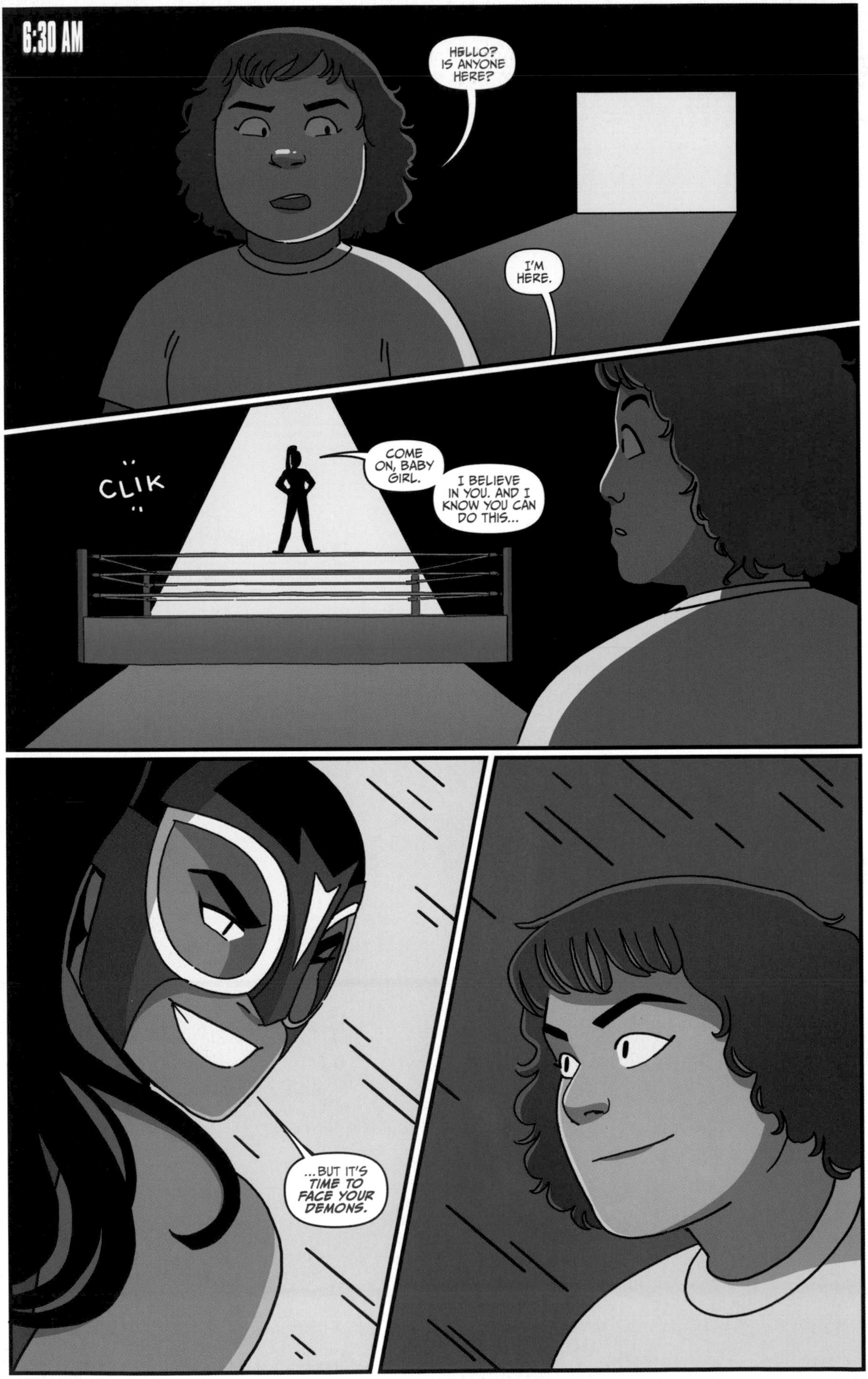
6:30 AM
HELLO? IS ANYONE HERE?
I'M HERE.
CLIK
COME ON, BABY GIRL.
I BELIEVE IN YOU. AND I KNOW YOU CAN DO THIS...
...BUT IT'S TIME TO FACE YOUR DEMONS.

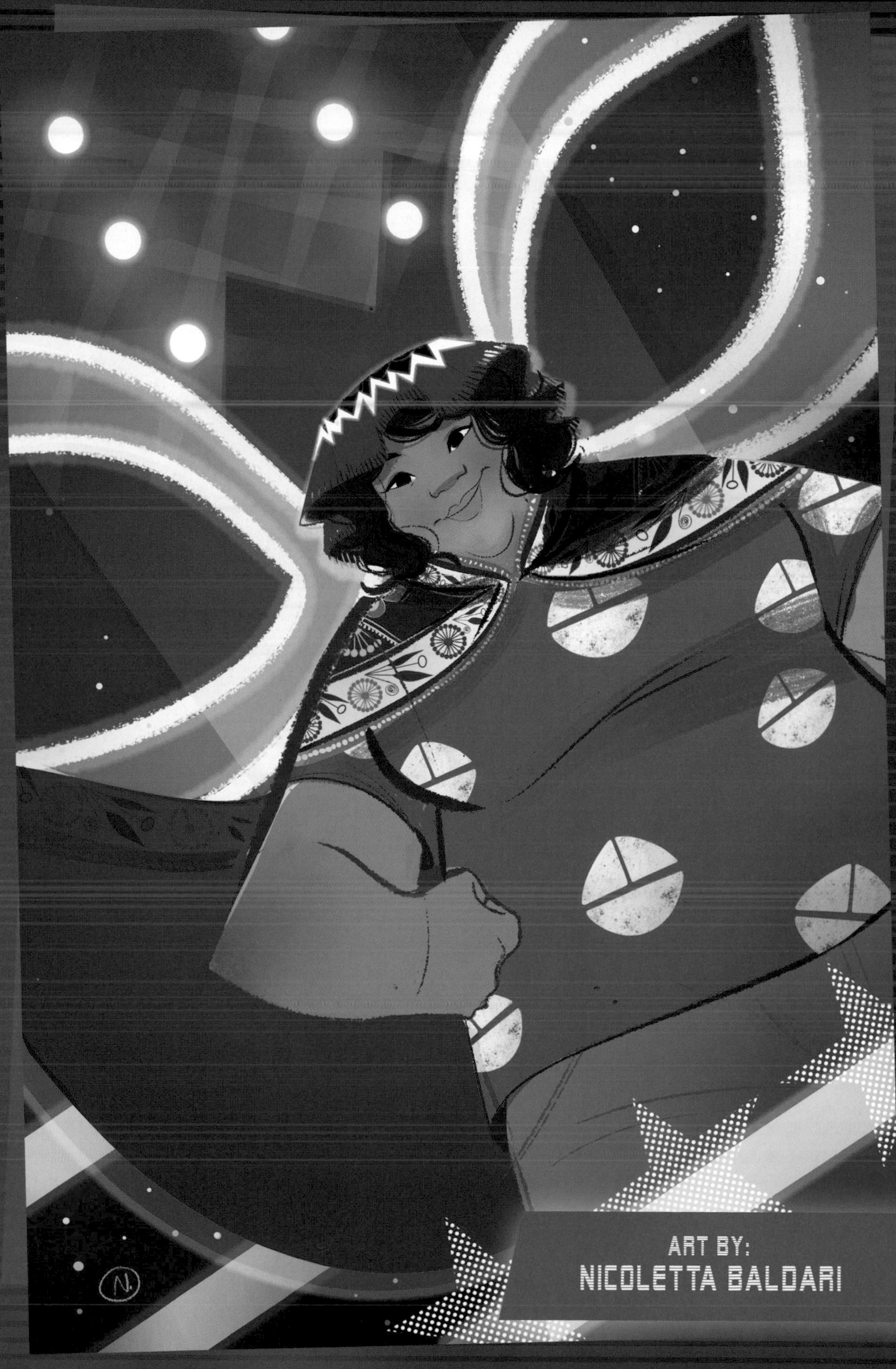
ART BY:
NICOLETTA BALDARI

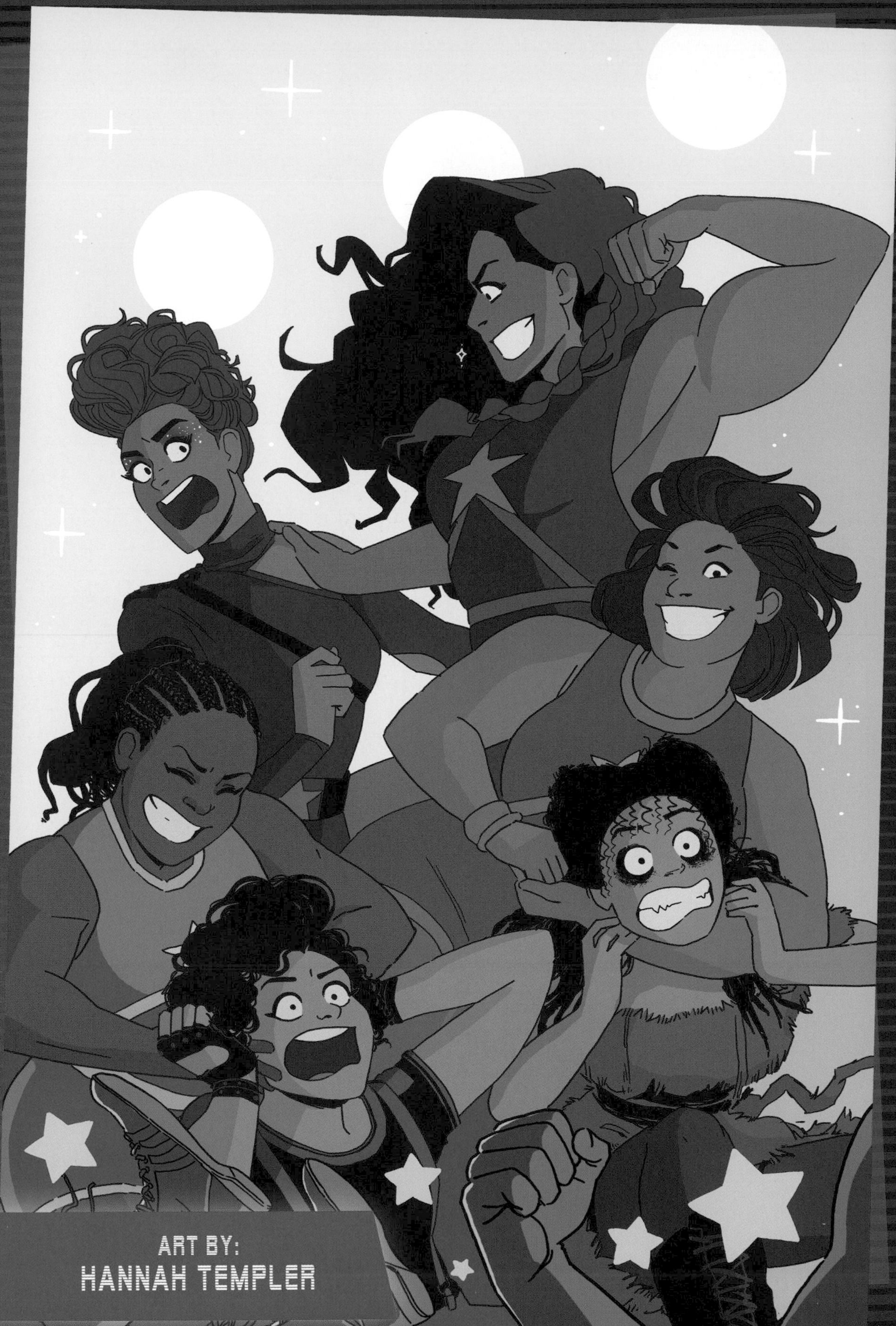
ART BY:
HANNAH TEMPLER

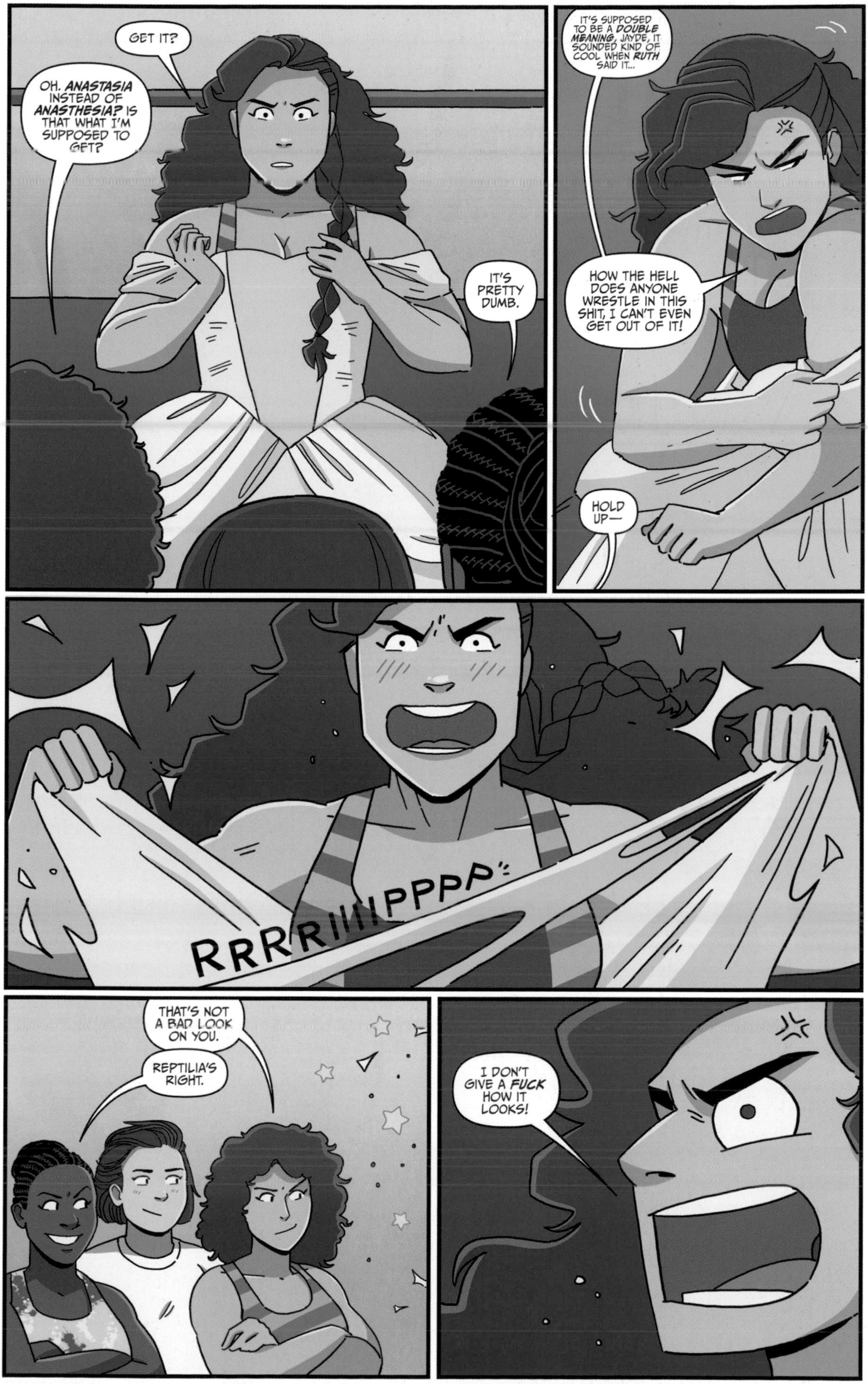
GET IT?
OH. ANASTASIA INSTEAD OF ANASTHESIA? IS THAT WHAT I'M SUPPOSED TO GET?
IT'S PRETTY DUMB.
IT'S SUPPOSED TO BE A DOUBLE MEANING, JAYDE, IT SOUNDED KIND OF COOL WHEN RUTH SAID IT...
HOW THE HELL DOES ANYONE WRESTLE IN THIS SHIT, I CAN'T EVEN GET OUT OF IT!
HOLD UP—
RRRRIIIIPPPP
THAT'S NOT A BAD LOOK ON YOU.
REPTILIA'S RIGHT.
I DON'T GIVE A FUCK HOW IT LOOKS!

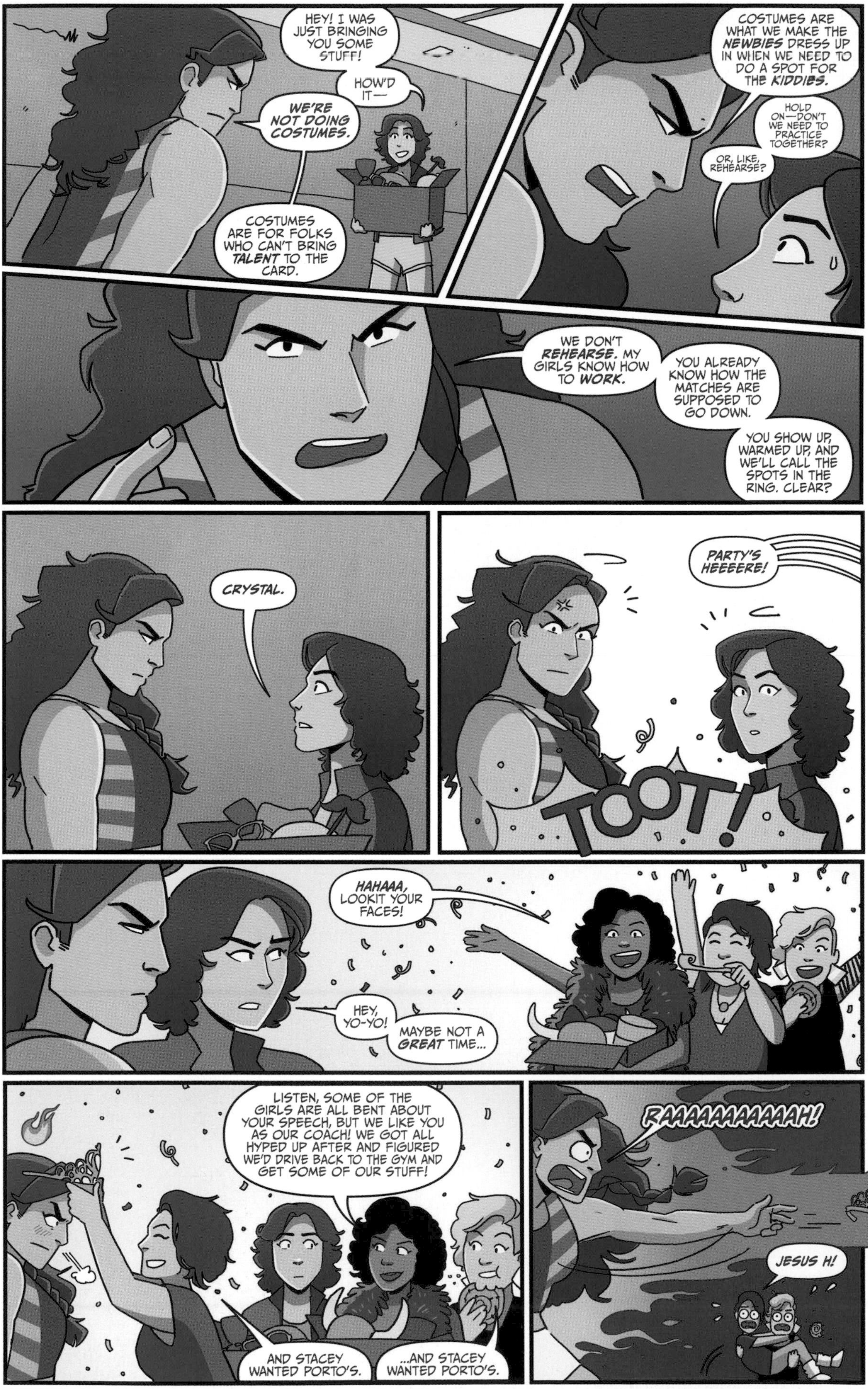

HEY! I WAS JUST BRINGING YOU SOME STUFF!
HOW'D IT—
WE'RE NOT DOING COSTUMES.
COSTUMES ARE FOR FOLKS WHO CAN'T BRING TALENT TO THE CARD.
COSTUMES ARE WHAT WE MAKE THE NEWBIES DRESS UP IN WHEN WE NEED TO DO A SPOT FOR THE KIDDIES.
HOLD ON—DON'T WE NEED TO PRACTICE TOGETHER?
OR, LIKE, REHEARSE?
WE DON'T REHEARSE. MY GIRLS KNOW HOW TO WORK.
YOU ALREADY KNOW HOW THE MATCHES ARE SUPPOSED TO GO DOWN.
YOU SHOW UP, WARMED UP, AND WE'LL CALL THE SPOTS IN THE RING. CLEAR?
CRYSTAL.
PARTY'S HEEEERE!
TOOT!
HAHAAA, LOOKIT YOUR FACES!
HEY, YO-YO!
MAYBE NOT A GREAT TIME...
LISTEN, SOME OF THE GIRLS ARE ALL BENT ABOUT YOUR SPEECH, BUT WE LIKE YOU AS OUR COACH! WE GOT ALL HYPED UP AFTER AND FIGURED WE'D DRIVE BACK TO THE GYM AND GET SOME OF OUR STUFF!
AND STACEY WANTED PORTO'S.
...AND STACEY WANTED PORTO'S.
RAAAAAAAAAAAH!
JESUS H!

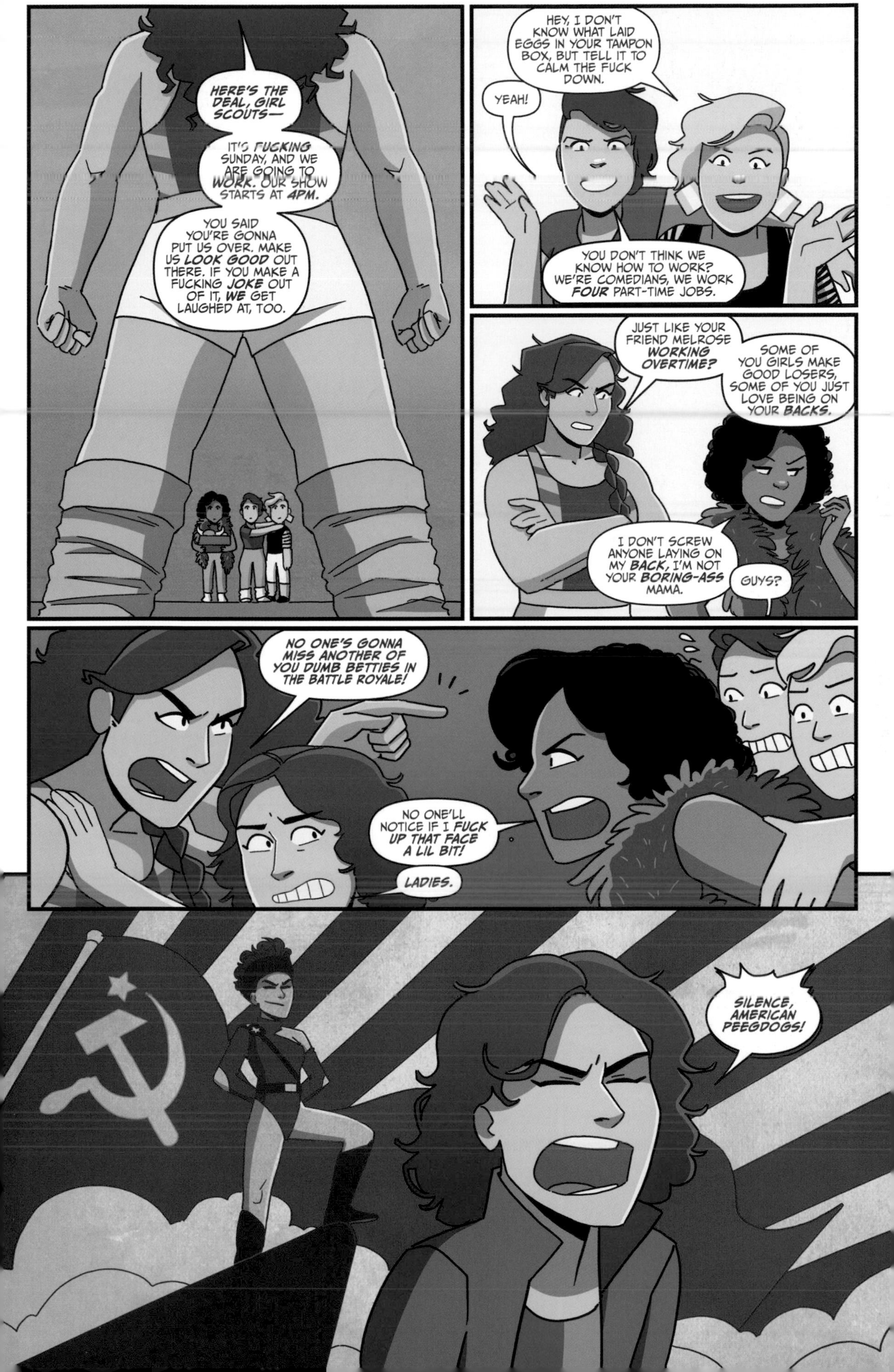

HERE'S THE DEAL, GIRL SCOUTS—
IT'S FUCKING SUNDAY, AND WE ARE GOING TO WORK. OUR SHOW STARTS AT 4PM.
YOU SAID YOU'RE GONNA PUT US OVER. MAKE US LOOK GOOD OUT THERE. IF YOU MAKE A FUCKING JOKE OUT OF IT, WE GET LAUGHED AT, TOO.
HEY, I DON'T KNOW WHAT LAID EGGS IN YOUR TAMPON BOX, BUT TELL IT TO CALM THE FUCK DOWN.
YEAH!
YOU DON'T THINK WE KNOW HOW TO WORK? WE'RE COMEDIANS, WE WORK FOUR PART-TIME JOBS.
JUST LIKE YOUR FRIEND MELROSE WORKING OVERTIME?
SOME OF YOU GIRLS MAKE GOOD LOSERS, SOME OF YOU JUST LOVE BEING ON YOUR BACKS.
I DON'T SCREW ANYONE LAYING ON MY BACK, I'M NOT YOUR BORING-ASS MAMA.
GUYS?
NO ONE'S GONNA MISS ANOTHER OF YOU DUMB BETTIES IN THE BATTLE ROYALE!
NO ONE'LL NOTICE IF I FUCK UP THAT FACE A LIL BIT!
LADIES.
SILENCE, AMERICAN PEEGDOGS!

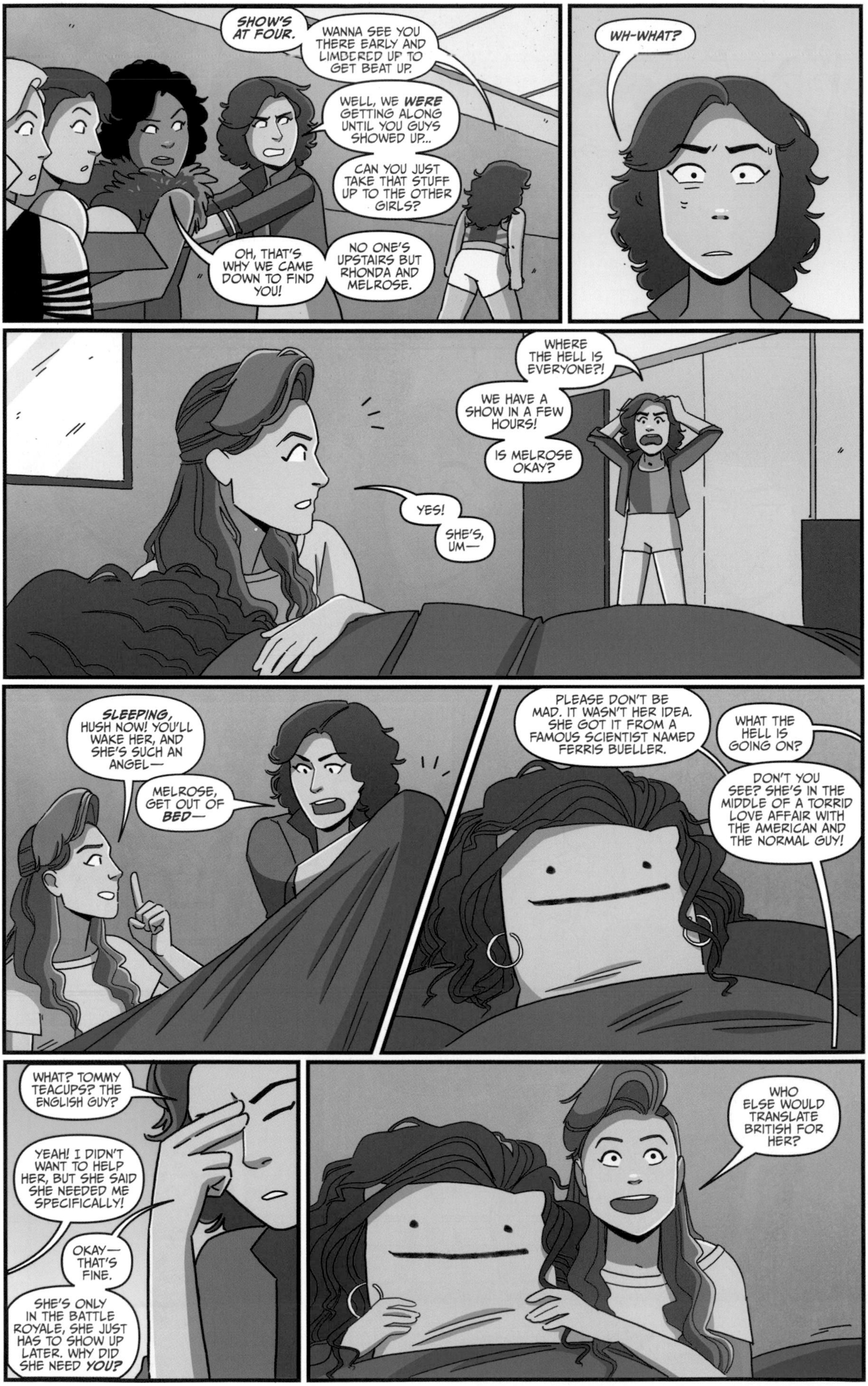
SHOW'S AT FOUR.
WANNA SEE YOU THERE EARLY AND LIMBERED UP TO GET BEAT UP.
WELL, WE *WERE* GETTING ALONG UNTIL YOU GUYS SHOWED UP...
CAN YOU JUST TAKE THAT STUFF UP TO THE OTHER GIRLS?
OH, THAT'S WHY WE CAME DOWN TO FIND YOU!
NO ONE'S UPSTAIRS BUT RHONDA AND MELROSE.
WH-WHAT?
WHERE THE HELL IS EVERYONE?!
WE HAVE A SHOW IN A FEW HOURS!
IS MELROSE OKAY?
YES!
SHE'S, UM—
SLEEPING, HUSH NOW! YOU'LL WAKE HER, AND SHE'S SUCH AN ANGEL—
MELROSE, GET OUT OF BED—
PLEASE DON'T BE MAD. IT WASN'T HER IDEA. SHE GOT IT FROM A FAMOUS SCIENTIST NAMED FERRIS BUELLER.
WHAT THE HELL IS GOING ON?
DON'T YOU SEE? SHE'S IN THE MIDDLE OF A TORRID LOVE AFFAIR WITH THE AMERICAN AND THE NORMAL GUY!
WHAT? TOMMY TEACUPS? THE ENGLISH GUY?
YEAH! I DIDN'T WANT TO HELP HER, BUT SHE SAID SHE NEEDED ME SPECIFICALLY!
OKAY— THAT'S FINE.
SHE'S ONLY IN THE BATTLE ROYALE, SHE JUST HAS TO SHOW UP LATER. WHY DID SHE NEED *YOU?*
WHO ELSE WOULD TRANSLATE BRITISH FOR HER?

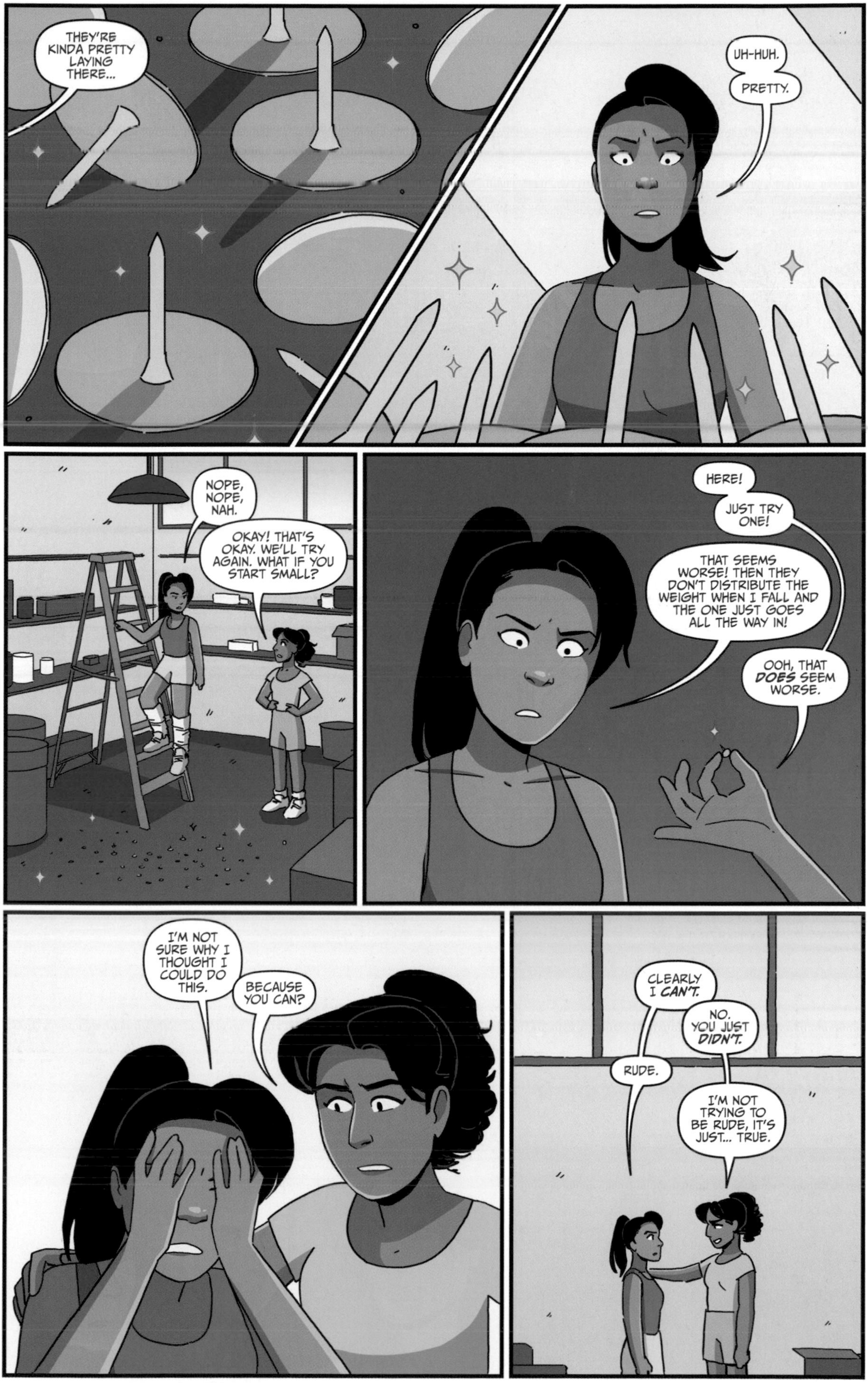
THEY'RE KINDA PRETTY LAYING THERE...
UH-HUH.
PRETTY.
NOPE, NOPE, NAH.
OKAY! THAT'S OKAY. WE'LL TRY AGAIN. WHAT IF YOU START SMALL?
HERE!
JUST TRY ONE!
THAT SEEMS WORSE! THEN THEY DON'T DISTRIBUTE THE WEIGHT WHEN I FALL AND THE ONE JUST GOES ALL THE WAY IN!
OOH, THAT ***DOES*** SEEM WORSE.
I'M NOT SURE WHY I THOUGHT I COULD DO THIS.
BECAUSE YOU CAN?
CLEARLY I ***CAN'T.***
NO. YOU JUST ***DIDN'T.***
RUDE.
I'M NOT TRYING TO BE RUDE, IT'S JUST... TRUE.

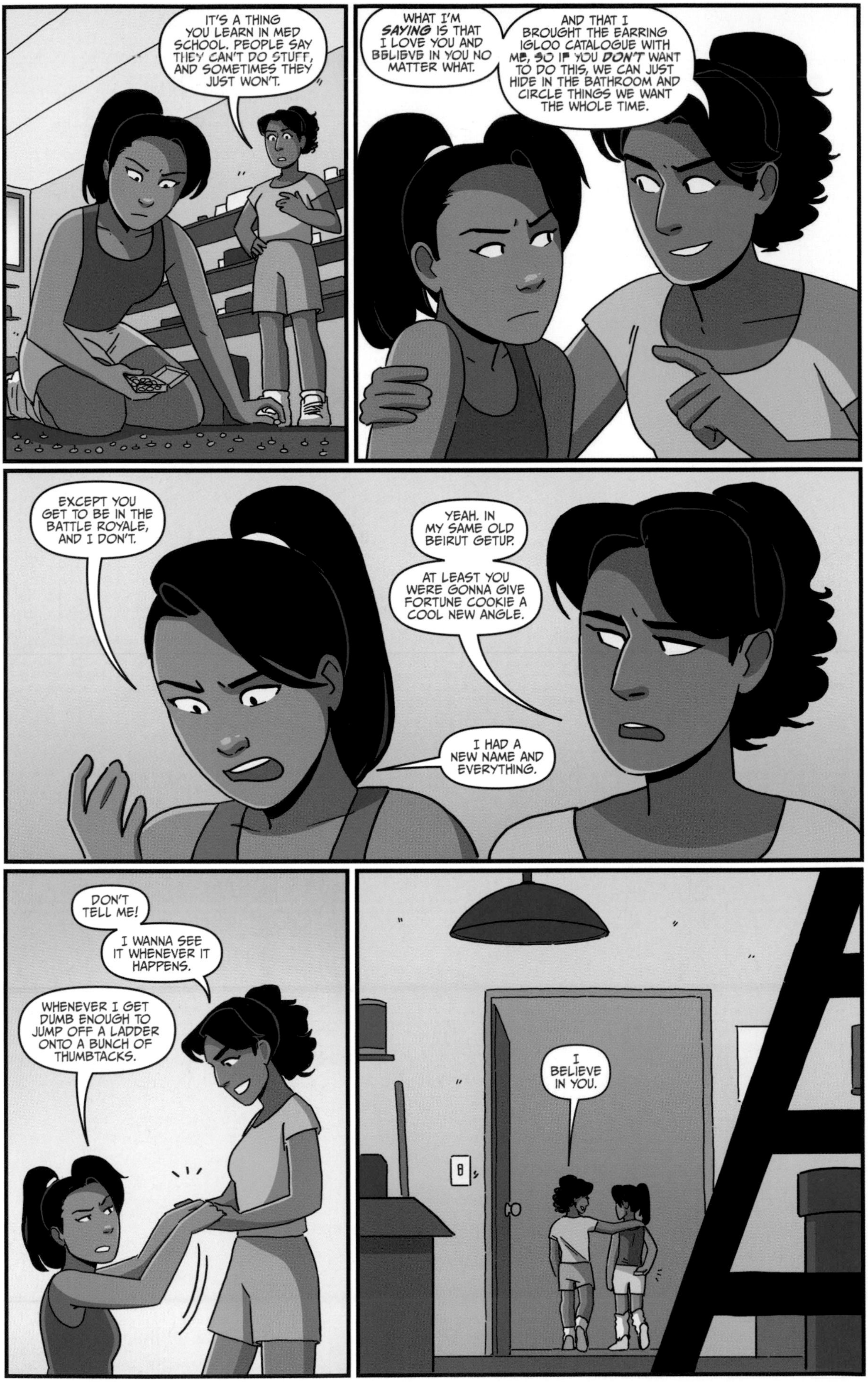
IT'S A THING YOU LEARN IN MED SCHOOL. PEOPLE SAY THEY CAN'T DO STUFF, AND SOMETIMES THEY JUST WON'T.
WHAT I'M SAYING IS THAT I LOVE YOU AND BELIEVE IN YOU NO MATTER WHAT.
AND THAT I BROUGHT THE EARRING IGLOO CATALOGUE WITH ME, SO IF YOU DON'T WANT TO DO THIS, WE CAN JUST HIDE IN THE BATHROOM AND CIRCLE THINGS WE WANT THE WHOLE TIME.
EXCEPT YOU GET TO BE IN THE BATTLE ROYALE, AND I DON'T.
YEAH. IN MY SAME OLD BEIRUT GETUP.
AT LEAST YOU WERE GONNA GIVE FORTUNE COOKIE A COOL NEW ANGLE.
I HAD A NEW NAME AND EVERYTHING.
DON'T TELL ME!
I WANNA SEE IT WHENEVER IT HAPPENS.
WHENEVER I GET DUMB ENOUGH TO JUMP OFF A LADDER ONTO A BUNCH OF THUMBTACKS.
I BELIEVE IN YOU.

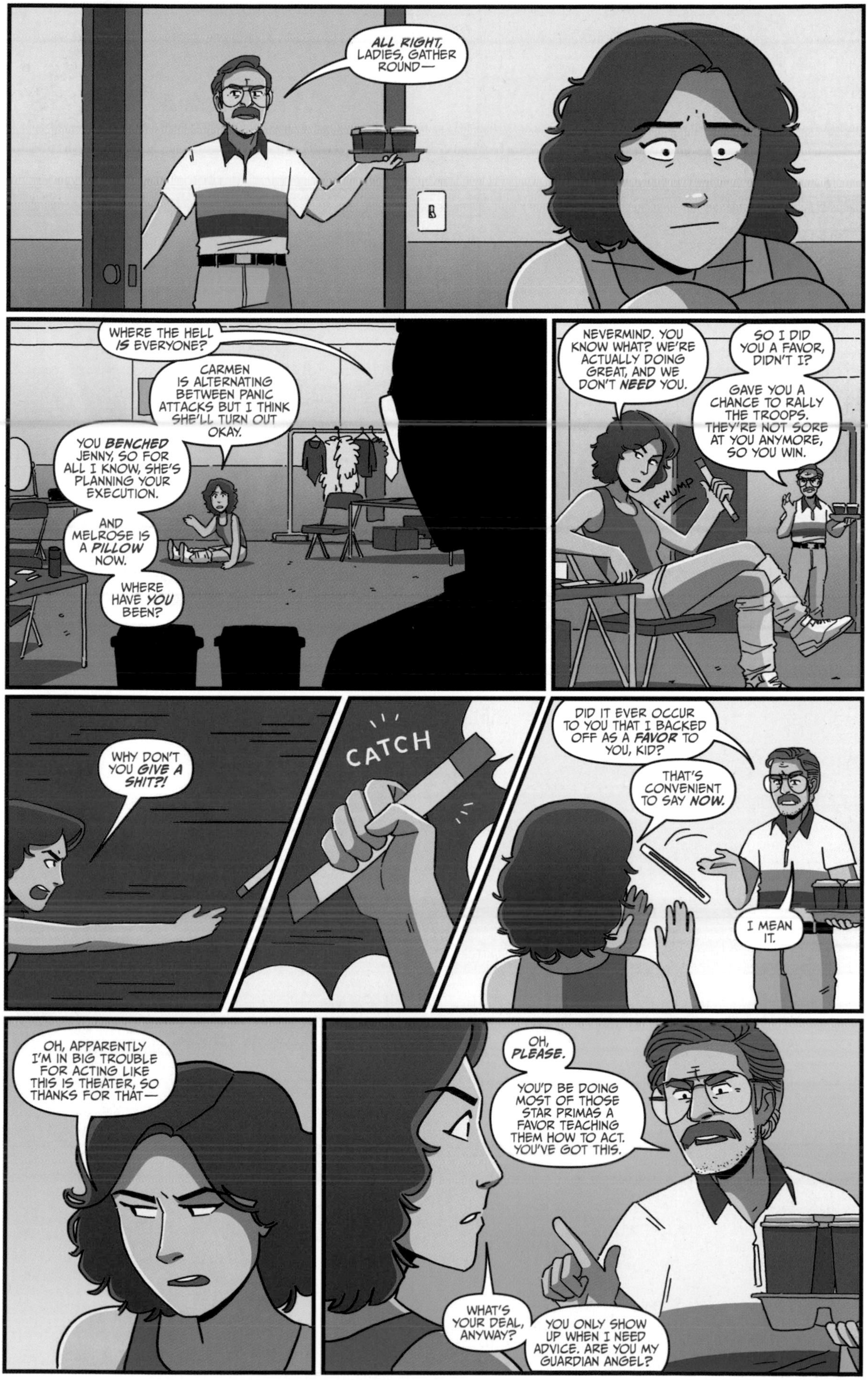

ALL RIGHT, LADIES, GATHER ROUND—
WHERE THE HELL IS EVERYONE?
CARMEN IS ALTERNATING BETWEEN PANIC ATTACKS BUT I THINK SHE'LL TURN OUT OKAY.
YOU BENCHED JENNY, SO FOR ALL I KNOW, SHE'S PLANNING YOUR EXECUTION.
AND MELROSE IS A PILLOW NOW.
WHERE HAVE YOU BEEN?
NEVERMIND. YOU KNOW WHAT? WE'RE ACTUALLY DOING GREAT, AND WE DON'T NEED YOU.
FWUMP
SO I DID YOU A FAVOR, DIDN'T I?
GAVE YOU A CHANCE TO RALLY THE TROOPS. THEY'RE NOT SORE AT YOU ANYMORE, SO YOU WIN.
WHY DON'T YOU GIVE A SHIT?!
CATCH
DID IT EVER OCCUR TO YOU THAT I BACKED OFF AS A FAVOR TO YOU, KID?
THAT'S CONVENIENT TO SAY NOW.
I MEAN IT.
OH, APPARENTLY I'M IN BIG TROUBLE FOR ACTING LIKE THIS IS THEATER, SO THANKS FOR THAT—
OH, PLEASE.
YOU'D BE DOING MOST OF THOSE STAR PRIMAS A FAVOR TEACHING THEM HOW TO ACT. YOU'VE GOT THIS.
WHAT'S YOUR DEAL, ANYWAY?
YOU ONLY SHOW UP WHEN I NEED ADVICE. ARE YOU MY GUARDIAN ANGEL?

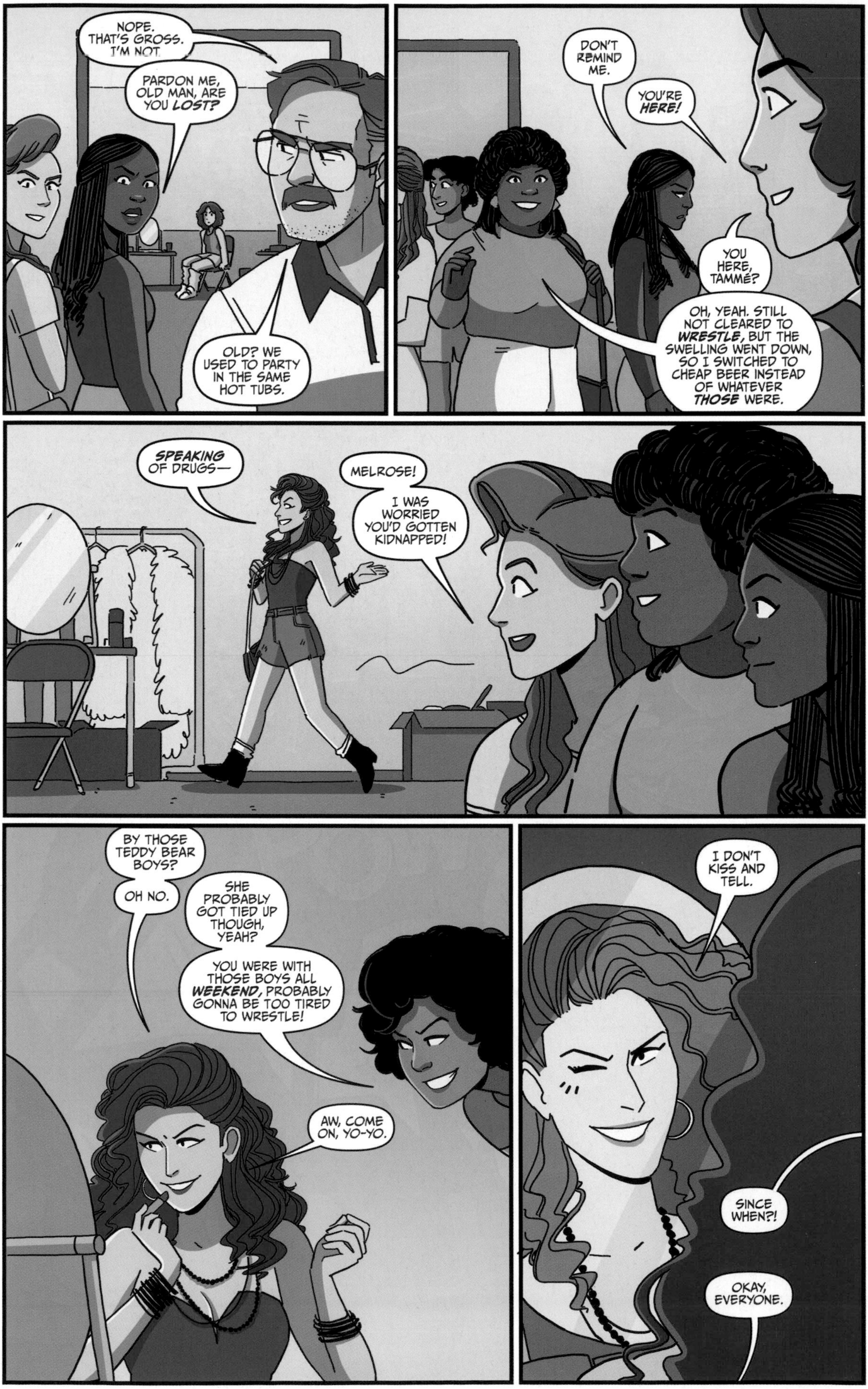

NOPE. THAT'S GROSS. I'M NOT.
PARDON ME, OLD MAN, ARE YOU LOST?
OLD? WE USED TO PARTY IN THE SAME HOT TUBS.
DON'T REMIND ME.
YOU'RE HERE!
YOU HERE, TAMMÉ?
OH, YEAH. STILL NOT CLEARED TO WRESTLE, BUT THE SWELLING WENT DOWN, SO I SWITCHED TO CHEAP BEER INSTEAD OF WHATEVER THOSE WERE.
SPEAKING OF DRUGS—
MELROSE!
I WAS WORRIED YOU'D GOTTEN KIDNAPPED!
BY THOSE TEDDY BEAR BOYS?
OH NO.
SHE PROBABLY GOT TIED UP THOUGH, YEAH?
YOU WERE WITH THOSE BOYS ALL WEEKEND, PROBABLY GONNA BE TOO TIRED TO WRESTLE!
AW, COME ON, YO-YO.
I DON'T KISS AND TELL.
SINCE WHEN?!
OKAY, EVERYONE.

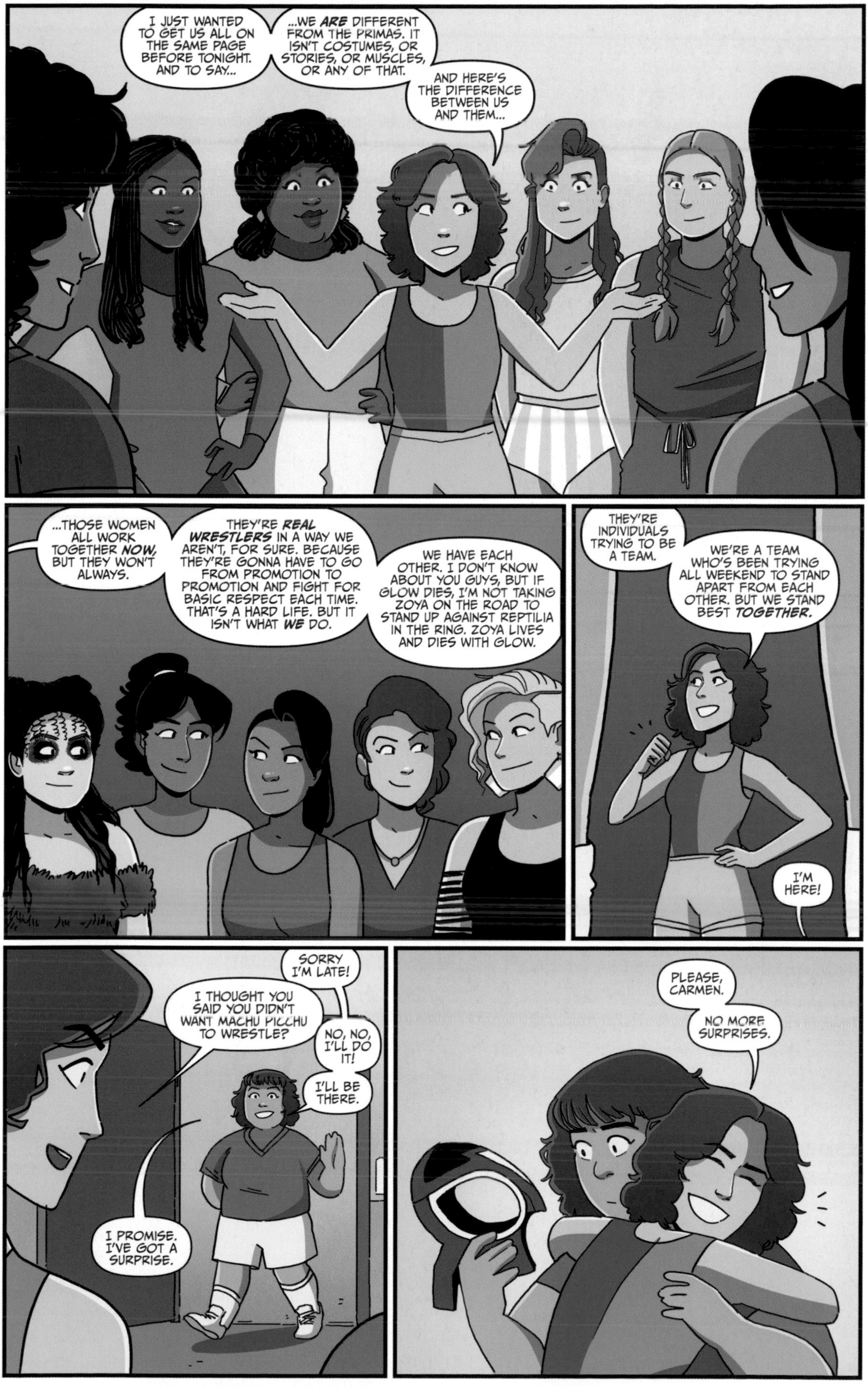
I JUST WANTED TO GET US ALL ON THE SAME PAGE BEFORE TONIGHT. AND TO SAY...
...WE ARE DIFFERENT FROM THE PRIMAS. IT ISN'T COSTUMES, OR STORIES, OR MUSCLES, OR ANY OF THAT.
AND HERE'S THE DIFFERENCE BETWEEN US AND THEM...
...THOSE WOMEN ALL WORK TOGETHER NOW, BUT THEY WON'T ALWAYS.
THEY'RE REAL WRESTLERS IN A WAY WE AREN'T, FOR SURE. BECAUSE THEY'RE GONNA HAVE TO GO FROM PROMOTION TO PROMOTION AND FIGHT FOR BASIC RESPECT EACH TIME. THAT'S A HARD LIFE. BUT IT ISN'T WHAT WE DO.
WE HAVE EACH OTHER. I DON'T KNOW ABOUT YOU GUYS, BUT IF GLOW DIES, I'M NOT TAKING ZOYA ON THE ROAD TO STAND UP AGAINST REPTILIA IN THE RING. ZOYA LIVES AND DIES WITH GLOW.
THEY'RE INDIVIDUALS TRYING TO BE A TEAM.
WE'RE A TEAM WHO'S BEEN TRYING ALL WEEKEND TO STAND APART FROM EACH OTHER. BUT WE STAND BEST TOGETHER.
I'M HERE!
SORRY I'M LATE!
I THOUGHT YOU SAID YOU DIDN'T WANT MACHU PICCHU TO WRESTLE?
NO, NO, I'LL DO IT!
I'LL BE THERE.
I PROMISE. I'VE GOT A SURPRISE.
PLEASE, CARMEN.
NO MORE SURPRISES.

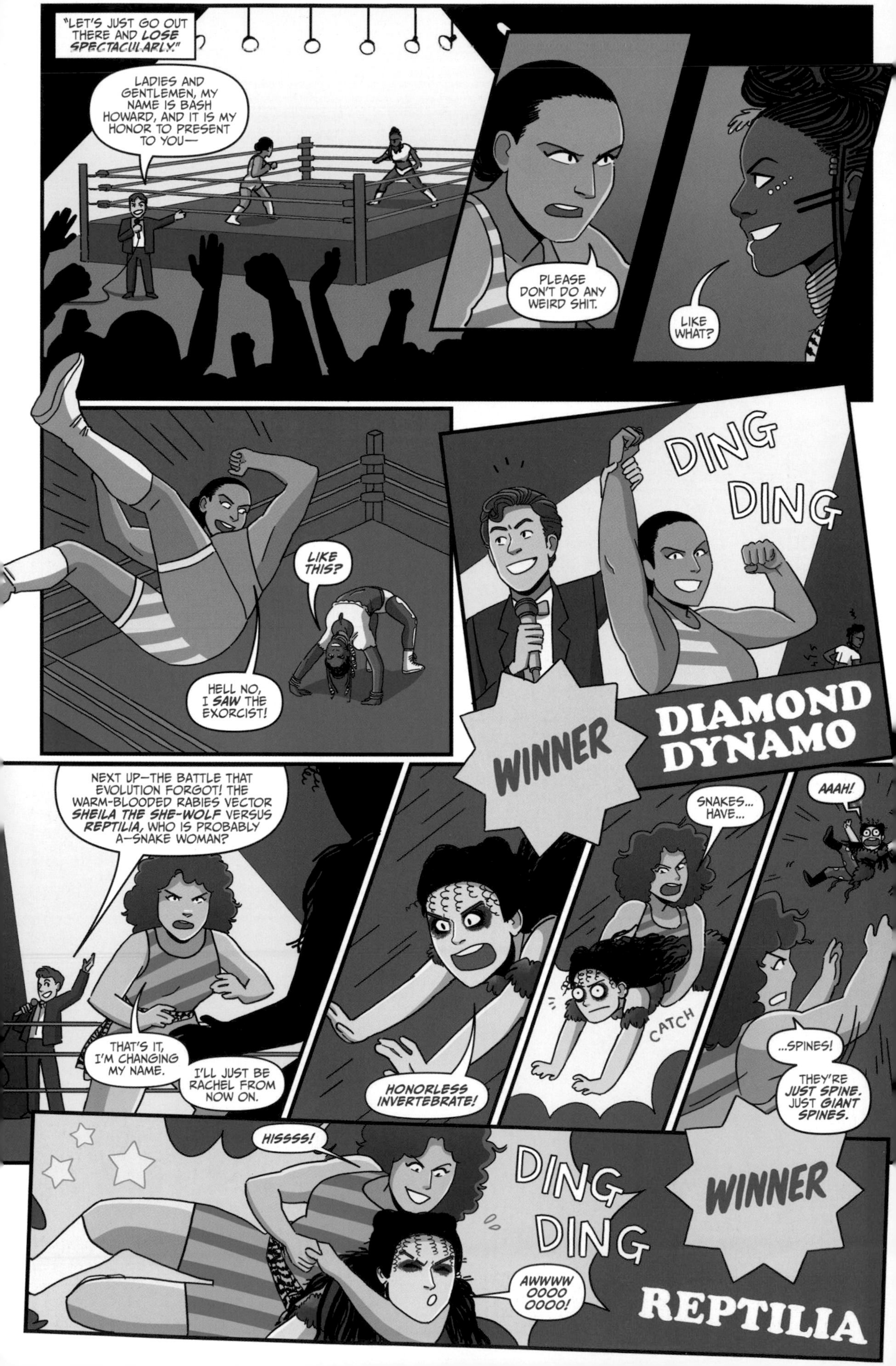
"LET'S JUST GO OUT THERE AND LOSE SPECTACULARLY."
LADIES AND GENTLEMEN, MY NAME IS BASH HOWARD, AND IT IS MY HONOR TO PRESENT TO YOU—
PLEASE DON'T DO ANY WEIRD SHIT.
LIKE WHAT?
LIKE THIS?
HELL NO, I SAW THE EXORCIST!
DING
DING
WINNER
DIAMOND DYNAMO
NEXT UP—THE BATTLE THAT EVOLUTION FORGOT! THE WARM-BLOODED RABIES VECTOR SHEILA THE SHE-WOLF VERSUS REPTILIA, WHO IS PROBABLY A—SNAKE WOMAN?
THAT'S IT, I'M CHANGING MY NAME.
I'LL JUST BE RACHEL FROM NOW ON.
HONORLESS INVERTEBRATE!
SNAKES... HAVE...
CATCH
AAAH!
...SPINES!
THEY'RE JUST SPINE. JUST GIANT SPINES.
HISSSS!
DING
DING
AWWWW OOOO OOOO!
WINNER
REPTILIA

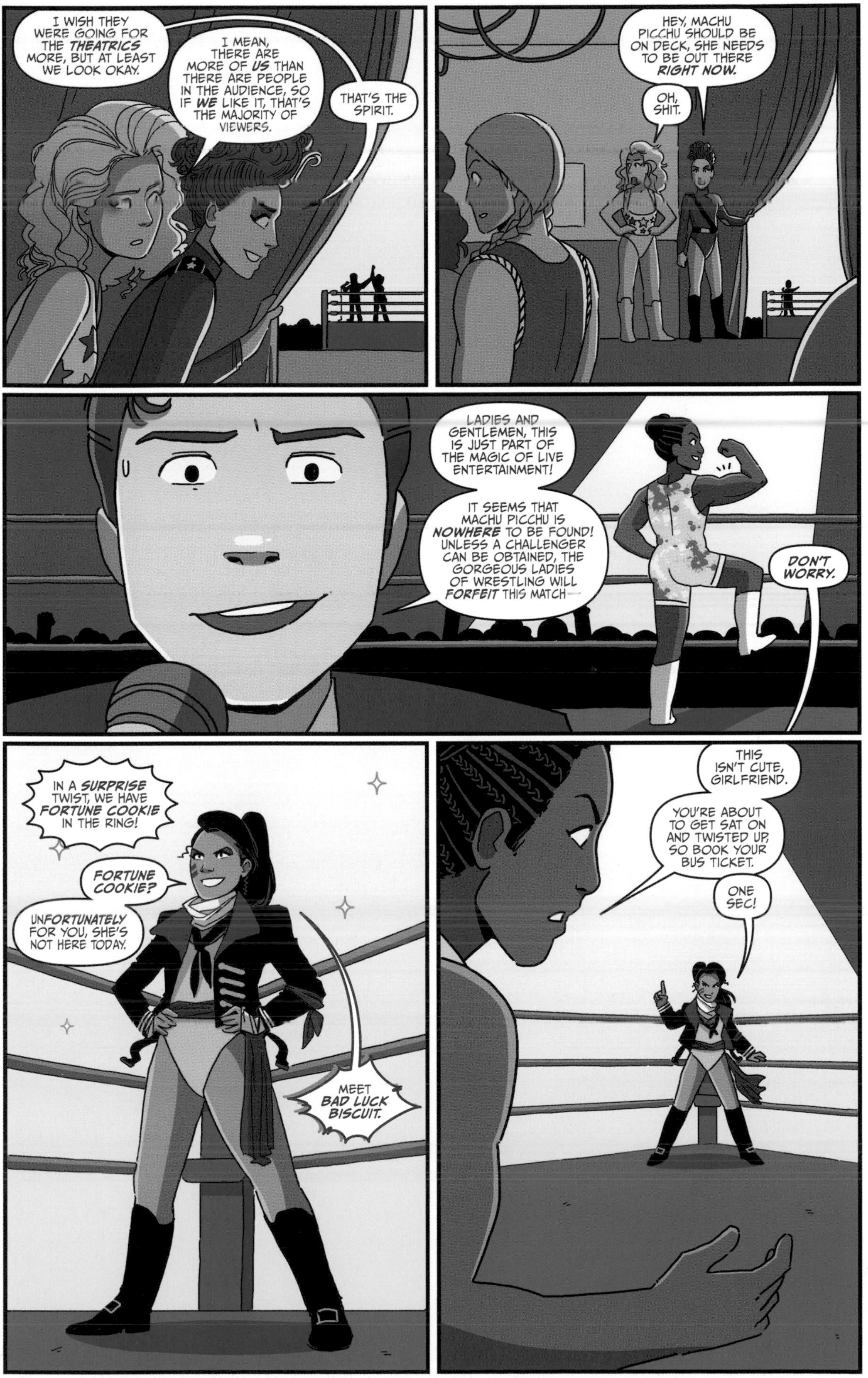
I WISH THEY WERE GOING FOR THE THEATRICS MORE, BUT AT LEAST WE LOOK OKAY.
I MEAN, THERE ARE MORE OF US THAN THERE ARE PEOPLE IN THE AUDIENCE, SO IF WE LIKE IT, THAT'S THE MAJORITY OF VIEWERS.
THAT'S THE SPIRIT.
HEY, MACHU PICCHU SHOULD BE ON DECK, SHE NEEDS TO BE OUT THERE RIGHT NOW.
OH, SHIT.
LADIES AND GENTLEMEN, THIS IS JUST PART OF THE MAGIC OF LIVE ENTERTAINMENT!
IT SEEMS THAT MACHU PICCHU IS NOWHERE TO BE FOUND! UNLESS A CHALLENGER CAN BE OBTAINED, THE GORGEOUS LADIES OF WRESTLING WILL FORFEIT THIS MATCH—
DON'T WORRY.
IN A SURPRISE TWIST, WE HAVE FORTUNE COOKIE IN THE RING!
FORTUNE COOKIE?
UNFORTUNATELY FOR YOU, SHE'S NOT HERE TODAY.
MEET BAD LUCK BISCUIT.
THIS ISN'T CUTE, GIRLFRIEND.
YOU'RE ABOUT TO GET SAT ON AND TWISTED UP, SO BOOK YOUR BUS TICKET.
ONE SEC!

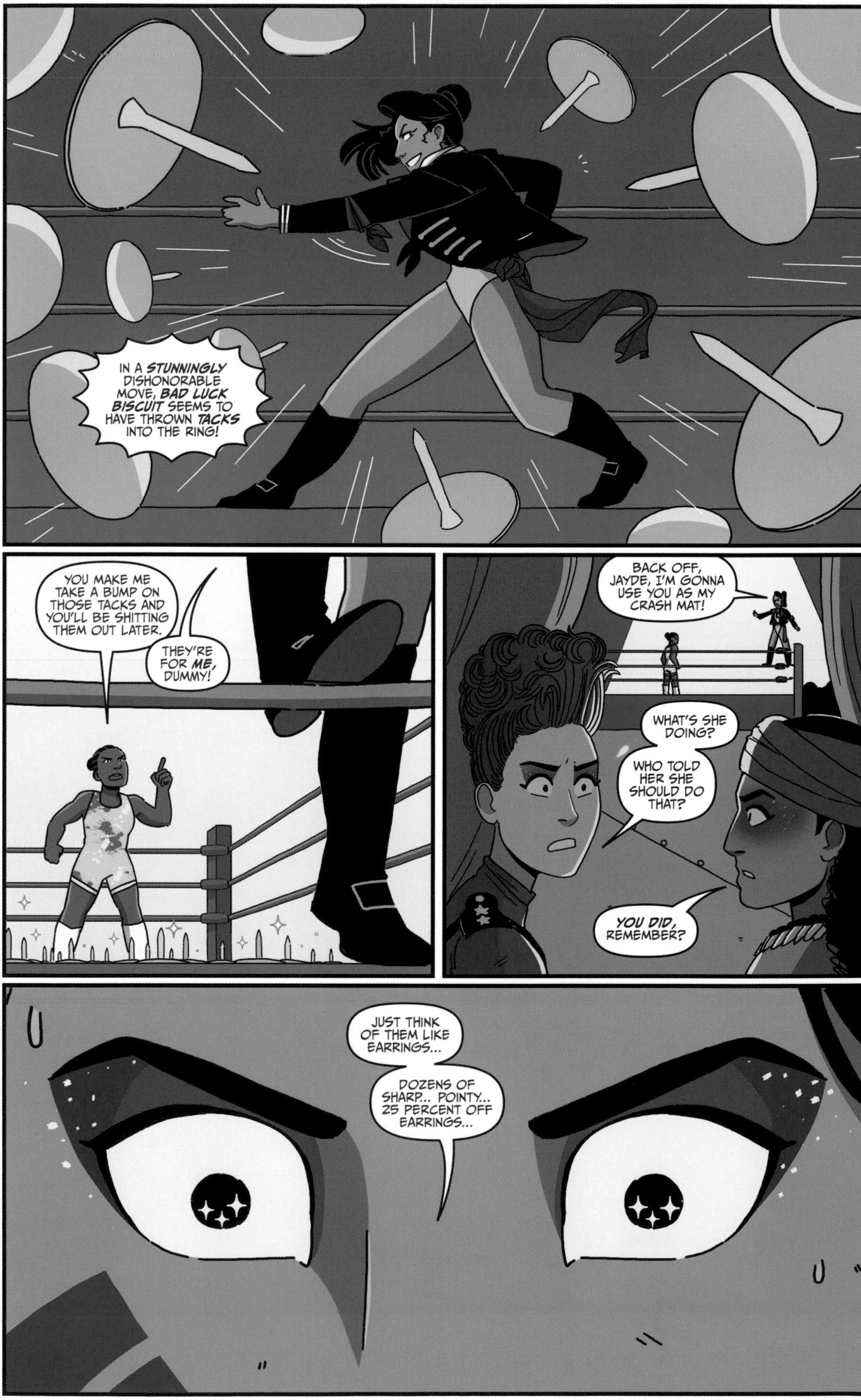
IN A STUNNINGLY DISHONORABLE MOVE, BAD LUCK BISCUIT SEEMS TO HAVE THROWN TACKS INTO THE RING!
YOU MAKE ME TAKE A BUMP ON THOSE TACKS AND YOU'LL BE SHITTING THEM OUT LATER.
THEY'RE FOR ME, DUMMY!
BACK OFF, JAYDE, I'M GONNA USE YOU AS MY CRASH MAT!
WHAT'S SHE DOING?
WHO TOLD HER SHE SHOULD DO THAT?
YOU DID, REMEMBER?
JUST THINK OF THEM LIKE EARRINGS...
DOZENS OF SHARP... POINTY... 25 PERCENT OFF EARRINGS...

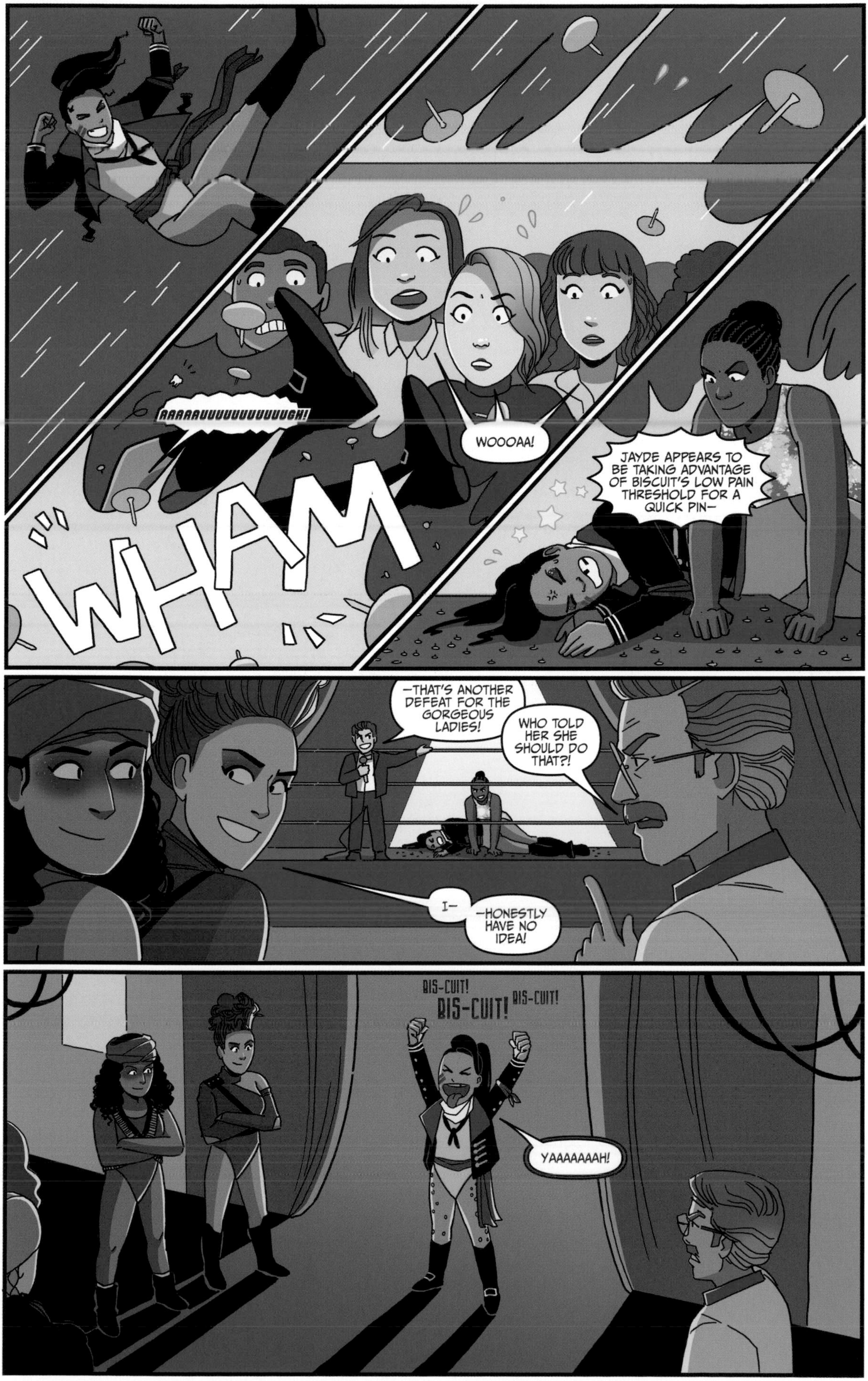
AAAAAUUUUUUUUUUUGH!
WOOOAA!
WHAM
JAYDE APPEARS TO BE TAKING ADVANTAGE OF BISCUIT'S LOW PAIN THRESHOLD FOR A QUICK PIN—
—THAT'S ANOTHER DEFEAT FOR THE GORGEOUS LADIES!
WHO TOLD HER SHE SHOULD DO THAT?!
I—
—HONESTLY HAVE NO IDEA!
BIS-CUIT!
BIS-CUIT!
BIS-CUIT!
YAAAAAAAH!

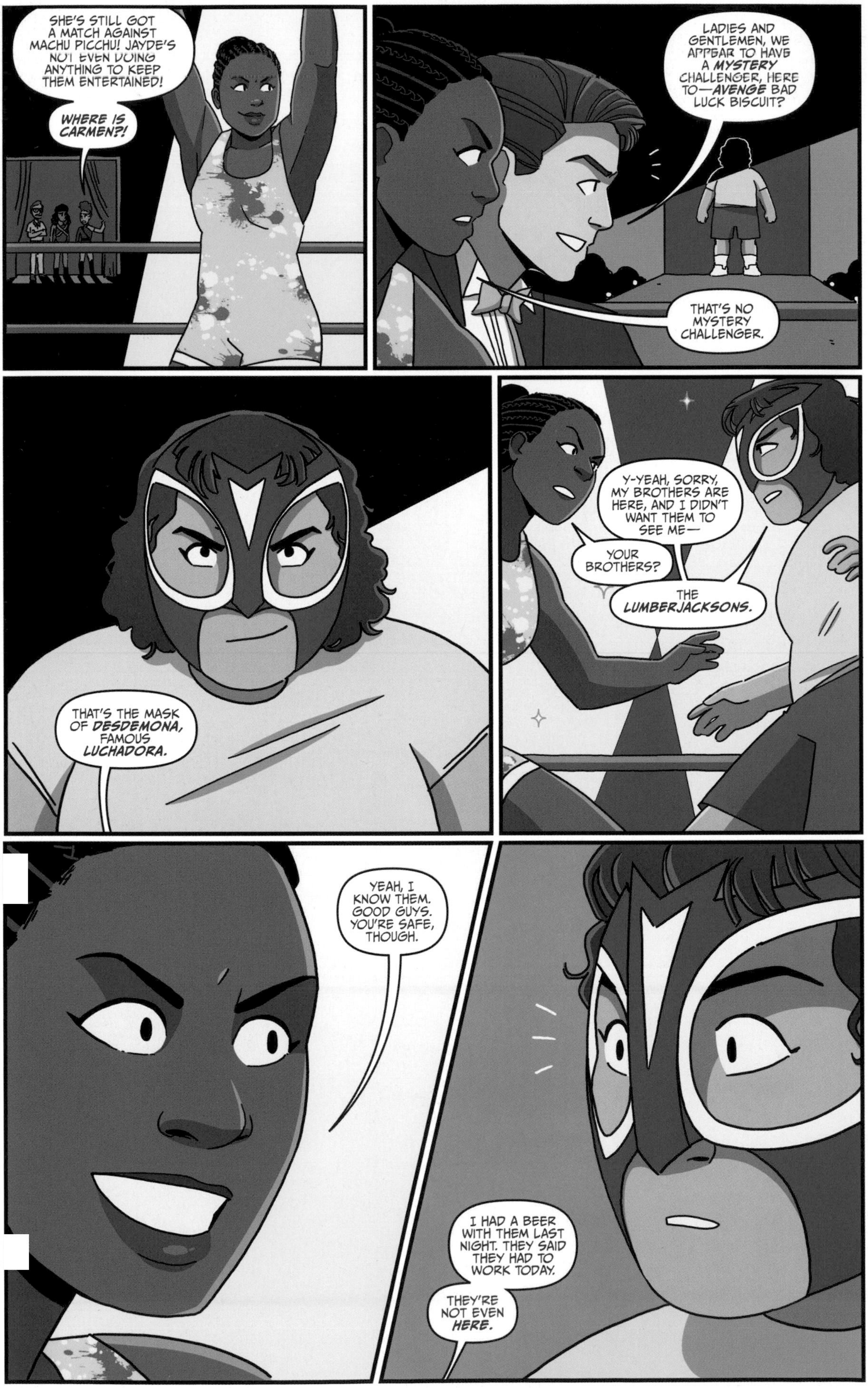
SHE'S STILL GOT A MATCH AGAINST MACHU PICCHU! JAYDE'S NOT EVEN DOING ANYTHING TO KEEP THEM ENTERTAINED!
WHERE IS CARMEN?!
LADIES AND GENTLEMEN, WE APPEAR TO HAVE A MYSTERY CHALLENGER, HERE TO—AVENGE BAD LUCK BISCUIT?
THAT'S NO MYSTERY CHALLENGER.
THAT'S THE MASK OF DESDEMONA, FAMOUS LUCHADORA.
Y-YEAH, SORRY, MY BROTHERS ARE HERE, AND I DIDN'T WANT THEM TO SEE ME—
YOUR BROTHERS?
THE LUMBERJACKSONS.
YEAH, I KNOW THEM. GOOD GUYS. YOU'RE SAFE, THOUGH.
I HAD A BEER WITH THEM LAST NIGHT. THEY SAID THEY HAD TO WORK TODAY.
THEY'RE NOT EVEN HERE.

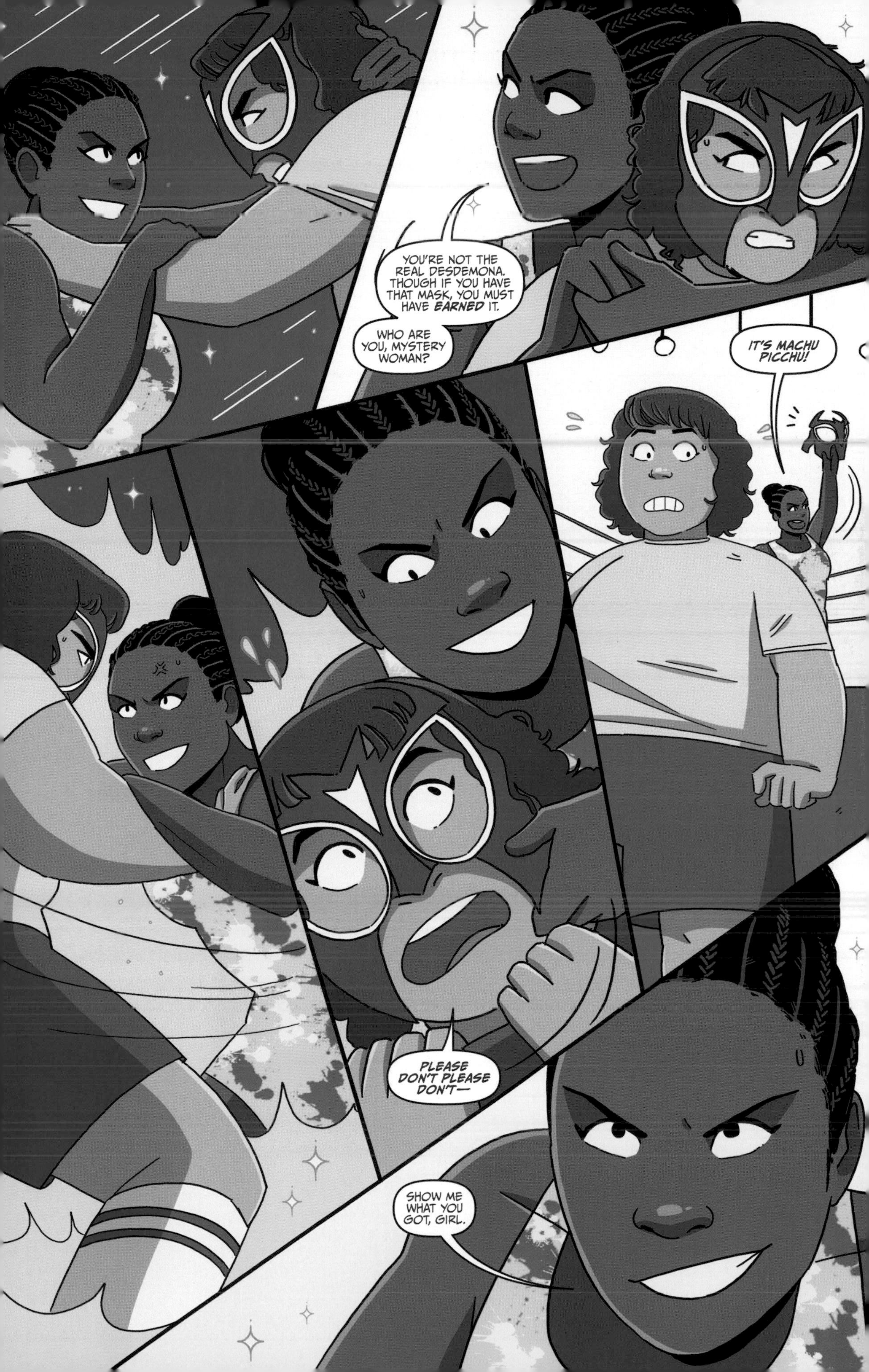
YOU'RE NOT THE REAL DESDEMONA. THOUGH IF YOU HAVE THAT MASK, YOU MUST HAVE *EARNED* IT.
WHO ARE YOU, MYSTERY WOMAN?
IT'S MACHU PICCHU!
PLEASE DON'T PLEASE DON'T—
SHOW ME WHAT YOU GOT, GIRL.

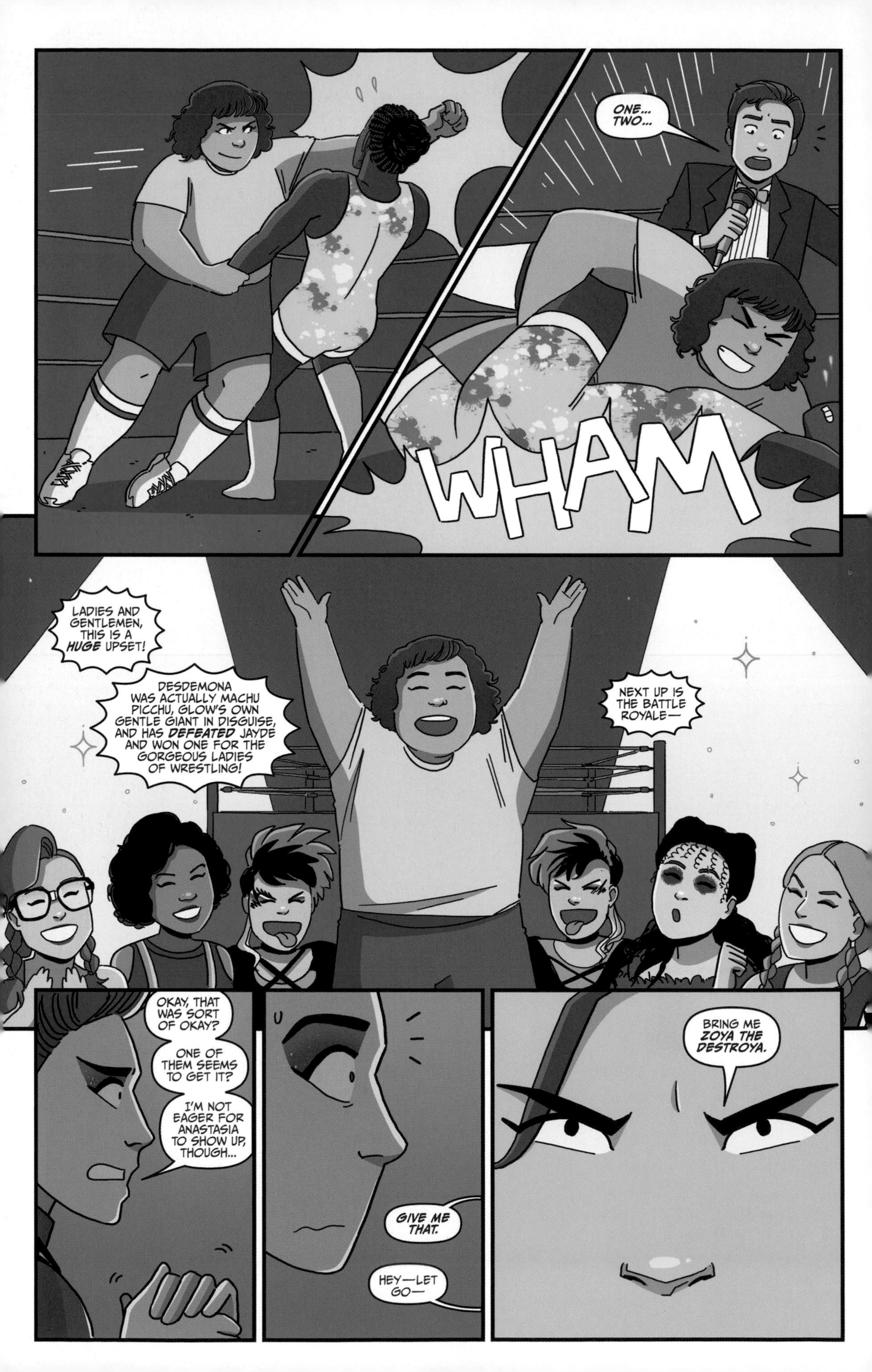
ONE... TWO...
WHAM
LADIES AND GENTLEMEN, THIS IS A HUGE UPSET!
DESDEMONA WAS ACTUALLY MACHU PICCHU, GLOW'S OWN GENTLE GIANT IN DISGUISE, AND HAS DEFEATED JAYDE AND WON ONE FOR THE GORGEOUS LADIES OF WRESTLING!
NEXT UP IS THE BATTLE ROYALE—
OKAY, THAT WAS SORT OF OKAY?
ONE OF THEM SEEMS TO GET IT?
I'M NOT EAGER FOR ANASTASIA TO SHOW UP, THOUGH...
GIVE ME THAT.
HEY—LET GO—
BRING ME ZOYA THE DESTROYA.

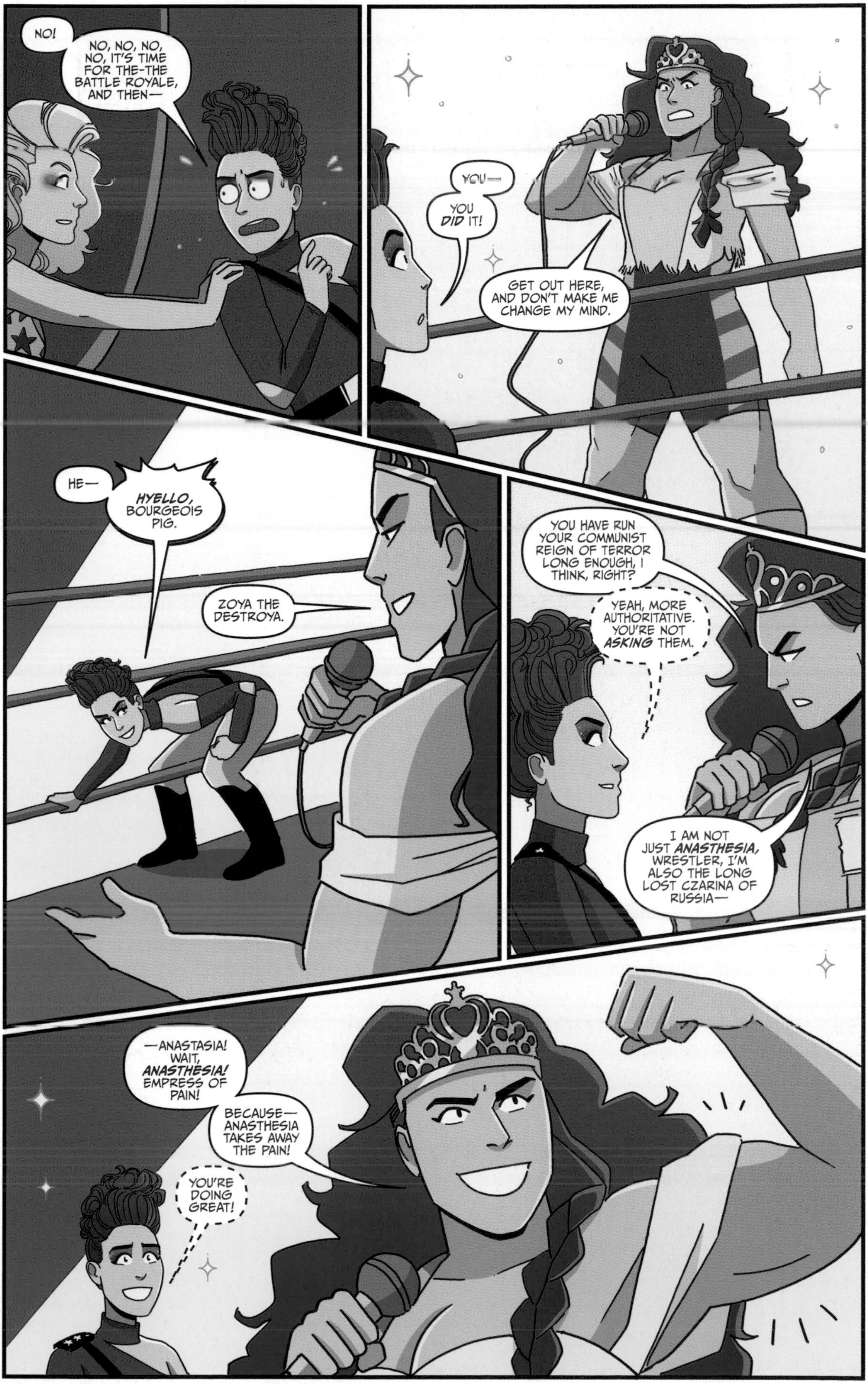
NO!
NO, NO, NO, NO, IT'S TIME FOR THE-THE BATTLE ROYALE, AND THEN—
YOU—
YOU *DID* IT!
GET OUT HERE, AND DON'T MAKE ME CHANGE MY MIND.
HE—
HYELLO, BOURGEOIS PIG.
ZOYA THE DESTROYA.
YOU HAVE RUN YOUR COMMUNIST REIGN OF TERROR LONG ENOUGH, I THINK, RIGHT?
YEAH, MORE AUTHORITATIVE. YOU'RE NOT *ASKING* THEM.
I AM NOT JUST *ANASTHESIA,* WRESTLER, I'M ALSO THE LONG LOST CZARINA OF RUSSIA—
—ANASTASIA! WAIT, *ANASTHESIA!* EMPRESS OF PAIN!
BECAUSE— ANASTHESIA TAKES AWAY THE PAIN!
YOU'RE DOING GREAT!

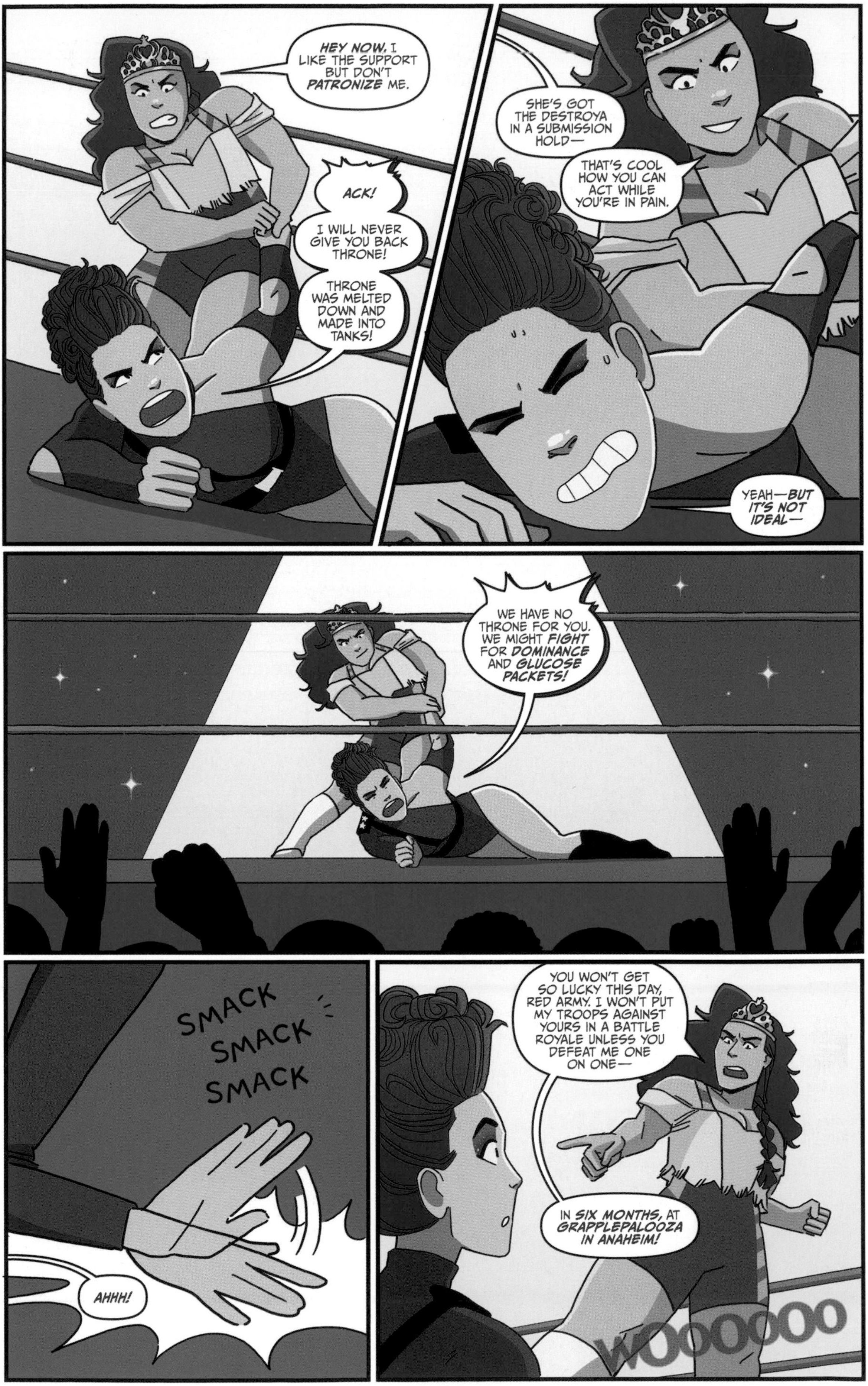
HEY NOW, I LIKE THE SUPPORT BUT DON'T PATRONIZE ME.
ACK!
I WILL NEVER GIVE YOU BACK THRONE!
THRONE WAS MELTED DOWN AND MADE INTO TANKS!
SHE'S GOT THE DESTROYA IN A SUBMISSION HOLD—
THAT'S COOL HOW YOU CAN ACT WHILE YOU'RE IN PAIN.
YEAH—BUT IT'S NOT IDEAL—
WE HAVE NO THRONE FOR YOU. WE MIGHT FIGHT FOR DOMINANCE AND GLUCOSE PACKETS!
SMACK SMACK SMACK
AHHH!
YOU WON'T GET SO LUCKY THIS DAY, RED ARMY. I WON'T PUT MY TROOPS AGAINST YOURS IN A BATTLE ROYALE UNLESS YOU DEFEAT ME ONE ON ONE—
IN SIX MONTHS, AT GRAPPLEPALOOZA IN ANAHEIM!
WOOOOOO

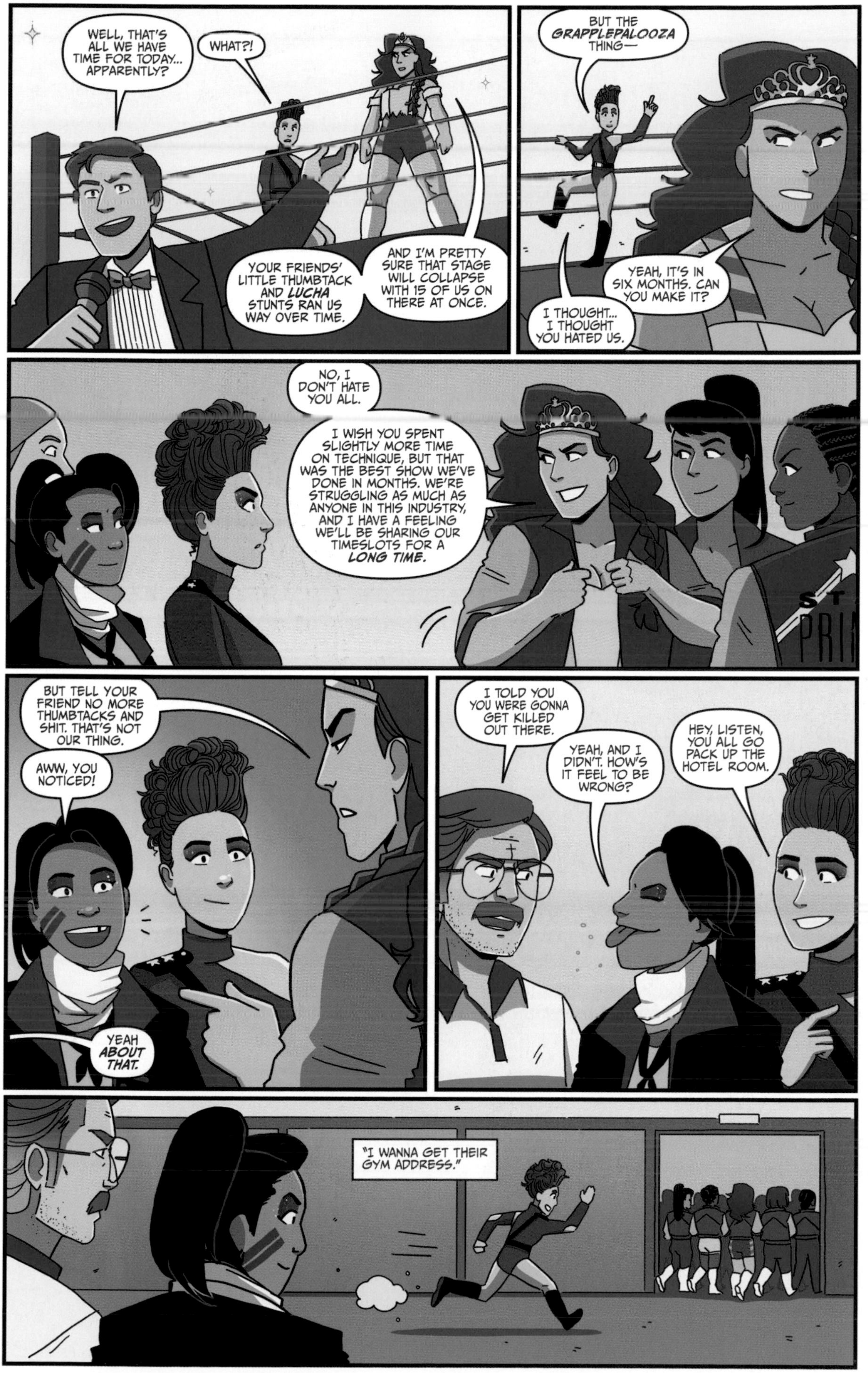
WELL, THAT'S ALL WE HAVE TIME FOR TODAY... APPARENTLY?
WHAT?!
YOUR FRIENDS' LITTLE THUMBTACK AND LUCHA STUNTS RAN US WAY OVER TIME.
AND I'M PRETTY SURE THAT STAGE WILL COLLAPSE WITH 15 OF US ON THERE AT ONCE.
BUT THE GRAPPLEPALOOZA THING—
YEAH, IT'S IN SIX MONTHS. CAN YOU MAKE IT?
I THOUGHT... I THOUGHT YOU HATED US.
NO, I DON'T HATE YOU ALL.
I WISH YOU SPENT SLIGHTLY MORE TIME ON TECHNIQUE, BUT THAT WAS THE BEST SHOW WE'VE DONE IN MONTHS. WE'RE STRUGGLING AS MUCH AS ANYONE IN THIS INDUSTRY, AND I HAVE A FEELING WE'LL BE SHARING OUR TIMESLOTS FOR A LONG TIME.
BUT TELL YOUR FRIEND NO MORE THUMBTACKS AND SHIT. THAT'S NOT OUR THING.
AWW, YOU NOTICED!
YEAH ABOUT THAT.
I TOLD YOU YOU WERE GONNA GET KILLED OUT THERE.
YEAH, AND I DIDN'T. HOW'S IT FEEL TO BE WRONG?
HEY, LISTEN, YOU ALL GO PACK UP THE HOTEL ROOM.
"I WANNA GET THEIR GYM ADDRESS."

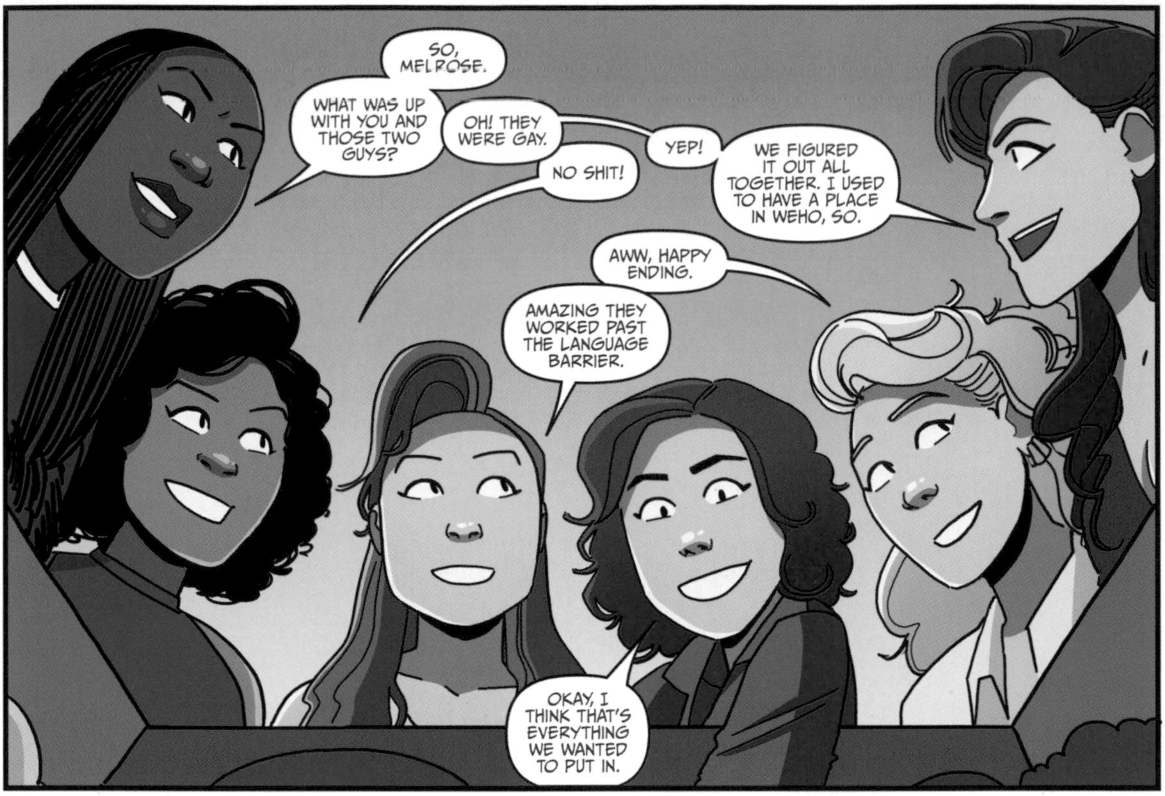
SO, MELROSE.
WHAT WAS UP WITH YOU AND THOSE TWO GUYS?
OH! THEY WERE GAY.
NO SHIT!
YEP!
WE FIGURED IT OUT ALL TOGETHER. I USED TO HAVE A PLACE IN WEHO, SO.
AWW, HAPPY ENDING.
AMAZING THEY WORKED PAST THE LANGUAGE BARRIER.
OKAY, I THINK THAT'S EVERYTHING WE WANTED TO PUT IN.

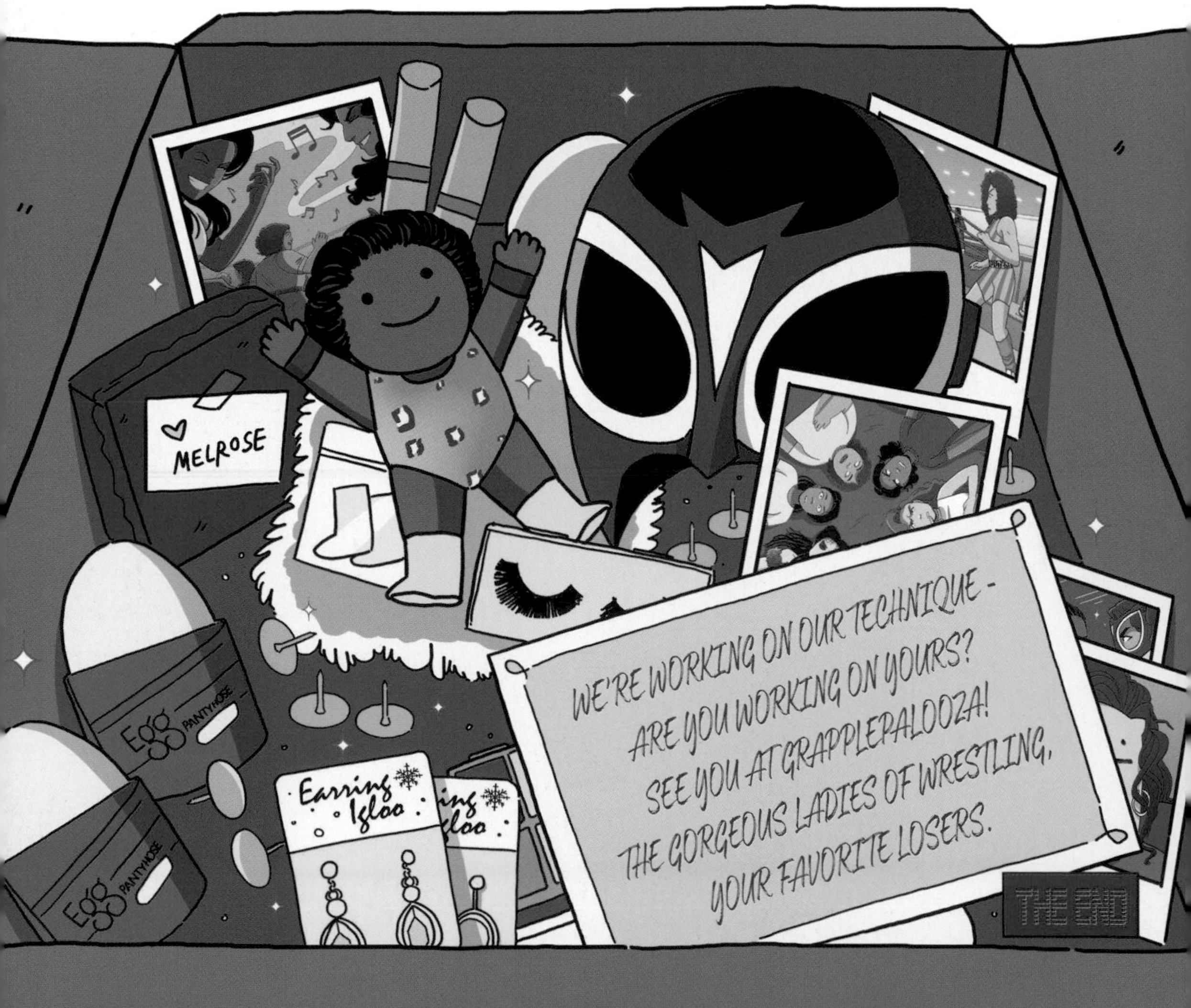
MELROSE
Earring Igloo
Egg PANTYHOSE
WE'RE WORKING ON OUR TECHNIQUE - ARE YOU WORKING ON YOURS? SEE YOU AT GRAPPLERALOOZA! THE GORGEOUS LADIES OF WRESTLING, YOUR FAVORITE LOSERS.
THE END

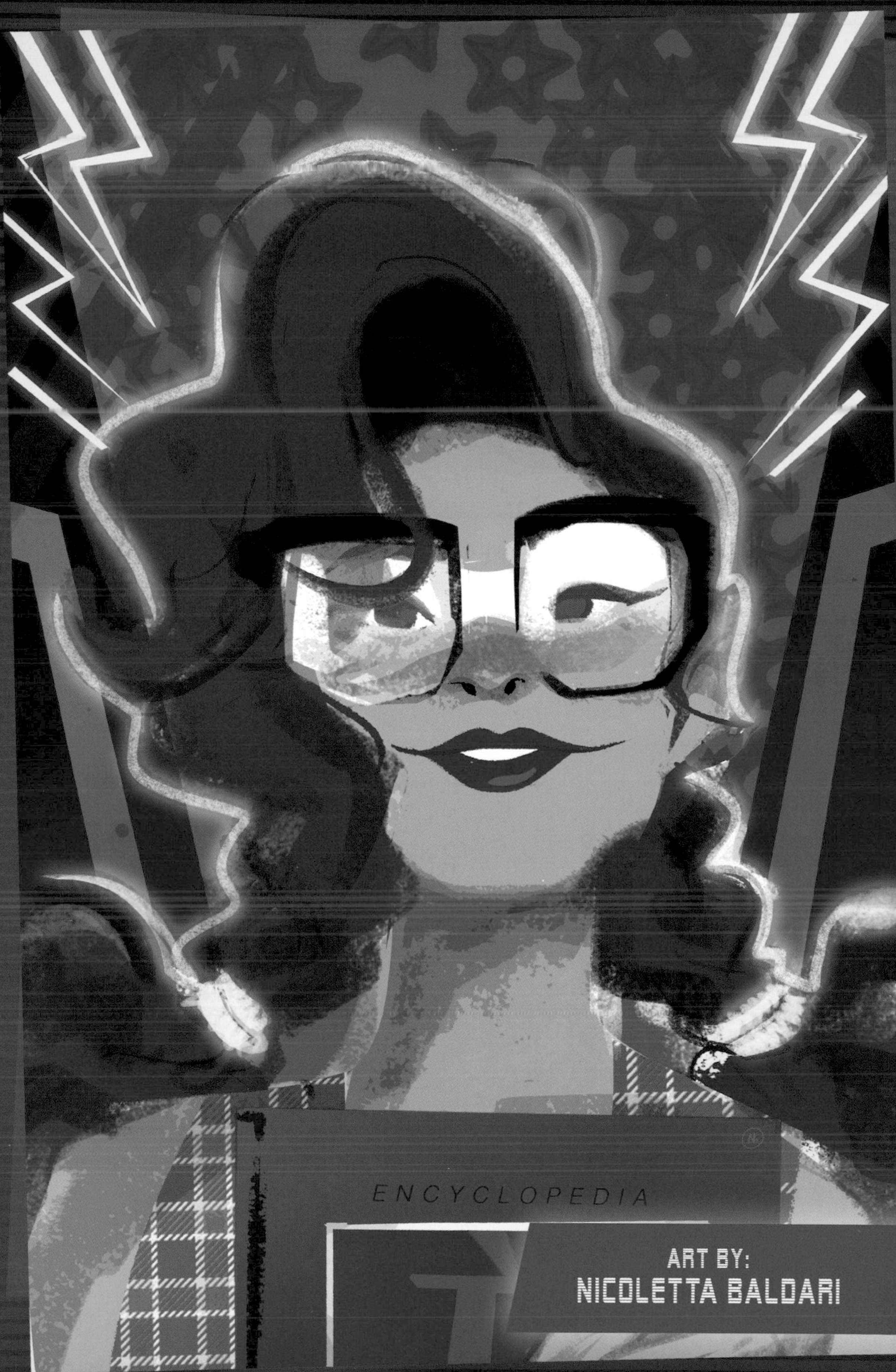
ENCYCLOPEDIA
ART BY:
NICOLETTA BALDARI

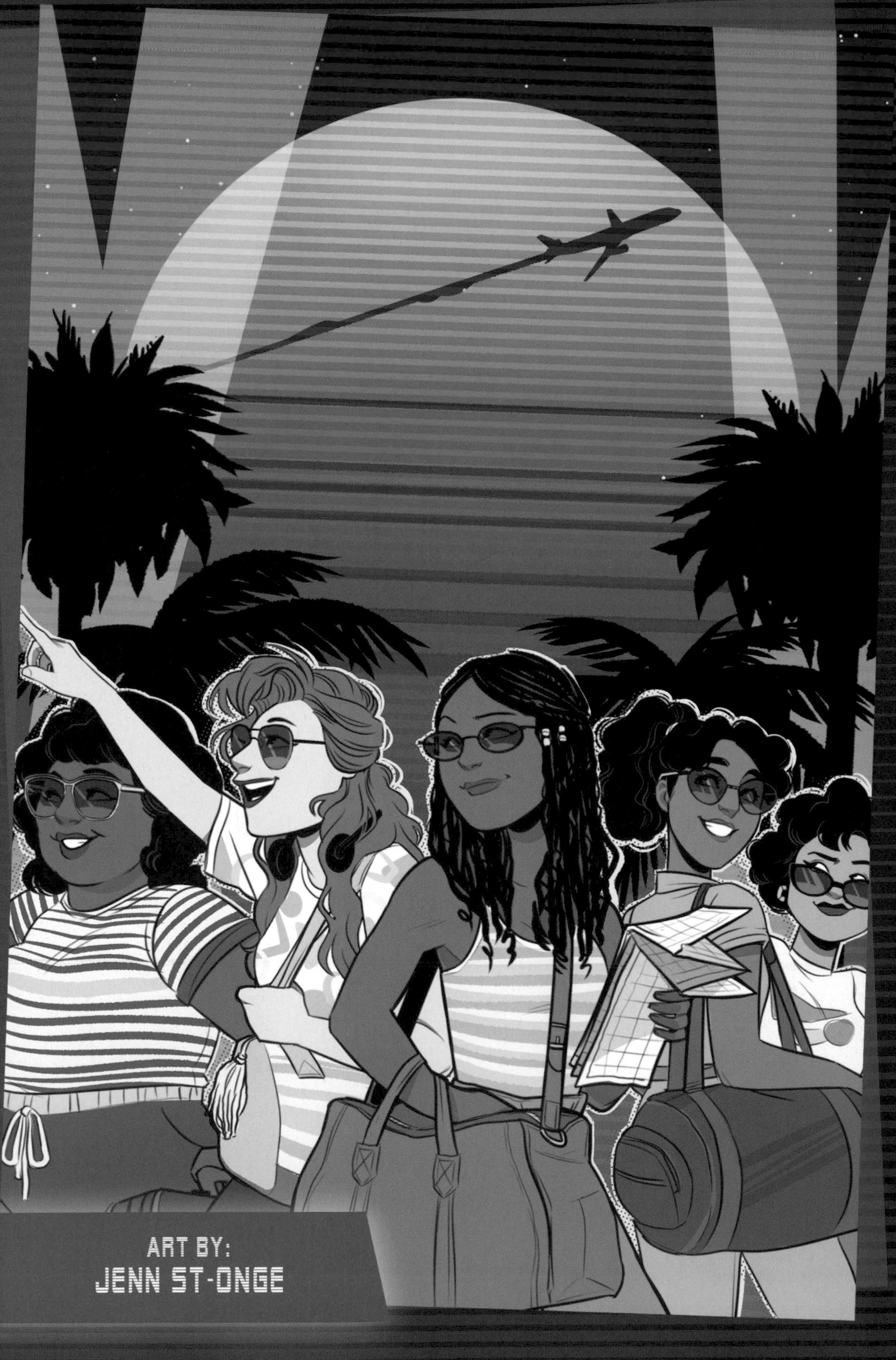

ART BY:
JENN ST-ONGE

RUTH WILDER
A.K.A. ZOYA THE DESTROYA

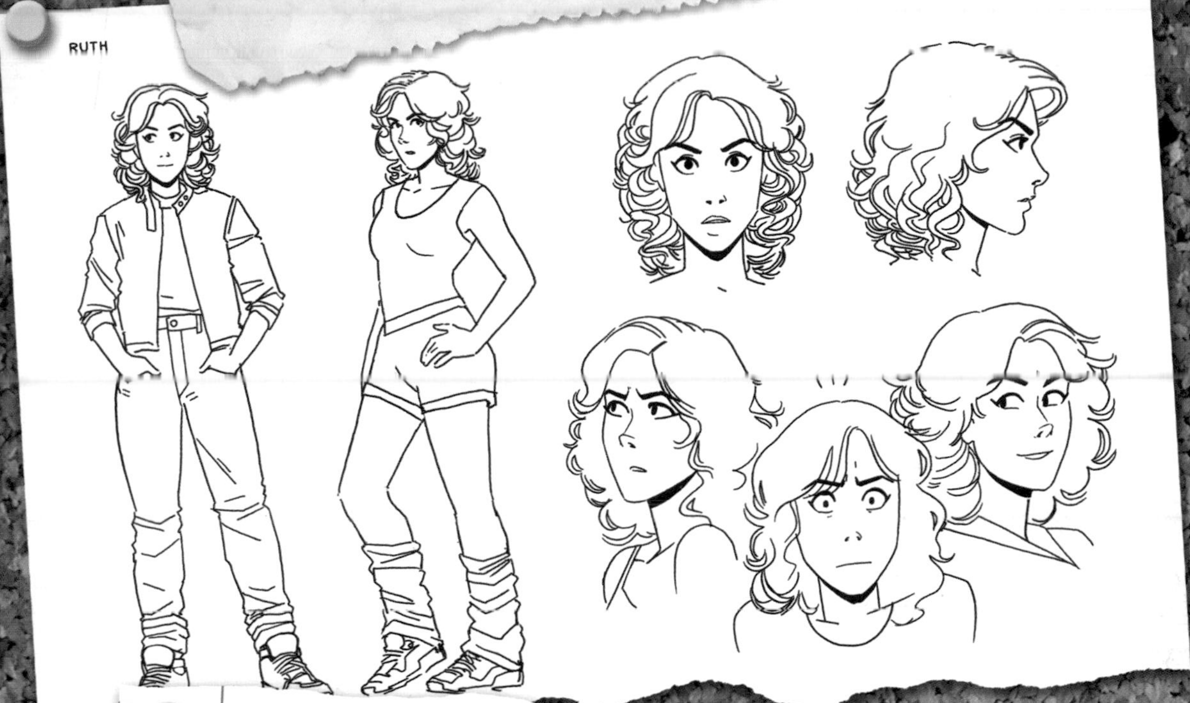
RUTH

RUTH IS THE SELF-PROCLAIMED LEADER OF THE GORGEOUS LADIES OF WRESTLING, AND SHE DOESN'T CORRECT ANA WHEN THE OTHER WOMAN MISTAKES HER FOR THEIR COACH. WHEN NO ONE THINKS THEY CAN SHARE THE RING WITH THE STAR PRIMAS, RUTH SETS OUT TO PROVE EVERYONE WRONG—AND PISSES OFF ALL OF HER FRIENDS IN THE PROCESS.

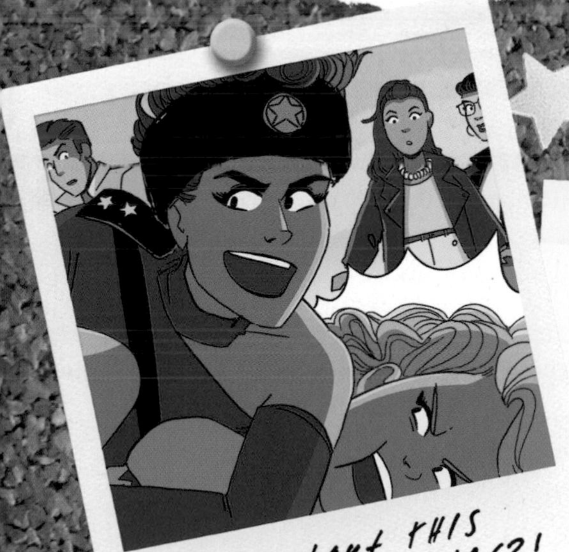

How bout THIS for an ARMS RACE?!

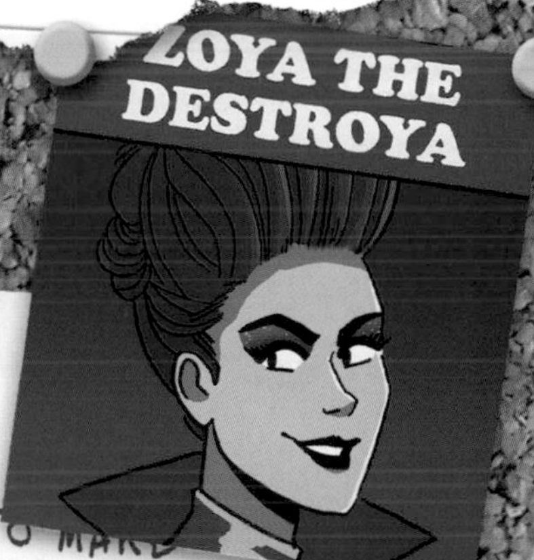
ZOYA THE DESTROYA

REMEMBER TO MAKE EYE CONTACT AND SPEAK FROM THE DIAPHRAGM

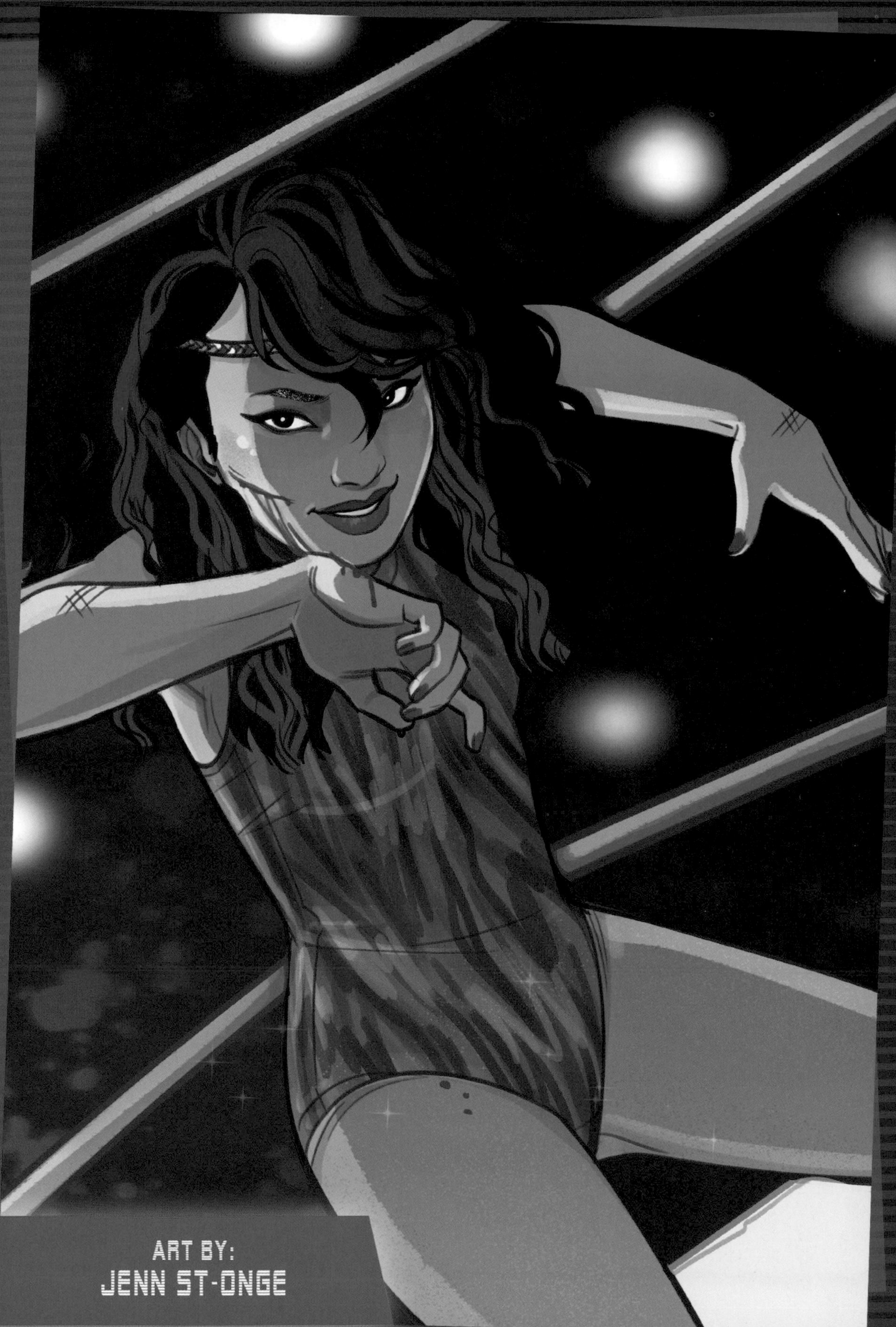
ART BY:
JENN ST-ONGE

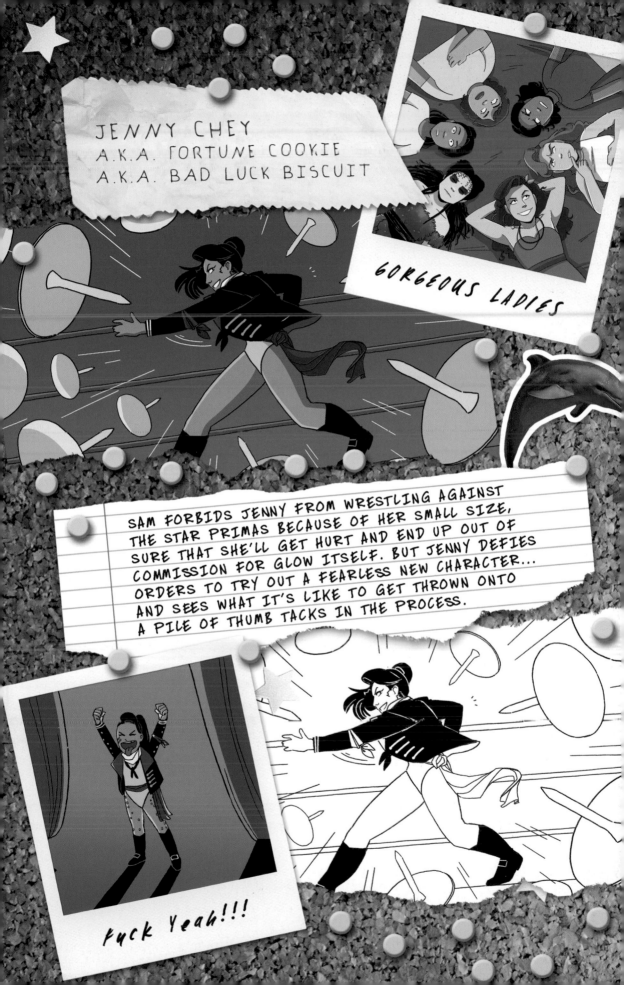

JENNY CHEY
A.K.A. FORTUNE COOKIE
A.K.A. BAD LUCK BISCUIT

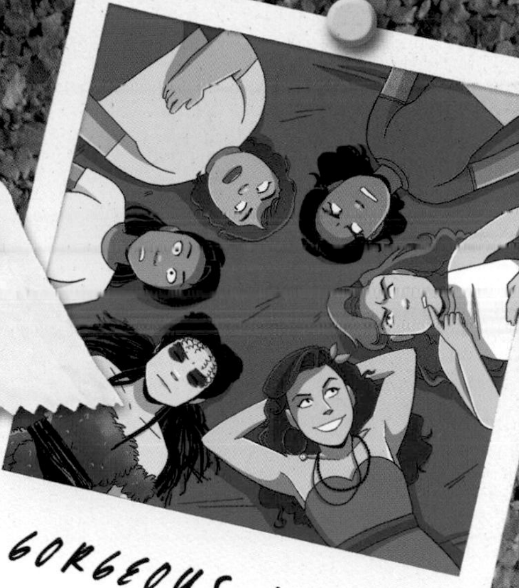

GORGEOUS LADIES

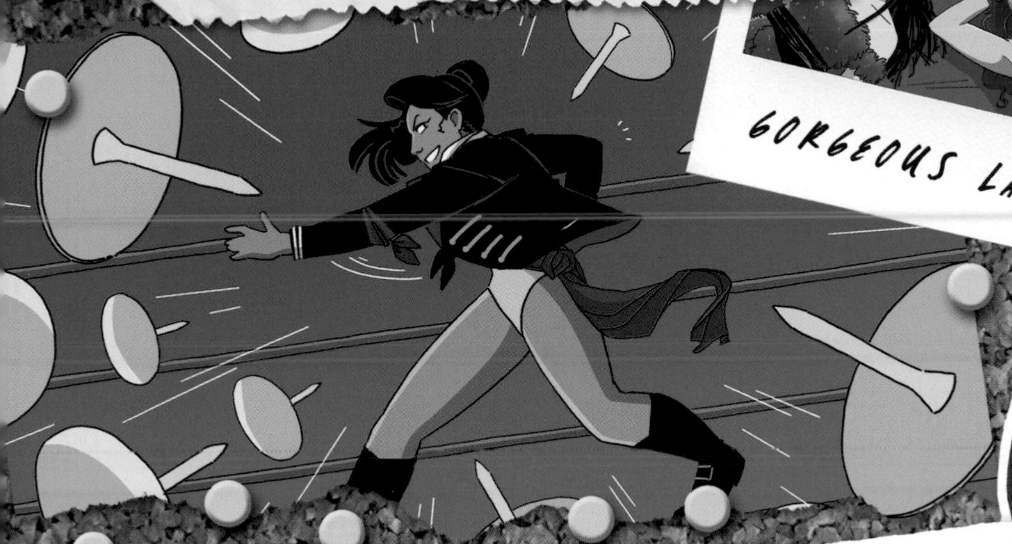

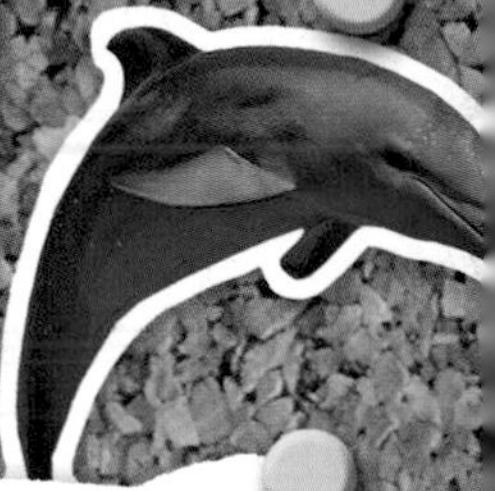

SAM FORBIDS JENNY FROM WRESTLING AGAINST THE STAR PRIMAS BECAUSE OF HER SMALL SIZE, SURE THAT SHE'LL GET HURT AND END UP OUT OF COMMISSION FOR GLOW ITSELF. BUT JENNY DEFIES ORDERS TO TRY OUT A FEARLESS NEW CHARACTER... AND SEES WHAT IT'S LIKE TO GET THROWN ONTO A PILE OF THUMB TACKS IN THE PROCESS.

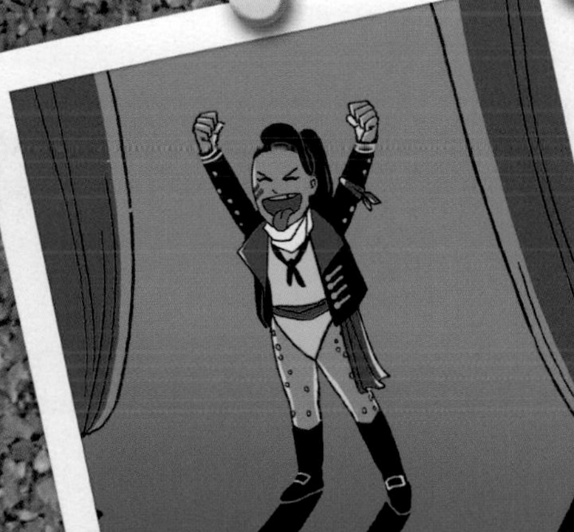

Fuck Yeah!!!

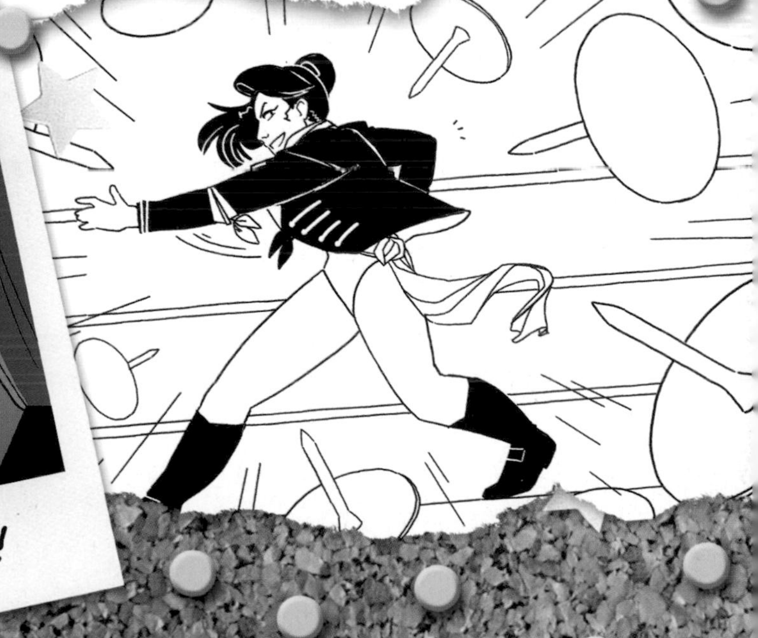

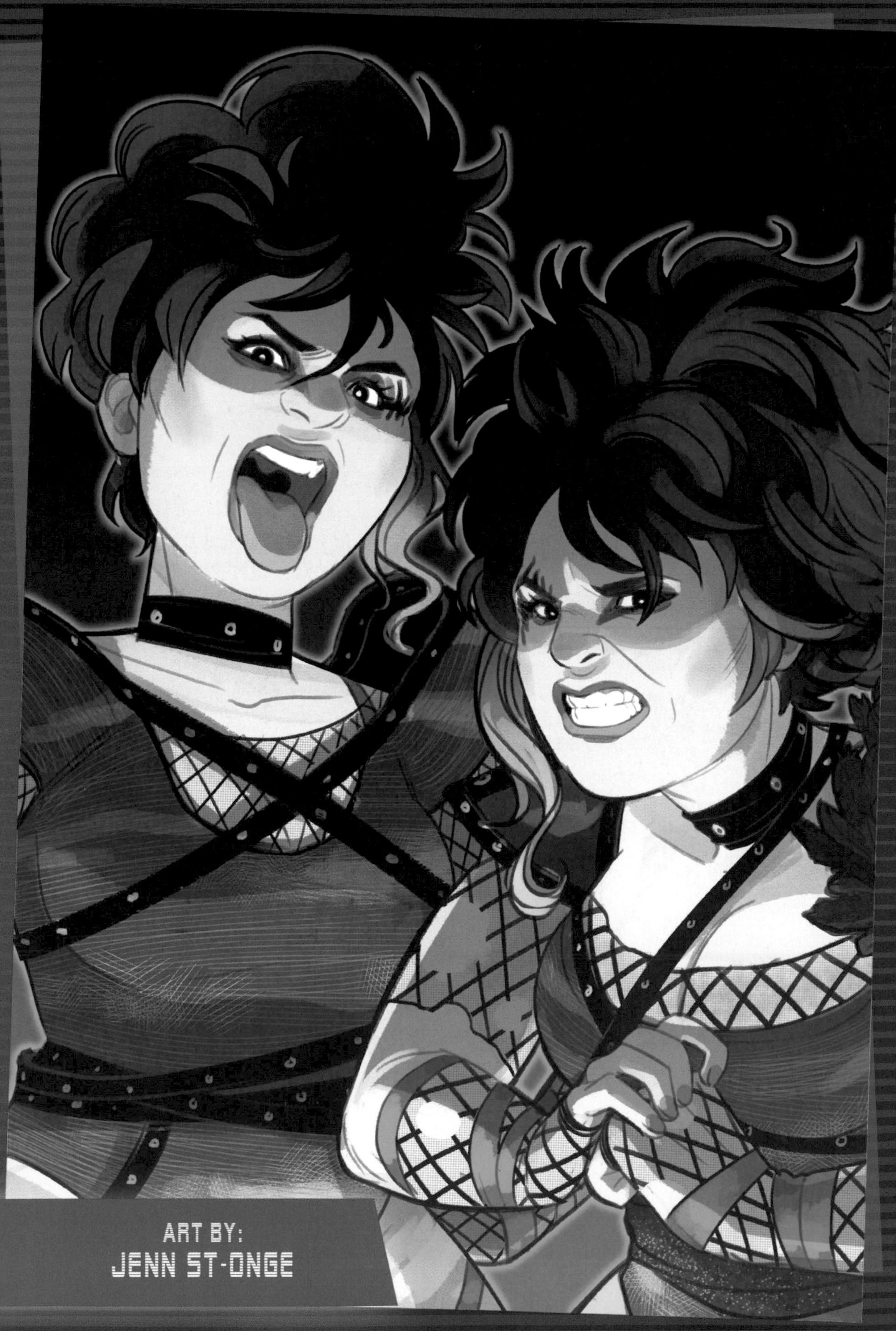
ART BY:
JENN ST-ONGE

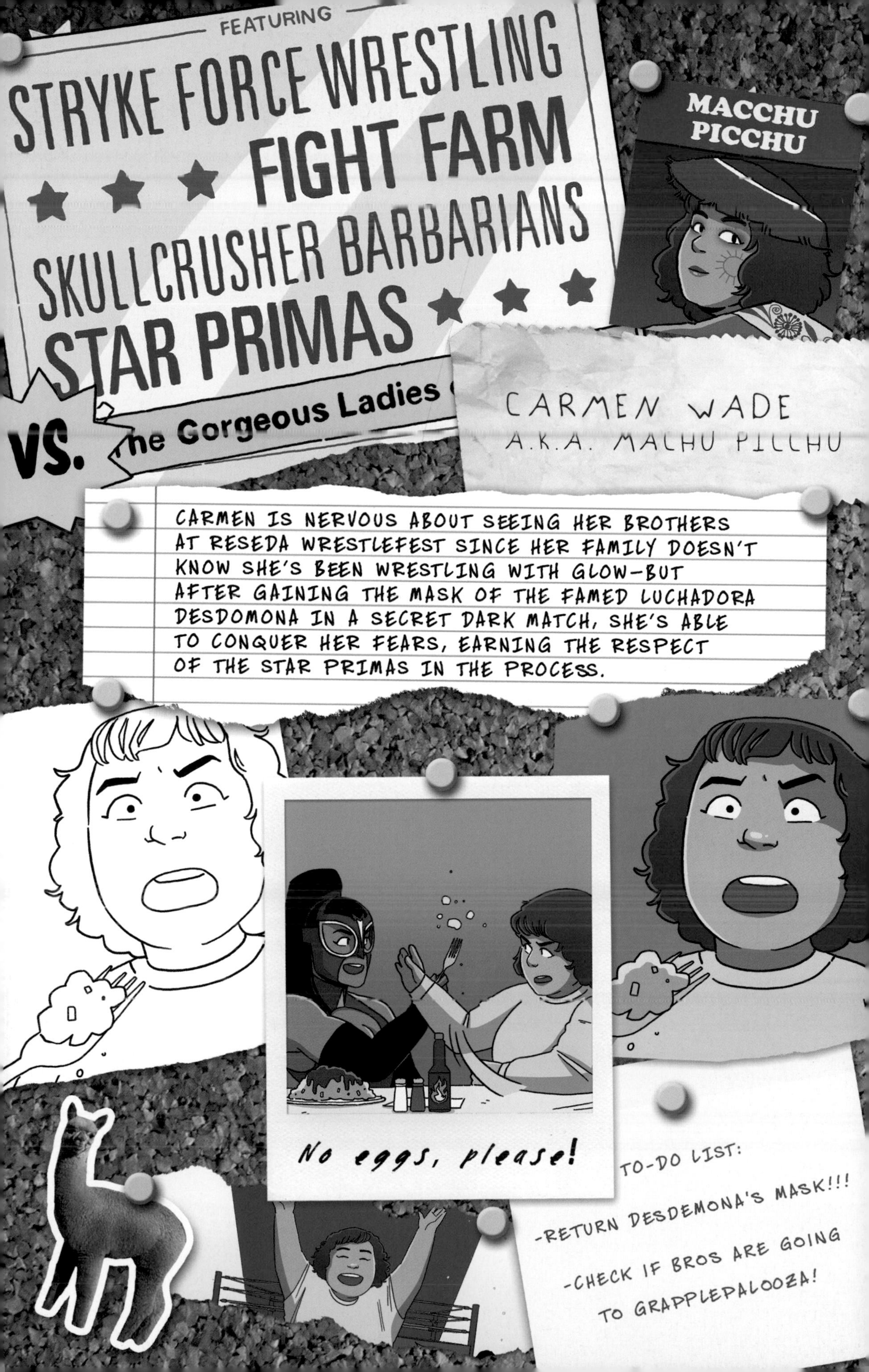
FEATURING
STRYKE FORCE WRESTLING
FIGHT FARM
SKULLCRUSHER BARBARIANS
STAR PRIMAS
VS.
The Gorgeous Ladies
MACCHU PICCHU
CARMEN WADE
A.K.A. MACHU PICCHU
CARMEN IS NERVOUS ABOUT SEEING HER BROTHERS AT RESEDA WRESTLEFEST SINCE HER FAMILY DOESN'T KNOW SHE'S BEEN WRESTLING WITH GLOW—BUT AFTER GAINING THE MASK OF THE FAMED LUCHADORA DESDOMONA IN A SECRET DARK MATCH, SHE'S ABLE TO CONQUER HER FEARS, EARNING THE RESPECT OF THE STAR PRIMAS IN THE PROCESS.
No eggs, please!
TO-DO LIST:
-RETURN DESDEMONA'S MASK!!!
-CHECK IF BROS ARE GOING TO GRAPPLEPALOOZA!

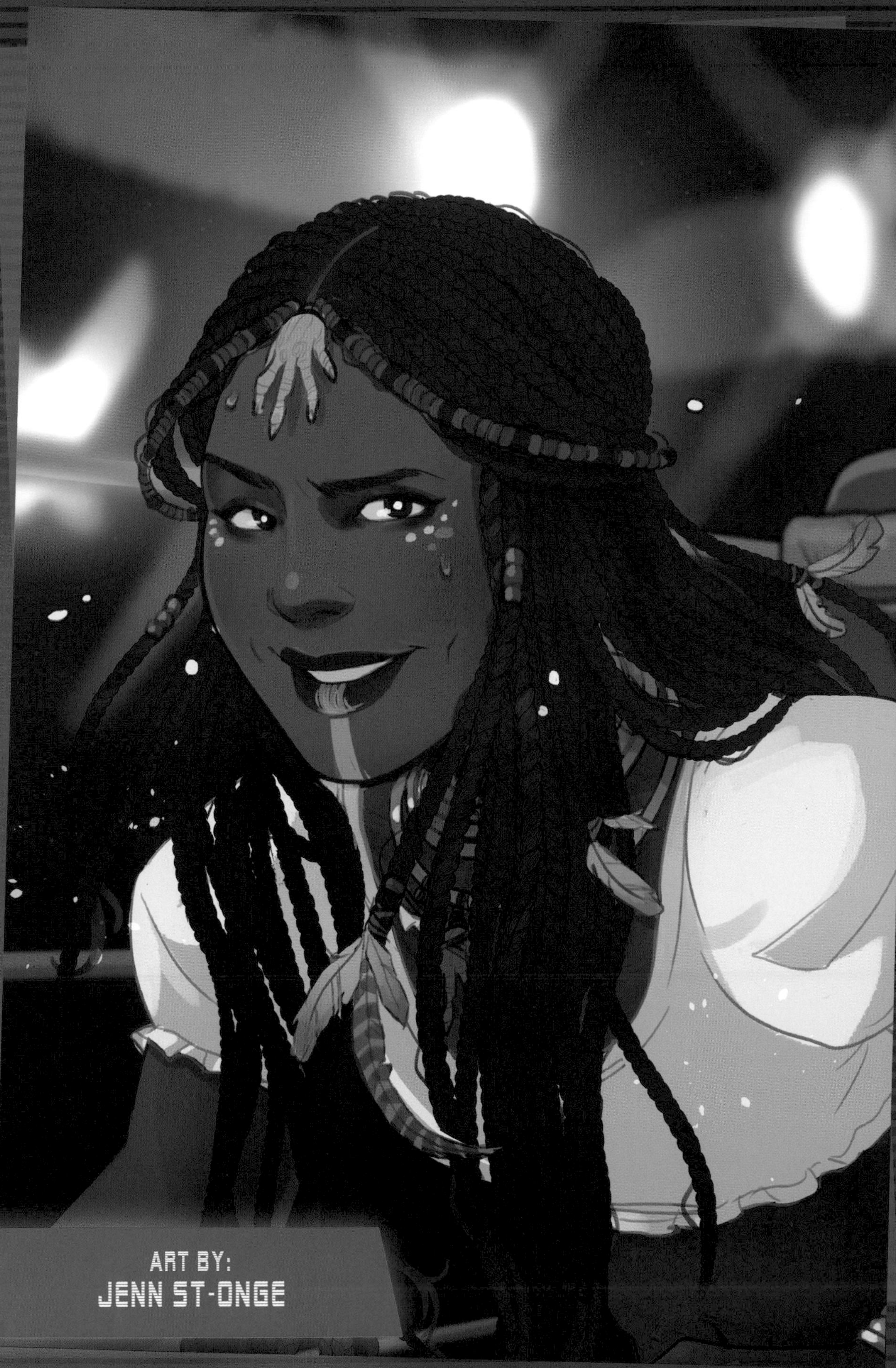
ART BY:
JENN ST-ONGE

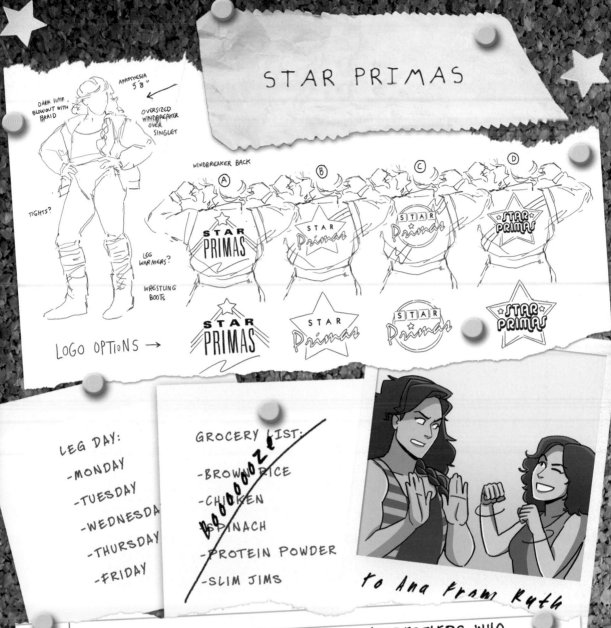

STAR PRIMAS

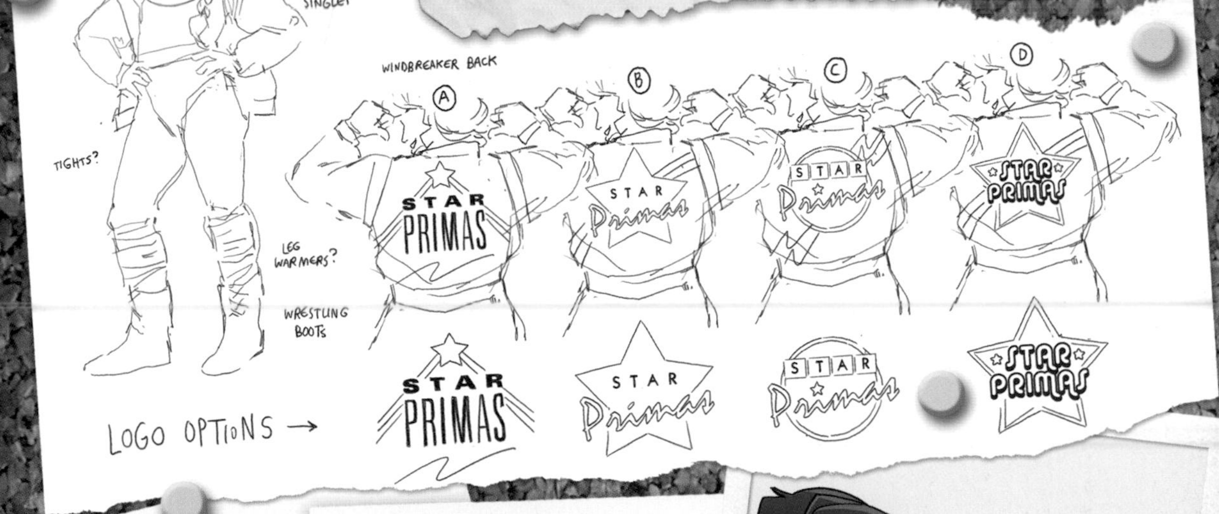

ANASTHESIA 5'8"
DARK HAIR, BLOWOUT WITH BRAID
OVERSIZED WINDBREAKER OVER SINGLET
TIGHTS?
LEG WARMERS?
WRESTLING BOOTS
WINDBREAKER BACK
A
B
C
D
STAR PRIMAS
STAR Primas
STAR Primas
STAR PRIMAS
LOGO OPTIONS →
STAR PRIMAS
STAR Primas
STAR Primas
STAR PRIMAS

LEG DAY:

- MONDAY
- TUESDAY
- WEDNESDAY
- THURSDAY
- FRIDAY

GROCERY LIST:

- BROWN RICE
- CHICKEN
- SPINACH
- PROTEIN POWDER
- SLIM JIMS

booooooze

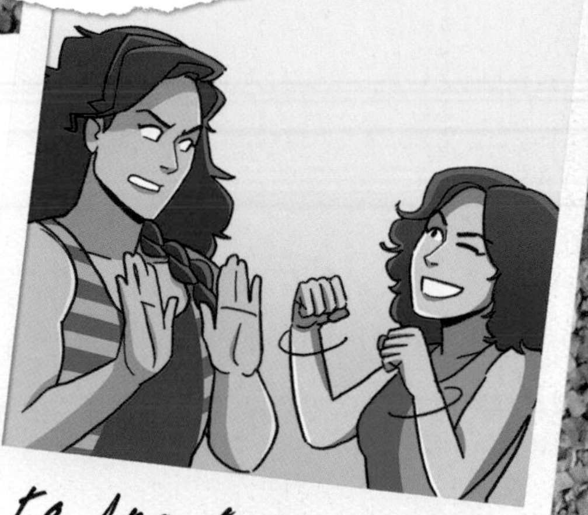

to Ana from Ruth

THE STAR PRIMAS ARE BADASS LADY WRESTLERS WHO
ACTUALLY KICK BUTT AND THE GLOW GIRLS ARE NOT
SCARED OF THEM AT ALL, NOPE! AT FIRST, THEY DON'T
WANT TO WORK WITH GLOW, AND WHAT THEY PERCEIVE
AS FAKE AND UNPROFESSIONAL WRESTLING, BUT THEY
HAVE A CHANGE OF HEART WHEN THE GORGEOUS LADIES
OF WRESTLING SHOW THEY'RE ENTHUSIASTICALLY READY
TO LOSE LIKE CHAMPS.

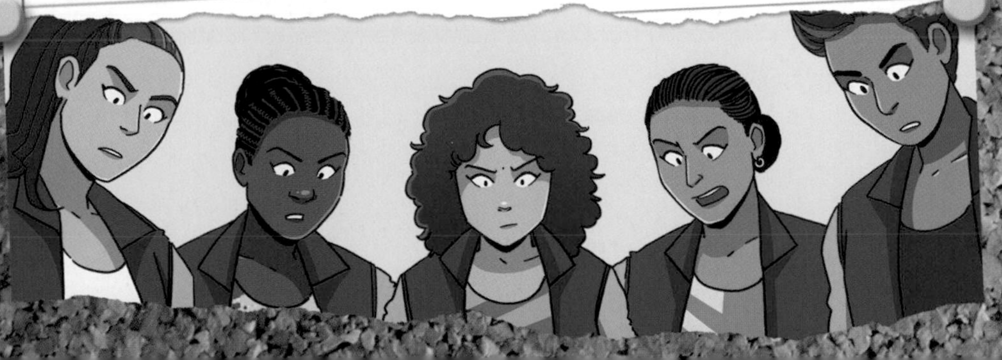

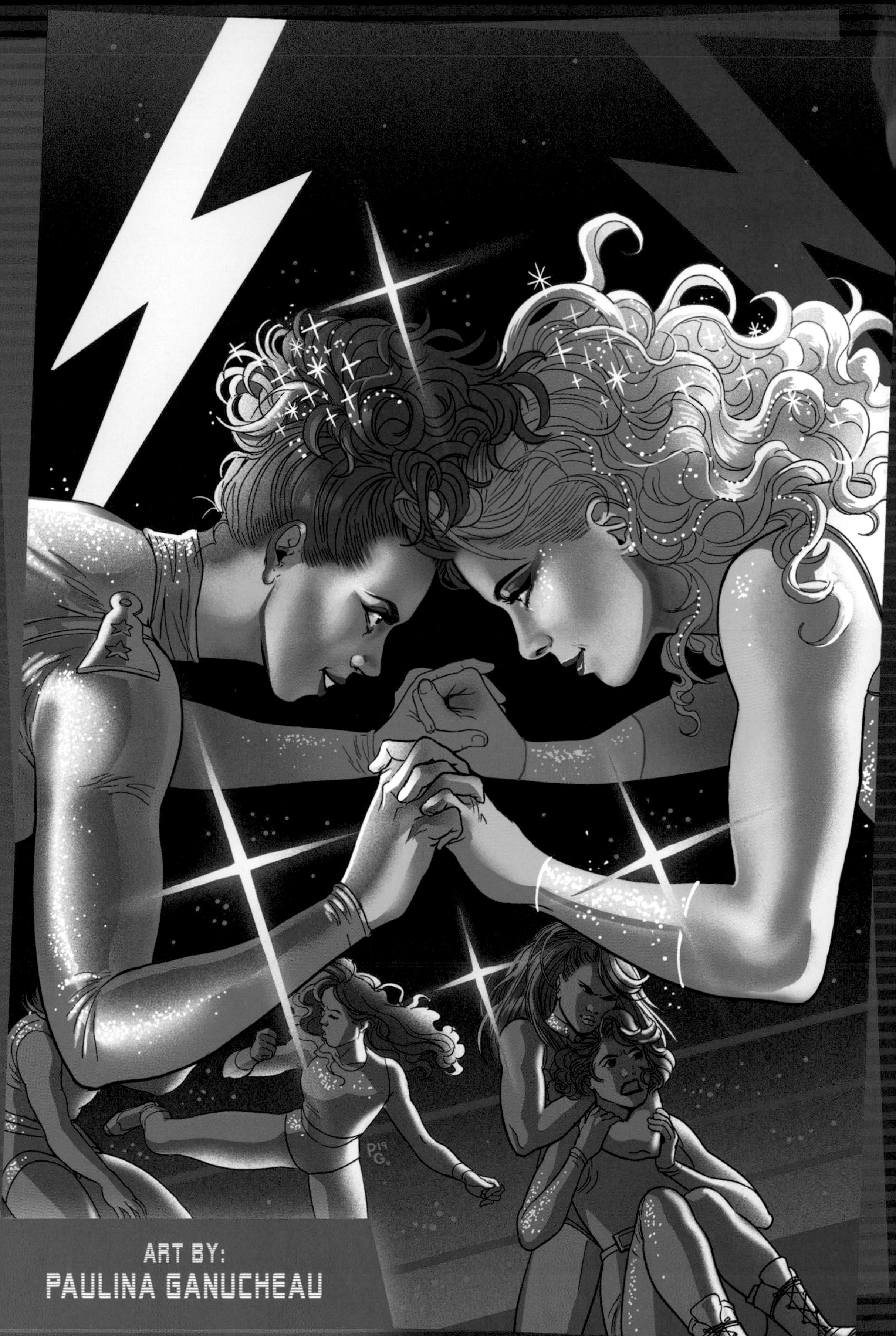

ART BY:
PAULINA GANUCHEAU